RESPLENDENT FAITH

THE SACRED LANDMARKS SERIES

Michael J. Tevesz, Editor

Revelations: Photographs of Cleveland's African American Churches

MICHAEL STEPHEN LEVY

Resplendent Faith: Liturgical Treasuries of the Middle Ages

STEPHEN N. FLIEGEL

The Sacred Landmarks Series includes both works of scholarship and general interest titles that preserve the history and increase understanding of religious sites, structures, and organizations in northeast Ohio, the United States, and around the world.

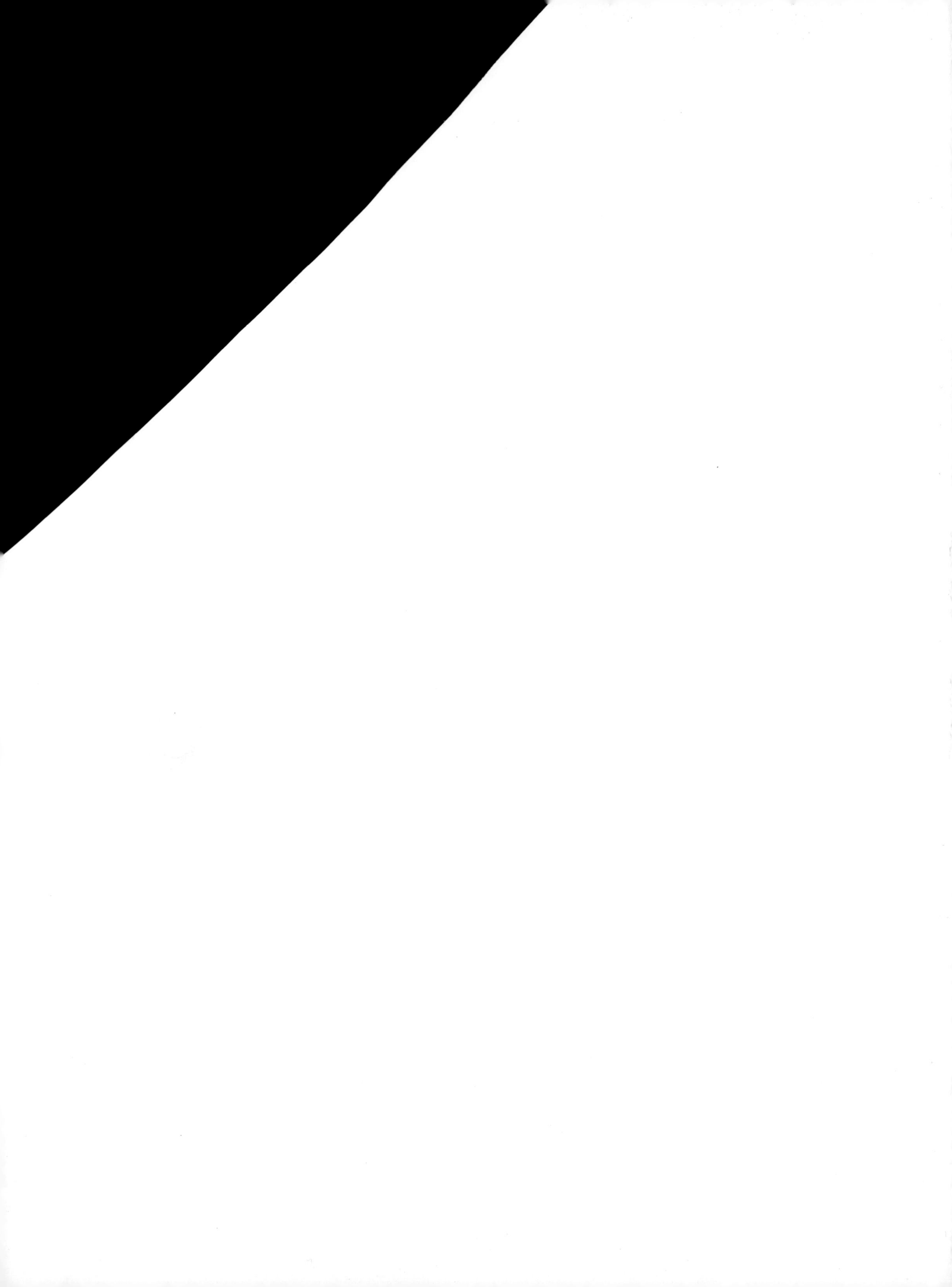

RESPLENDENT FAITH

Liturgical Treasuries of the Middle Ages

Stephen N. Fliegel

Published in cooperation with Cleveland State University's Maxine
Goodman Levin College of Urban Affairs' Center for Sacred Landmarks

THE KENT STATE UNIVERSITY PRESS KENT, OHIO

Library of Congress Catalog Card Number 2008037400
ISBN 978-0-87338-979-2
Manufactured in China

Designed by Dave Kuhar and set in 11/14 Adobe Garamond Pro.

Published in cooperation with Cleveland State University's Maxine Goodman Levin College of Urban Affairs' Center for Sacred Landmarks.

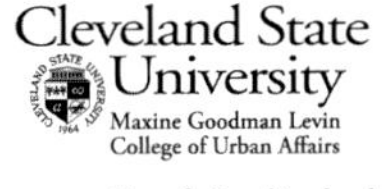

LIBRARY OF CONGRESS CATALOGING-IN-PUBLICATION DATA
Fliegel, Stephen N., 1950–
Resplendent faith : liturgical treasuries of the Middle Ages / Stephen N. Fliegel.
p. cm. — (Sacred landmarks series)
Includes bibliographical references and index.
ISBN 978-0-87338-979-2 (hardcover : alk. paper) ∞
1. Liturgical objects. 2. Church history—Middle Ages, 600–1500. I. Title.
BV195.F55 2009
246—dc22 2008037400

British Library Cataloging-in-Publication data are available.

13 12 11 10 09 5 4 3 2 1

Contents

Preface

The subject of medieval church treasuries can be accessed in any number of ways. The art historical approach, with its emphasis on style, technique, and iconography, is but one of these. Other approaches may focus on the liturgy, contemporary piety, social history, and even the medieval political condition. Indeed, the objects found in ecclesiastical treasuries are frequently exquisite examples of medieval craftsmanship. Therefore the artistic aspects of these objects cannot be divorced from their consideration. Their fabrication from sumptuous and costly materials continues to captivate and fascinate us many centuries after their creation. In a sense, objects like the *Ardagh Chalice*, the *Reichenau Crosier*, or the enameled *Shrine of the Three Kings* are emblematic of an age of faith so unlike the secular world of today. Scarcely any object was as ubiquitous to the material culture of the Middle Ages as sacral objects intended for use in public worship or private devotion. Additionally, such objects are representative of the best medieval craftsmanship, the medieval concept of the cosmos, and the contemporary approach to the spiritual and ethereal.

When invited to write this book, a subject of deep interest to me for many years, I felt that the only viable approach for the interested general reader was to place these extraordinary objects within a historical framework while at the same time to emphasize their sumptuous artistry. In doing so, I endeavor to describe the principal medieval sacral objects against a backdrop of contemporary liturgical practice, medieval piety, and devotion. I also sought to elucidate the functionality of objects that can only seem abstruse to the modern reader.

The subject of medieval treasure objects is vast and complex, and its corresponding literature is extensive. Therein lies the problem for the general reader seeking an introduction to the subject. The challenge of navigating the copious literature, mainly produced for the academic scholar or museum professional, can be daunting for the nonspecialist. And it should be added that much of this specialist literature is published in languages other than English. Additionally, most of the current scholarly literature takes a highly focused approach by concentrating on a specific medium, technique, style, form, period, place of production, or location of the treasury.

This publication was not planned for the specialist, academic, or professional reader. Nor was it intended to introduce new scholarship or new arguments to an already broad subject. This book's intended audience is the general reader who aspires to know more about the subject in a publication of reasonable length. That said, I believe that the present book may include some features of interest to both the educator and student, particularly those interested in the Middle Ages, art history, liturgy, and the history of religion. My desire is to encourage those who read this book to delve more deeply into the specialized literature. To that end, a selected bibliography is provided at the back. No work of art can be fully appreciated if divorced from the culture that produced it. I therefore endeavor to provide a survey of the medieval treasury against a useful historical framework that considers not only artistic technique and method but also medieval liturgical practice, piety, and pilgrimage. I also provide a compendium of the typical objects found within medieval church treasuries with corresponding discussion of their form and functionality. The challenge was doing this in a reasonable length and using superior illustrations. Since the range of liturgical objects is so vast and the quantity of treasuries so great, any study of them must be limited in scope.

The Middle Ages was subject to a dominant force in the working out of human destiny. This was the spiritual and temporal power of the Christian Church. The medieval treasury was produced because of a universal belief and a common spiritual center. The liturgical objects that have survived have done so because they are generally made from precious or opulent materials and are things of beauty—ironically the same criteria that caused the destruction of others. Thus the artistic legacy of these sacral objects is what ties the modern viewer to the past and to one's deeply held spiritual values. The surviving objects from the treasury serve as a mirror of another age and are intrinsically charged with didactic, narrative, and symbolic meaning.

In every marvelously wrought object, we discover those servants of God who occasionally revealed their name or otherwise made their presence known. We are also reminded of those prelates who commissioned such works of art, like Suger of Saint-Denis. Following Suger, perhaps we might posit a similar response: "We profess that we must do homage also through the outward ornaments of sacred vessels...Thus, when—out of my delight in the beauty of the house of God—the loveliness of the many-colored gems has called me away from external cares, and worthy meditation has induced me to reflect, transferring that which is material to that which is immaterial."[1]

We approach those objects that survived amid all that were destroyed with awe, both for their artistic beauty and for their ability to reveal a deeper understanding of the history of the church, its artifacts, and its liturgy. These objects, whether contained in a museum collection or in use in a parish, are the patrimony of the church, its adherents, and those skilled artists and craftsmen who devoted their consummate skills in creating them. Increasing our knowledge of these objects and their provenance, how they were made, the materials used, and the liturgical function they served can only enhance our appreciation and sensitize us to their inherent sacredness.

Why the Middle Ages? Why medieval treasuries and not Baroque or later treasuries? Simply put, it is the epoch we know as the Middle Ages that saw the genesis of liturgical treasuries and the standardization of liturgical practice and ritual in the West. Notwithstanding the historical attrition of treasuries by fire, theft, and warfare, it was the end of the Middle Ages and later that saw the irreparable loss of their contents. This sad despoliation was brought about by the Reformation in England and Protestant Europe. Local rebellions during the sixteenth century and after also contributed to these losses, as did the revolution in France.

The restoration of ecclesiastical treasuries in many famous churches and cathedrals across Europe has provided beautiful objects in their own right for the visitor to behold. This was achieved through the addition of new liturgical objects in the seventeenth to twentieth centuries to replace the lost medieval examples. However worthy of study, the Baroque and nineteenth-century treasuries form a separate chapter from a liturgical, artistic, and social point of view. The earlier medieval treasury adheres to a common spirit and aesthetic that is the focus of this book.

Without doubt, there still exist liturgical treasuries in their original locations. Some of these, such as the treasuries of Notre Dame in Paris, the cathedrals of Chartres and Rouen, or Westminster Abbey in London, are today dominated by postmedieval objects. The treasury of San Marco in Venice, while essentially medieval, contains objects that were not originally produced for or commissioned by that church. Instead, the contents of San Marco's treasury were acquired as war booty from Constantinople by Venetian crusaders in the thirteenth century. Some of the oldest relatively intact medieval treasuries exist today in Germany at Aachen, Trier, and Hildesheim.

The contents of many treasuries have survived in dispersed form in the countless number of museums and libraries in Europe and North America, and it is here that the serious student of this material will be able to view and study them. In recent years, some scholars have begun the process of reconstructing dismantled medieval treasuries through the study of early inventories and other documents. These reconstructed treasuries may be viewed occasionally in exhibitions or studied in their catalogs.

Much of the recent important literature on medieval treasuries and liturgical objects, including illuminated manuscripts, has taken the form of exhibition catalogs. For the scholar, these are often the most important references. While some catalogs are focused on a particular medium, such as goldsmith work or enamels, others treat a localized center of production, such as Limoges, Hildeshiem, Cologne, or Magdeburg. Other exhibition catalogs provide a sweeping mixed media survey of a particular subject, like Romanesque England or Paris ca. 1400, while at the same time incorporating important medieval liturgical objects.

Given their importance to the subject, I have included the more recent exhibition catalogs in the bibliography, notwithstanding the fact that some are in languages other than English. For the most part, I have concentrated on the important recent literature. There have been few general introductions to the medieval treasury specifically written for the non-specialist reader in monograph form produced within the past four decades. Robert G. Calkins's *A Medieval Treasury* (1968), long out of print and illustrated in black and white, provided a short introductory essay on the subject, yet its primary function was as the catalog of an exhibition held at Cornell University. Also of interest is *The Medieval Treasury*, edited by Paul Williamson (1986), a catalog of this material in the Victoria and Albert Museum in London. Though well served by its introductory essay and catalog entries, the Victoria and Albert Museum publication suffers from its largely black-and-white illustrations.

The bibliography is arranged by topic. And while I do include some original source material, I generally avoid listing tourist guidebooks to historic treasuries, publications that are usually cursory in nature and, while they sometimes provide interesting synopses of a particular treasury, suffer from poor illustration and limited discussion of the objects themselves. The illustrations included in this book were carefully selected to support the text and to present some of the finest examples of medieval treasure objects.

Finally, I provide a basic glossary of terms, where I describe most liturgical terminology, objects, and techniques referred to in the text. I realize that nomenclature is often a problem for understanding the broader subject.

It is my fervent hope that this book will inform and engage the reader.

Acknowledgments

When asked to contribute a book to this series I was both eager and honored to accept. I am a firm believer in the work of the Center for Sacred Landmarks of the Maxine Goodman Levin College of Urban Affairs at Cleveland State University and its educational mission. As an art historian and museum professional, I am aware of the importance of the study and preservation of our sacred heritage. Our modern artistic, cultural, and religious traditions found their inception in our distant past. With respect to the Christian tradition in particular, the Middle Ages was the crucible that produced the template for ecclesiastical architecture, painting, and the liturgical arts.

I wish to thank Dr. Michael J. Tevesz, director of the Center for Sacred Landmarks, for proposing this book and for his warm personal support throughout its writing. I also thank my editor, Douglas R. Hoffman. I am grateful to my friend, Reverend David A. Novak, Pastor of Holy Trinity Church in Lorain, Ohio. Father Novak was kind enough to read the current book in manuscript and provide a critical review. I thank Father Novak for generously sharing his extensive liturgical knowledge and for suggesting refinements to my text.

I would also like to express my appreciation to the other readers of my text and their suggested improvements. The present book has benefited greatly from their comments. I would like to thank the editorial board of the Kent State University Press and particularly Joanna Hildebrand Craig, former assistant director/editor-in-chief, and Mary D. Young, managing editor. At the Cleveland Museum of Art, I wish to thank Elizabeth Saluk, curatorial assistant in the Department of Medieval Art, for her consummate help in securing the images and reproduction rights.

Stephen N. Fliegel
Curator of Medieval Art
The Cleveland Museum of Art

Bright is the noble work; but being nobly bright, the work should brighten minds, so that they may travel … to the True Light where Christ is the true door … the dull mind rises to truth through that which is material.

—Suger, Abbot of the Royal Monastery of Saint-Denis, Paris

CHAPTER ONE

The Medieval Liturgical Treasury

Exhibiting small-scale, highly sumptuous works of art produced for the liturgical needs of the church is a tradition of considerable antiquity. Today's churches have modern variants of these objects, such as reliquaries, censers, monstrances, chalices, patens, and vestments, while the objects from the Middle Ages are seen today primarily in museums or ancient European church treasuries. That many such precious objects were dispersed over the centuries through warfare, revolution, and of course, the Reformation accounts for their presence in today's museums. Others have been lost forever, returned to the goldsmith's melting pot. The original function of these liturgical objects is not always clear to the modern layperson, and their nomenclatures may be equally enigmatic. The terms "ostensorium" and

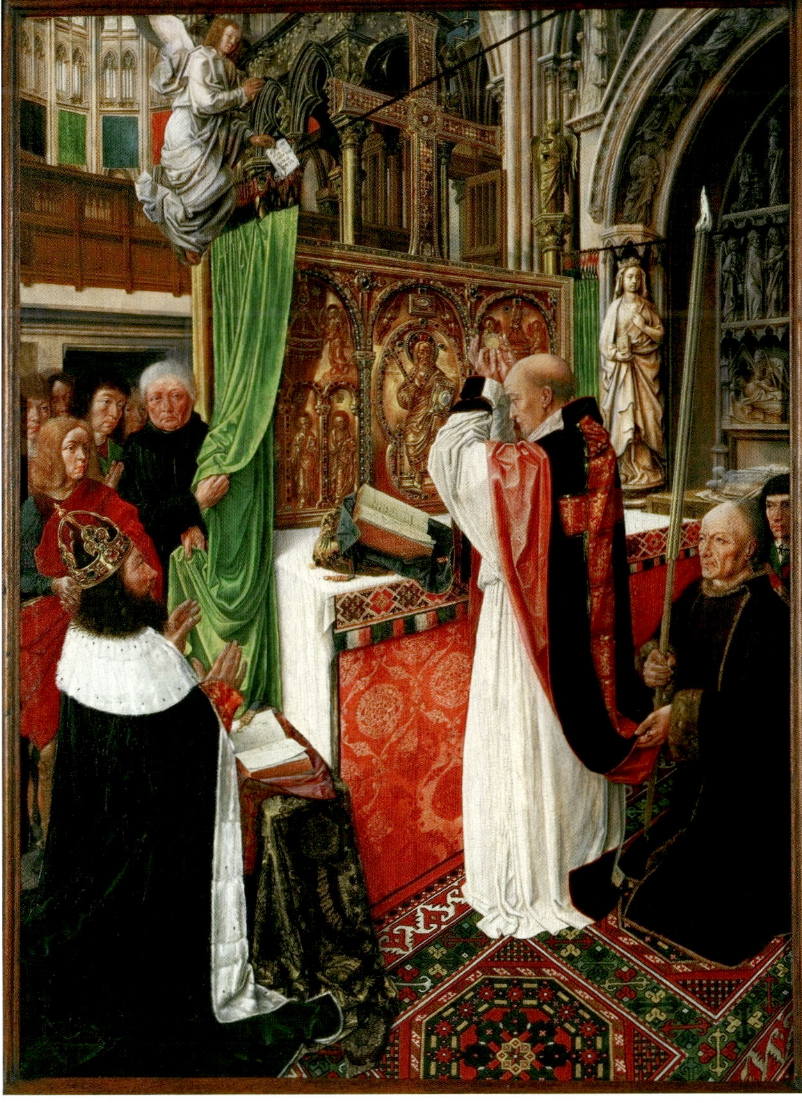

Figure 1. Mass of Saint Giles in the Church of Saint-Denis.
Oil on wood panel. Master of Saint Giles, French(?) ca. 1500. National Gallery of Art, London.
Photo: Erich Lessing / Art Resource, NY

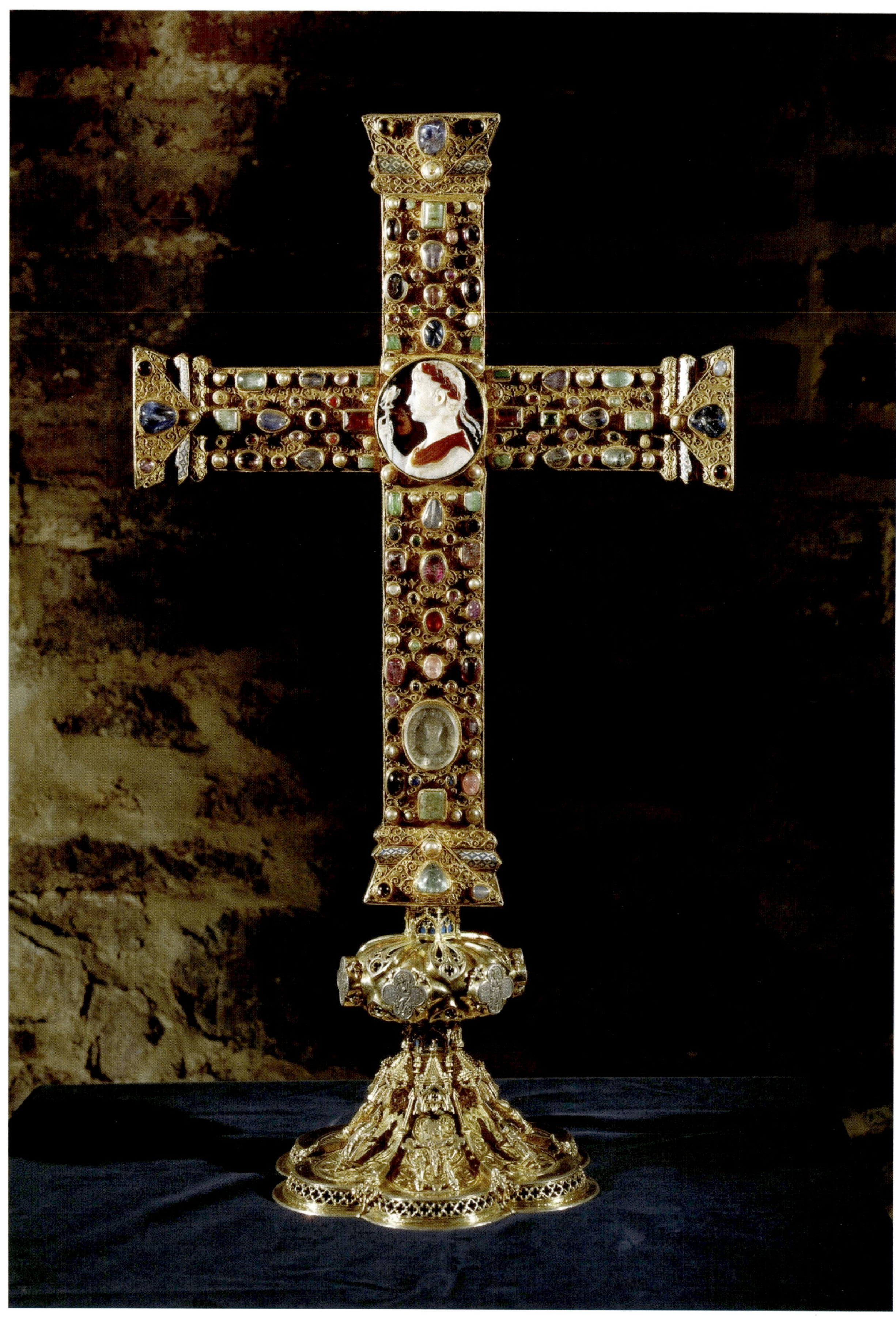

"pyx," "dalmatic" and "lectionary" are hardly familiar, even to contemporary Catholics. While many liturgical objects in use today would have been known and used by medieval Christians—the chalice and paten as perhaps the best examples—others have disappeared following the reforms to the liturgy arising from the Second Vatican Council from 1962–65.

During the Middle Ages, liturgical objects were usually crafted from precious metals, such as silver, gilt-silver, and gold, to which costly gemstones, enamels, and carved ivory plaques were often applied. Then, as now, they met specific liturgical functions, but, given their lavish decoration and artistry, they were often displayed only in a church sacristy or in a secure room known as a "treasury." Sometimes, important objects such as reliquaries and manuscripts were displayed openly on or near the altar for all to see. For the medieval mind, rich detail and superb execution were imperative for objects that were placed on the altar or held the relics of saints *(fig. 1)*. Likewise, the vestments required to serve the numerous seasons, occasions, and feast days within the church calendar were made from expensive silks and trimmed with elaborate embroideries of silver and gold thread. The many books produced during this period to celebrate the Mass, the administration of the sacraments, and the recitation or chanting of the Daily Office were handmade and costly to produce. Often decorated, or illuminated, with silver and gold leaf and colorful paint, these illustrated manuscripts were among the most prized possessions of any cathedral, parish church, or monastery. Manuscripts were sometimes bound between bejeweled covers of gilt-silver, befitting their function on the altar. Some of these great medieval treasuries have survived in situ in cities such as Venice, Hildesheim, Aachen, Trier, and elsewhere.

Within the sacred confines of the church, the medieval churchgoer would have been overwhelmed by the sensory richness of the setting—the diffused and colored light emanating from stained-glass windows, the flickering light from candles, and the smell of incense. Liturgical objects, such as crosses, reliquaries, and chalices, dazzled and inspired the faithful with the shimmer of their gold and silver surfaces and the luminescent glow of gems and enamels. In this ethereal world, embellished with sculpture, icons, and frescoes of God, the angels, and saints, the liturgical performance achieved an otherworldliness in a way now difficult to comprehend *(fig. 2)*.

The two constant features of medieval art are the use of precious materials and highly skilled execution. In this way, the Middle Ages identified formal beauty with the sacred. In other words, an object conveyed a sense of sacredness by its formal beauty. Rarity and shimmer or sparkle were deemed to be expressions of wealth and therefore were appropriately offered to God. However, to the medieval mind, precious materials achieved pious distillation only when skillfully worked. An object was rendered doubly sacred by its material value and the perfection of its execution, thus achieving a magical or spiritual quality. During the Middle Ages and later, Christian churches began collecting exquisite, skillfully wrought liturgical objects for their ecclesiastical treasuries.

Over time medieval ecclesiastical treasuries have suffered greatly as a result of warfare, looting, the Reformation of the sixteenth century,

Figure 2 (facing page). Cross of Lothar (with Antique Cameo of Emperor Augustus). Gold, gems, pearls, and enamels. Cologne(?), Germany, ca. 985–91. Aachen, Palace Chapel, Treasury.

Photo: Erich Lessing / Art Resource, NY

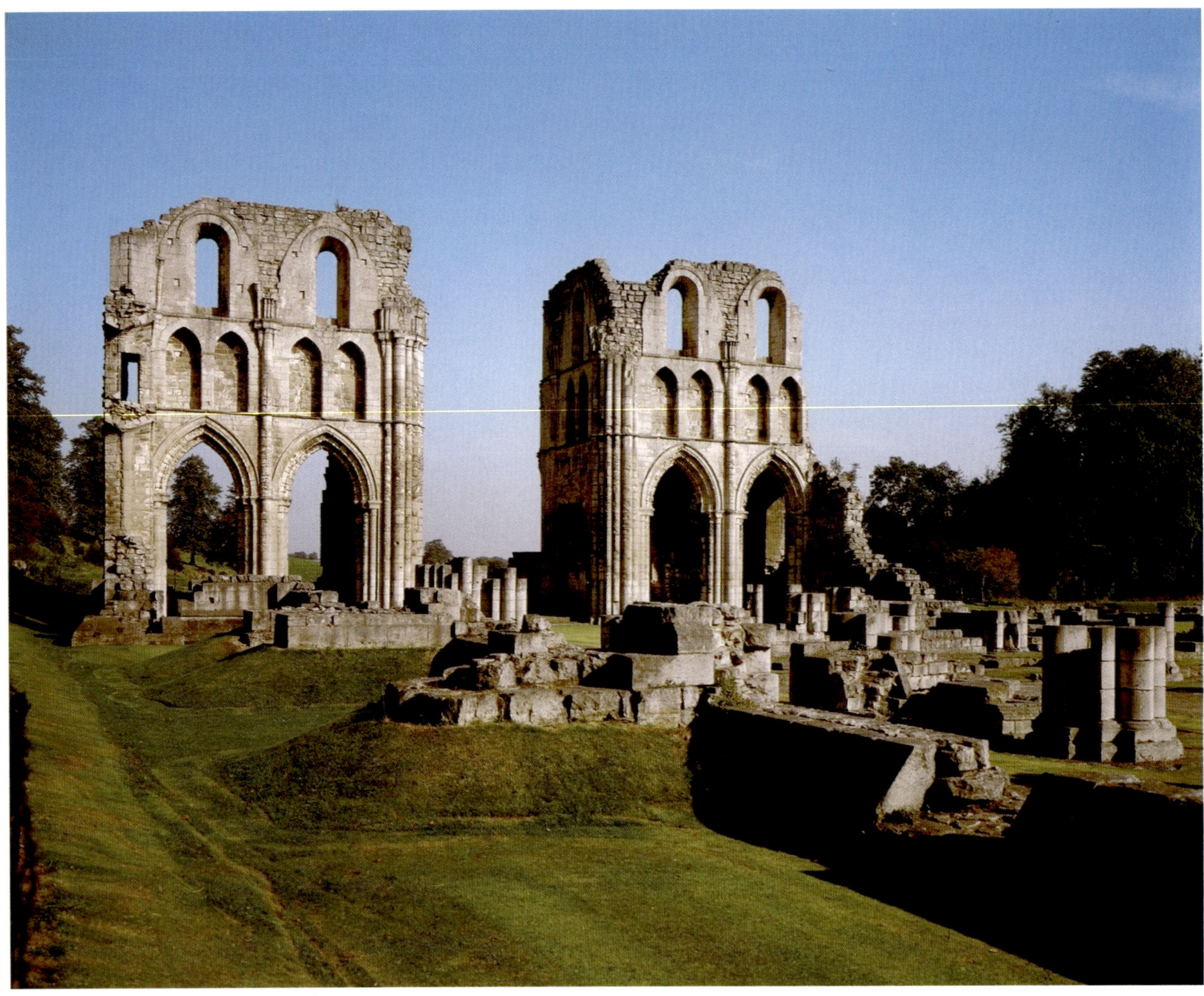

Figure 3. Ruins of the Cistercian Abbey of Roche (founded 1147). South Yorkshire, England. View of the Transepts, ca. 1170. The abbey was dissolved by Henry VIII.

Photo: Erich Lessing / Art Resource, NY

civil disturbances and revolution, and natural calamities, such as fires and floods. Sadly, the vicissitudes of history have resulted in the complete destruction of many of these liturgical objects, while others survive today in only fragmentary condition and are housed in museums, private collections, or new liturgical treasuries. Today we must often rely on inventory evidence or sales records to trace provenance and reconstruct the original context for lost medieval treasuries, but the context of many objects has been lost or obscured.

Among the earliest despoliations of medieval treasuries was the dissolution of the English monasteries following the break of King Henry VIII (r. 1509–47) with the Roman Church in 1533–34. Failing to obtain a divorce from his first wife, Catherine of Aragon, Henry resolved to break with the Catholic religion and refused to accept papal authority on the matter. The closure of the monasteries was initiated by the Act of Suppression of 1536, which transferred all the lands and property of religious houses within Britain to the crown. Henry closed down more than 850 monasteries between 1536 and 1540 *(fig. 3)*.

Those monks and nuns who did not oppose Henry's policies were given small pensions, but most found themselves in a state of extreme poverty. Those who actively opposed Henry's reformation of the English Church, such as the abbots of Glastonbury, Colchester, and Reading, were tortured or executed. "Before the winter of 1540 had set in," one writer observed, "the last of the abbeys had been added to the ruins with which the land was strewn from one end to the other."[1] The king expelled from the major monasteries an estimated 3,200 monks and regular canons, 1,800 friars, and 1,600 nuns.

The Dissolution, or Suppression, of the Monasteries was a sad episode in English history, resulting in the destruction of much of the country's artistic legacy from the Middle Ages. The treasuries were confiscated, and liturgical silver and gold were melted down and sent to the royal mint. Other works of art—altarpieces, manuscripts, vestments, furniture—were reused for their raw materials or destroyed. The monastic buildings and convents were often demolished and the stone used as construction material for other buildings. The lead from their roofs was frequently melted down and sold.

In 1538 Thomas Cromwell, the king's designate charged with the suppression of the religious houses, turned his attention to religious shrines in England. For centuries pilgrims had visited shrines that contained important religious relics. As an expression of personal faith and to maintain the shrines, wealthy pilgrims often left expensive jewels and ornaments to the religious orders who looked after these shrines. Henry VIII decided that the shrines should be closed down and the wealth confiscated for the crown.

The pope and Catholic Europe were shocked in 1538 when they learned of the destruction of the treasury of Canterbury Cathedral, including the shrine of Saint Thomas Becket, one of England's most beloved saints. A vivid description of the confiscation of the Canterbury treasury noted that some twenty-four carts were required to transport the precious objects to the London mint, where they undoubtedly were broken up and melted down in the years before 1540. The embellishments from Saint Thomas Becket's tomb reportedly filled two huge chests and required six men to lift them.[2] The loss of so much important medieval English religious art as a result of the Dissolution and the later civil war has left an enormous gap in art history for late medieval England.

Similar losses to the ecclesiastical treasury occurred in other regions of Europe following the Middle Ages. As in England, the Reformation on the continent resulted in the breakup and dispersal or secularization of many important treasuries. The Guelph Treasure, the former liturgical treasure of Braunschweig's Church of Saint Blaise, gradually reverted to the possession of the Dukes of Brunswick-Lüneburg during the late seventeenth century *(see figs. 20, 35, 37, 47)*. In 1528 the citizens of Braunschweig had embraced the principles of the Reformation, and in 1540 the town council demanded the suppression of the church as a Catholic collegiate chapter. The Church of Saint Blaise was subsequently replaced by a new constitution favoring Lutheran beliefs and rendering anachronistic those medieval objects that once served the Roman liturgy. In 1930 the Guelph Treasure was placed on the international art market by its secular owner, Ernst August II, Duke of Brunswick-Lüneburg, and has since been dispersed by direct sale among many public institutions in the United States and Germany.[3]

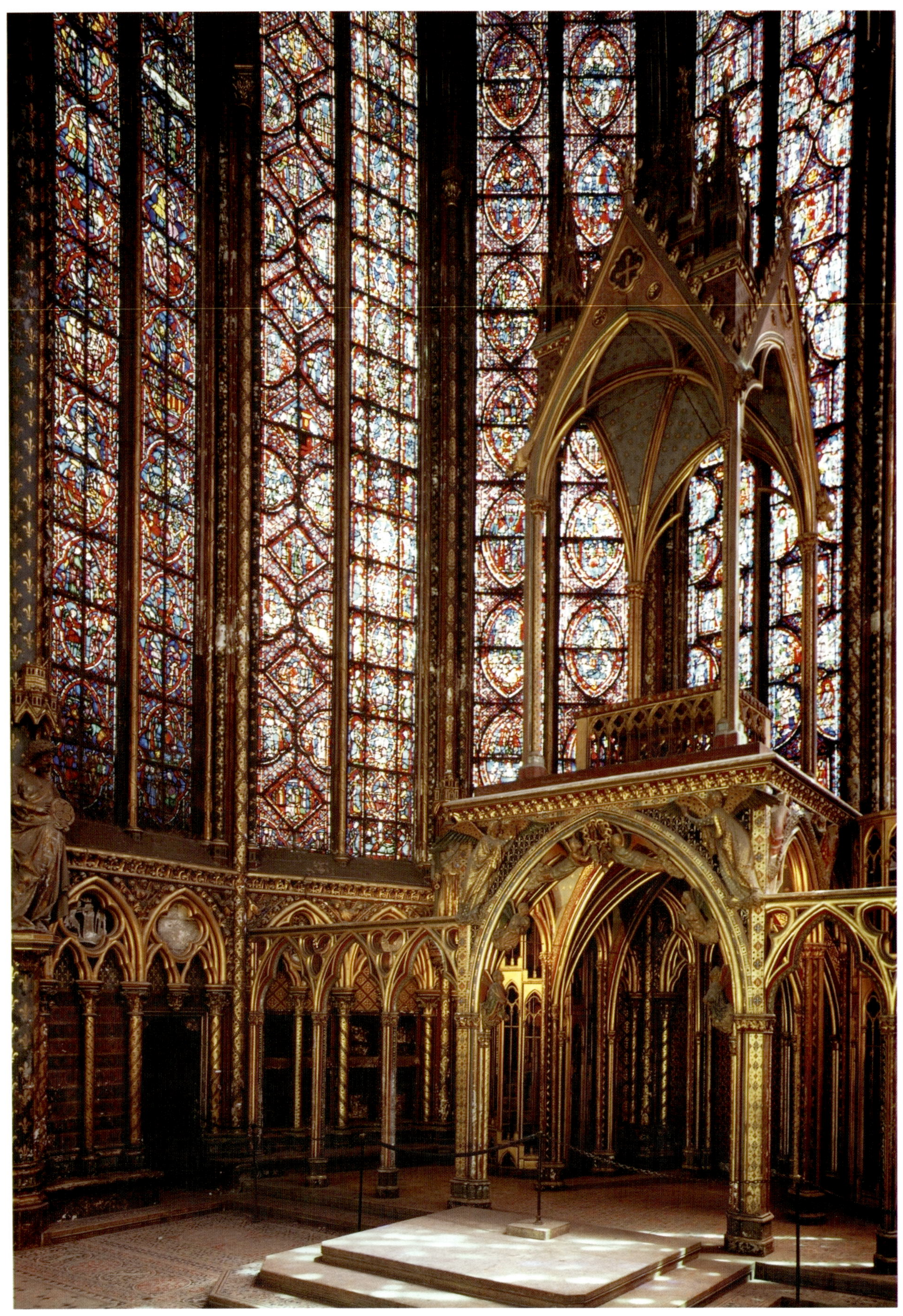

In Switzerland the Treasury of the Cathedral of Basel met with a similar fate. All of its precious objects were used on the high altar of the cathedral until 1529. The Bishop of Basel had lost his jurisdiction over the city in 1501 when Basel joined the Swiss Confederation. By 1525 the town's Roman Catholic clergy was being taxed, and on April 1, 1529, the town council officially adopted the principles of the Reformation, thus halting future growth of the Basel Treasury. Members of the council who were reluctant to abandon Catholicism were forced to leave the city. In an effort to hasten the decision of the council, some two hundred men marched to the Basel Cathedral and other churches in the city and burned altarpieces, paintings, and sculptures that were now regarded as idolatrous. In the case of Basel's Treasury, history was kinder; virtually all of its precious objects survived and are now housed in the Historisches Museum in Basel as well as in a few churches and major European museums.[4]

Figure 4 (facing page). Sainte-Chapelle, Paris. Apse, Upper Chapel, 1241–48. The great reliquary was housed under the architectural canopy just above the altar.

Photo: Scala/Art Resource, New York

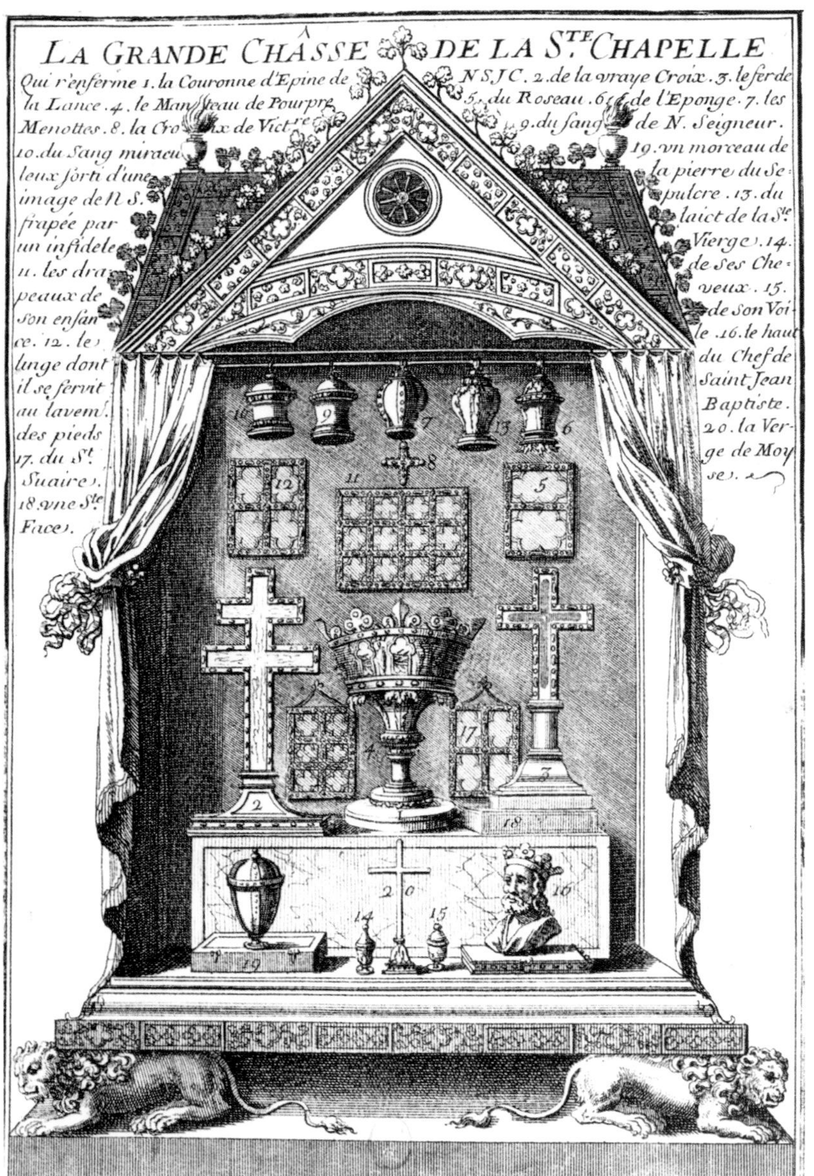

Figure 5. The Great Reliquary of Sainte-Chapelle. Print. France, early 18th century. Bibliothèque nationale de France, Paris, Arch. Nat. LL 630, fol. 17.

Photo: Snark/Art Resource, New York

Figure 6 (facing page). Kneeling Prophet (supporting figure from The Reliquary of Saint-Germain-des-Prés). Gilt bronze. Paris, 1409. The Cleveland Museum of Art, Leonard C. Hanna Jr. Fund, 1964.360.

The tragic losses to the medieval treasury within France were extensive, largely due to the French Revolution (1789–99). At the same time, the French Roman Catholic Church was forced to undergo radical restructuring. Many churches became the property of the state and were sold or demolished. Others were converted into "temples of reason." In 1383 the Duke of Burgundy, Philip the Bold, and his wife, Margaret, the Countess of Flanders, founded the Chartreuse de Champmol, just outside Dijon, which held many major works of art, including altarpieces, devotional sculptures, paintings, manuscripts, vestments, and liturgical objects. The monastery was sold and then demolished in 1791, with its contents and furnishings stripped as state property. While some of the original sculpture survived in situ and some of the paintings have been preserved in museums, most of the original furnishings and treasure objects have been irretrievably lost to the revolutionaries who associated such ecclesiastical buildings with the ancient régime.

Similarly, great cathedrals, such Notre Dame in Paris and Reims, lost much of their original sculpture and stained glass. Even the Cathedral of Chartres, southwest of Paris, which managed to retain its sculpture and glass, lost its liturgical treasure during the Revolution. At the Royal Abbey of Saint-Denis, north of Paris, many of the great liturgical objects described by its venerable Abbot Suger disappeared forever. These included the Great Cross of gold, gems, and enamel, which the abbot had erected in the new choir between 1145 and 1147. Though it had been partially dismembered during the seventeenth century, it completely vanished during the Revolution. Also lost were the Carolingian altar frontal of Charles the Bald, adapted as an altarpiece by Suger and illustrated in the painting *The Mass of Saint Giles (fig. 1)*, and Le Tombeau des Corps-Saints, the shrine that contained the relics of Saints Denis, Rusticus, and Eleutherius.[5]

The Sainte-Chapelle, the royal chapel built by King Louis IX (1226–70) on the Ile-de-France between 1241 and 1248, housed the notable Crown of Thorns and other relics acquired by Louis while on crusade and suffered serious despoliations during the Revolution. In the upper chapel, the Crown of Thorns and a fragment of the True Cross were preserved in a large, richly decorated reliquary—a grand chasse—made of gilt-silver *(figs. 4, 5)*. The relics were exhibited to the faithful each year on Good Friday. This famous reliquary disappeared during the Revolution and the relics were scattered, though some were eventually transferred to Notre Dame. Perceived as religious and royal symbols, the furniture of the Sainte-Chapelle, as well as its choir stalls and screen, were removed and lost, but, fortunately, two-thirds of its stained glass and some of its sculpture survived.

Saint-Germain-des-Prés was a powerful Benedictine monastery in Paris, founded in the sixth century by the Merovingian King Childebert I. Its monastic community, whose wealth was drawn from its lands and royal patronage, flourished as a center of reformed monastic life and learning as late as the seventeenth and eighteenth centuries. Its notable treasury included a large reliquary of the remains of Saint Germain, the bishop-saint and patron of Paris. The only surviving fragments of the Reliquary Châsse of Saint-Germain are two supporting figures in the form

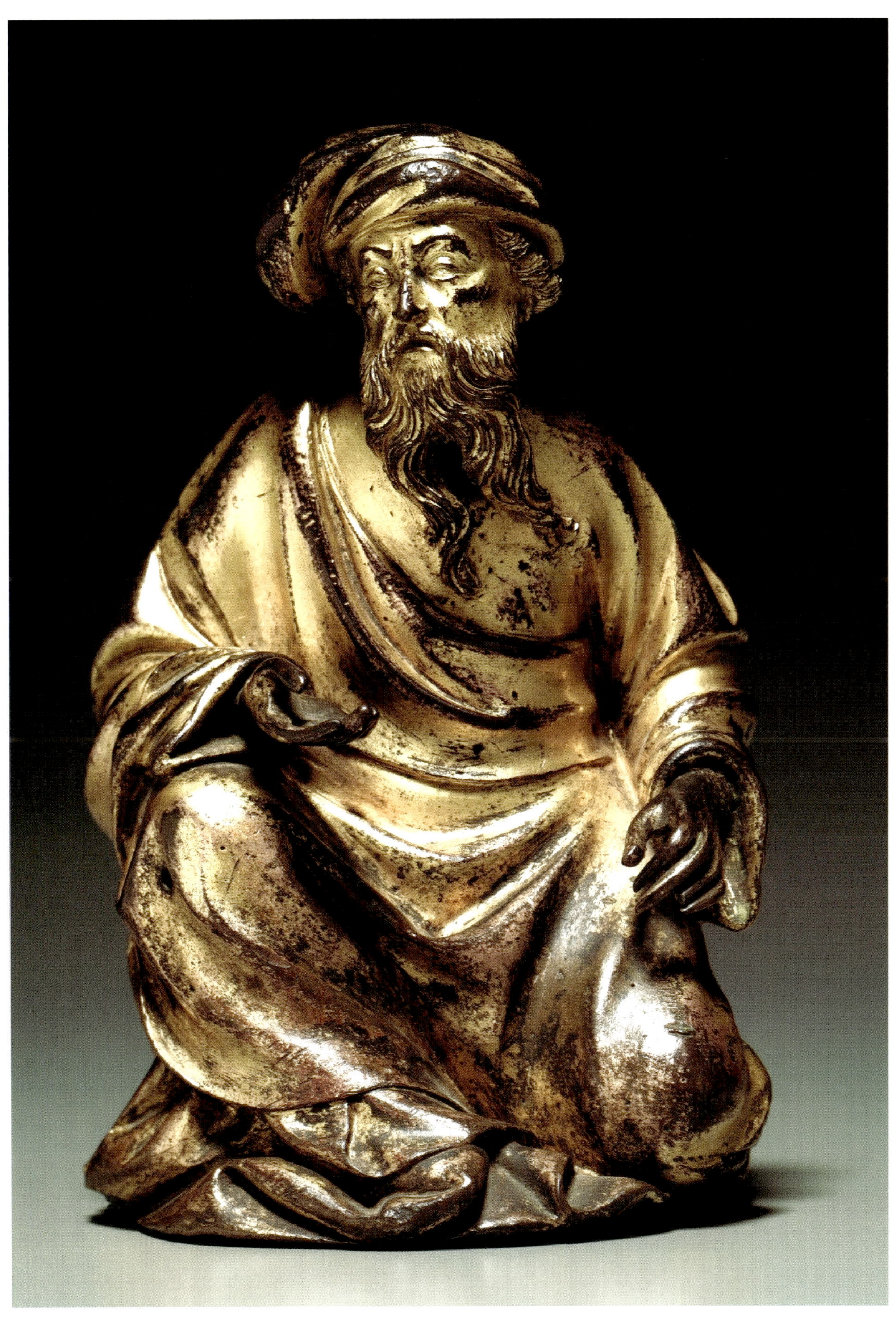

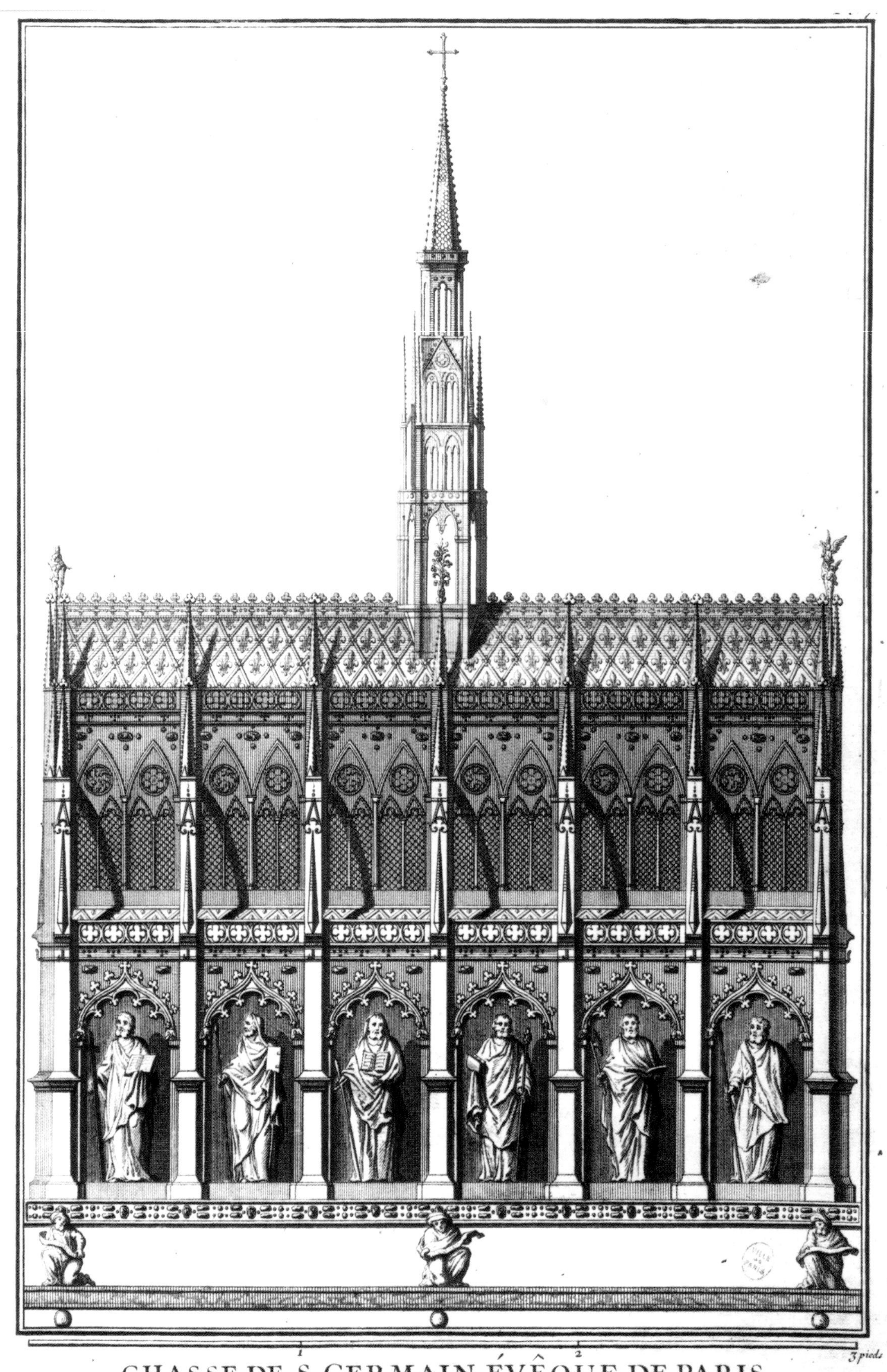
1
2
3 pieds
CHASSE DE S.GERMAIN ÉVÊQUE DE PARIS.
Chaufourier del.
Baquoy fec.

of kneeling prophets; today they are preserved in the Louvre and the Cleveland Museum of Art *(fig. 6)*. These objects represent two of the original six feet of the reliquary, a large chest. The reliquary, architectural in form and fashioned from silver and gold with precious stones, was designed to hold the body of this revered bishop-saint *(figs. 7, 8)*.

The Reliquary Châsse of Saint-Germain was housed in the ancient Benedictine Abbey of Saint-Germain-des-Prés in Paris and formed the monastery's great treasure until the French Revolution, when it was sent to the mint to be melted down. Documents relate that the deed was done on May 12, 1794, and produced 23 marcs of gold (about 6 kg) and 186 marcs of silver (about 46 kg). In addition, numerous precious stones were removed from the reliquary, including 77 sapphires and 50 emeralds.[6] The two kneeling prophets in gilt-bronze, now in Cleveland and Paris, represent the only surviving fragments of this important example of Parisian ecclesiastical goldsmithing.

Even the Holy See was not spared the indignities of looting. Luigi Celotti, an Italian abbot turned art dealer, acquired from Napoleon's soldiers a large number of illuminated manuscripts that they had looted from the Sistine Chapel in 1798. He dismembered these and sold them profitably at Christie's in London on May 26, 1825.

Such accounts illustrate both the vulnerability of medieval ecclesiastical treasuries across the centuries as well as the harsh indifference of history. Rather than lament these losses, we should probably rejoice in those objects that have escaped mutation or destruction through history. Indeed, many liturgical objects have survived and are today preserved in public institutions, such as museums and libraries, where they are revealed to new audiences and to people of various faiths. Some liturgical objects are still retained within a church setting, though perhaps not the one intended for their original function. In rare cases, some medieval

Figure 7 (facing page). The Reliquary Châsse of Saint-Germain-des-Prés. Engraving from **Dom Jacques Bouillart, Histoire de l'abbaye royale de Saint Germain des Prez**, 1724, illustrated by Jean Chaufourier. Musée Carnavalet, Cabinet des Estampes, Paris, G 30505. The supporting prophet figures are clearly visible in the engraving.

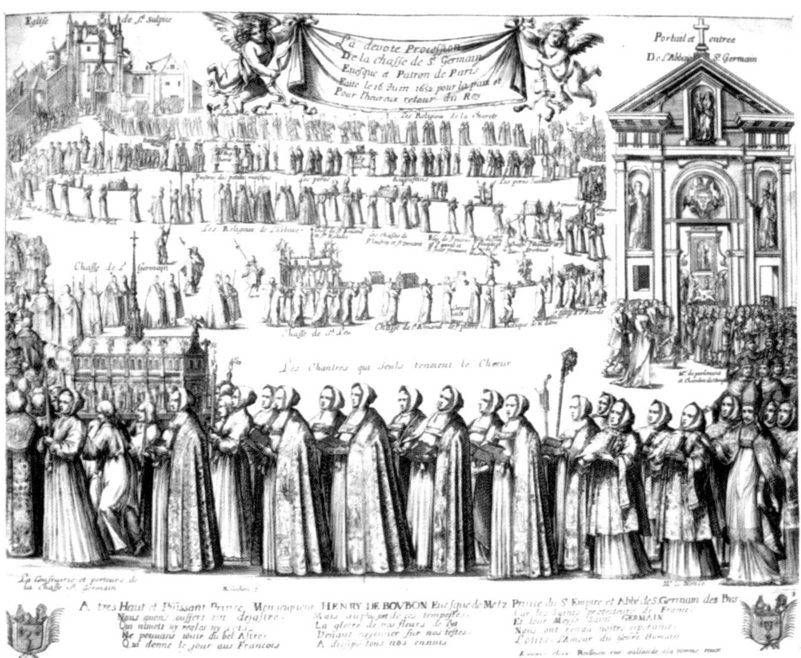

Figure 8. Procession of Saint Germain, Bishop and Patron of Paris, June 16, 1652. Engraving. Paris, late 17th century. Bibliothèque nationale de France, Cabinet des Estampes, Paris, 70 C 41546. The illustrious medieval reliquary continued to be processed well into the seventeenth century as shown here. The reliquary appears in the lower left followed by the chanting monks of the abbey. The reliquary was destroyed during the Revolution.

treasuries, such as San Marco in Venice and Aachen in Germany, have been preserved more or less intact and in situ.

For those liturgical objects preserved in museums, there is increasing sensitivity to their original purpose. Indeed, today's museums expend great effort to replicate in their displays the context of spirituality that produced them. The contents of the medieval treasury are clearly of great value as consummate works of art. However, such objects also reflect the culture of faith that originally produced and used them. The makers of the chalices, reliquaries, and vestments described here could hardly have envisioned that their creations would eventually become objects of awe and mystery to be admired hundreds of years later by a public audience.

CHAPTER TWO

Liturgy and Ritual

The liturgy is defined as the form of public worship with all of its formularies, particularly with regard to the sacramental service of the Eucharist. Even though Christian liturgy is not choreographed, it nevertheless implies precise organization of the movements of its participants. In this way, the ritual remained largely standardized and universal in its public and essential forms around the time of Pope Gregory I (590–604). There existed, however, variations within the rite according to local use during the Middle Ages. For example, the Roman Rite was observed throughout Italy and Flanders, but England observed the Sarum Rite. The North Netherlands followed the Use of Utrecht, and the Dominicans had their own rite.[1]

The liturgy's ceremonial side is a necessity, so that the liturgical rites can take place in absolute peace and communicate a sense of sacredness to the faithful. Such details were historically laid out in the rubrics contained with the missal and other service books. The rubrics were headings and explanatory notes written in red ink (from the Latin *rubrum,* meaning red). These included not only the spoken words of the priest but also details of his vesting and ceremonial directions.

According to this context, liturgical celebrations today require the worshipper to adopt the positions of standing, sitting, and kneeling. During the Middle Ages, the sitting position was uncommon, as churches were not furnished with pews. The faithful simply stood, knelt, or lay prostrate on the ground in supplication and humility on the stone or tiled floor of the church. Aristocratic worshippers, however, were often the exceptions. They would supply their own private pews or prie-dieux, which were often elaborate structures with kneeling rails, a lectern to support a devotional book, and sometimes curtains for privacy. Aristocratic worshippers could observe the priest celebrating Mass at the altar yet remain hidden from distractions and the view of other worshippers. Similarly, aristocrats were afforded a degree of comfort and warmth in the cold, unheated church of the period. Philip the Good (1419–67), the Duke of Burgundy, is depicted in a manuscript miniature worshipping in precisely this way *(fig. 9).* He is aided by his book of hours and a small devotional diptych. Such comforts were not available to average worshippers.

During the Middle Ages, numerous treatises and commentaries on the liturgy were written and widely circulated. Nearly all liturgical acts were explained in one or more of these treatises. One noted canonist was William Durandus (ca. 1237–96), who was born in southern France and studied canon law at Bologna. Durandus's most famous work was the *Rationale divinorum officiorum* written in 1286. Its eight books contain a detailed account of the laws, ceremonies, customs, and mystical interpretation of the Roman Rite. Durandus's *Rationale* is the most complete

Figure 9. **Duke Philip the Good of Burgundy attending Mass.** Fol. 9r. From **The Hours of Philip the Good.** Tempera and gold on vellum, 1457. Jean le Tavernier, Netherlandish. Bibliothèque royale de Belgique, Brussels, ms. 9092.

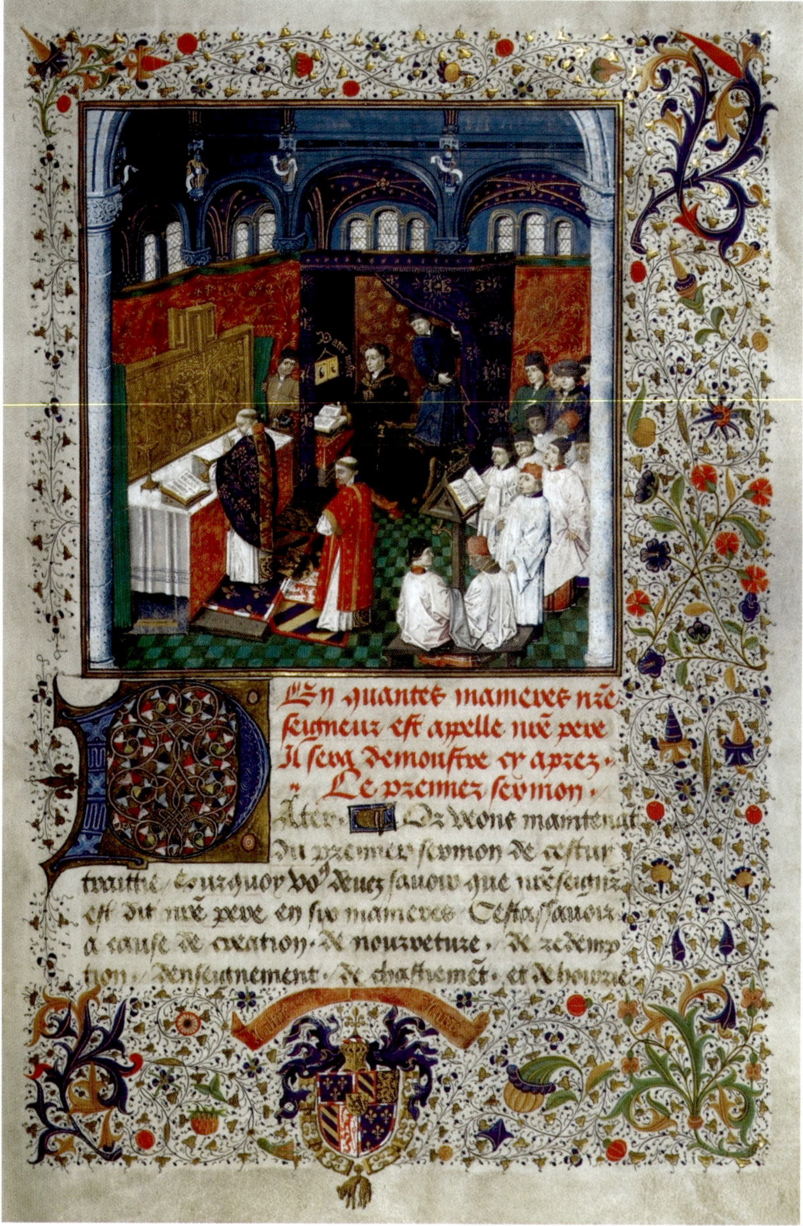

medieval treatise of its kind and is still the standard authority for the ritual of the thirteenth century and for the symbolism of rites and vestments.

The vast majority of early treatises dealt with the Mass, the Divine Office, baptism and confirmation, liturgical ministers or orders and vestments, dedication of churches, sickness, death, burial, and the liturgical calendar. The church fathers of the late first and second centuries frequently referred to liturgical matters, especially baptism and the Eucharist. By the third century, commentators such as Tertullian and Cyprian had described baptism, the manner of prayer, penance, fasting, and the consecration of virgins. In that same century, Origen wrote in detail on baptism, the creed, the Eucharist, Holy Orders, anointing the sick, and the liturgical year. Directives were given for different sacred rites, such as postures to be assumed, the duties of ministers, and the reading of Scriptures. Subsequent canonists and reformers continued to revise and refine the liturgy through the centuries, but the origins of the liturgy were born during early Christianity and late antiquity.

At the heart of the Christian liturgy is the Mass, which has perpetuated the unique sacrifice of Christ on the cross and serves as the key to individual redemption. By partaking of the Eucharist bread and wine, Christians become contemporaries of the Crucifixion. Fundamental to this is the acceptance—by both the medieval Christian Church and, following the Reformation, the Roman Catholic Church—that the bread and wine actually become the body and blood of Jesus. As far as the Catholic Church is concerned, a real transformation of substance occurs during the consecration of the bread and wine (transubstantiation).[2] Ordination allows a priest to consecrate the bread and wine, and in this way he renews Christ's sacrifice on the cross. The altar is the table on which the offering is laid out and remains the most elevated symbol of Christ and the church. The priest kisses it at the beginning and the end of Mass as a sign of respect.

The forms of liturgical vessels during the thirteenth century are suggestive of changes in liturgical practice that had begun earlier. Some of these changes had the effect of separating the congregation from full participation in the Mass. In the early church, the Mass was spoken in Greek, the universally recognized language of the liturgy. Starting in the third century, at least in Rome, the liturgy began its gradual transition to Latin.[3] By the thirteenth century, Europe was experiencing the ascendancy of its vernacular languages in diplomacy, commerce, government, and administration. However, the Mass remained in Latin throughout the West. Gradually, there was a shift away from the direct participation of the laity reciting prayers aloud in the Mass and toward the priest's secret recitation of prayers to God at the altar. Also fully accepted by the year 1000 was the practice of the priest celebrating Mass with his back toward the congregation, a feature that became universal.[4]

As these changes occurred during the Middle Ages and across the generations, by the thirteenth century the laity had only a vague recollection of what the rituals originally meant. Thus, the Mass became primarily a visual experience. At best, the congregation was occupied in its own private devotions during the celebration.

It is difficult to make the sounds and smells of medieval Christian worship come alive today even though the fundamental tenets of that worship have remained much the same. No medieval church had pews or, before the fifteenth century, an organ, much less air-conditioning or electric lights.[5] Churches were bitterly cold in winter. For much of the year, particularly in northern Europe, churches were fairly dark, illuminated by candles or oil lamps. The typical layperson through much of the Middle Ages would have been illiterate.

Only in the fourteenth and fifteenth centuries were advances made in lay literacy. The later medieval aristocracy was usually literate and sometimes schooled in Latin, the language of the church as well as that of scholarship and diplomacy.[6] Literacy was essential for the clergy, however, who were required to read the rubrics and instructions for liturgical ceremony as well as the spoken texts in the missal and other service books.

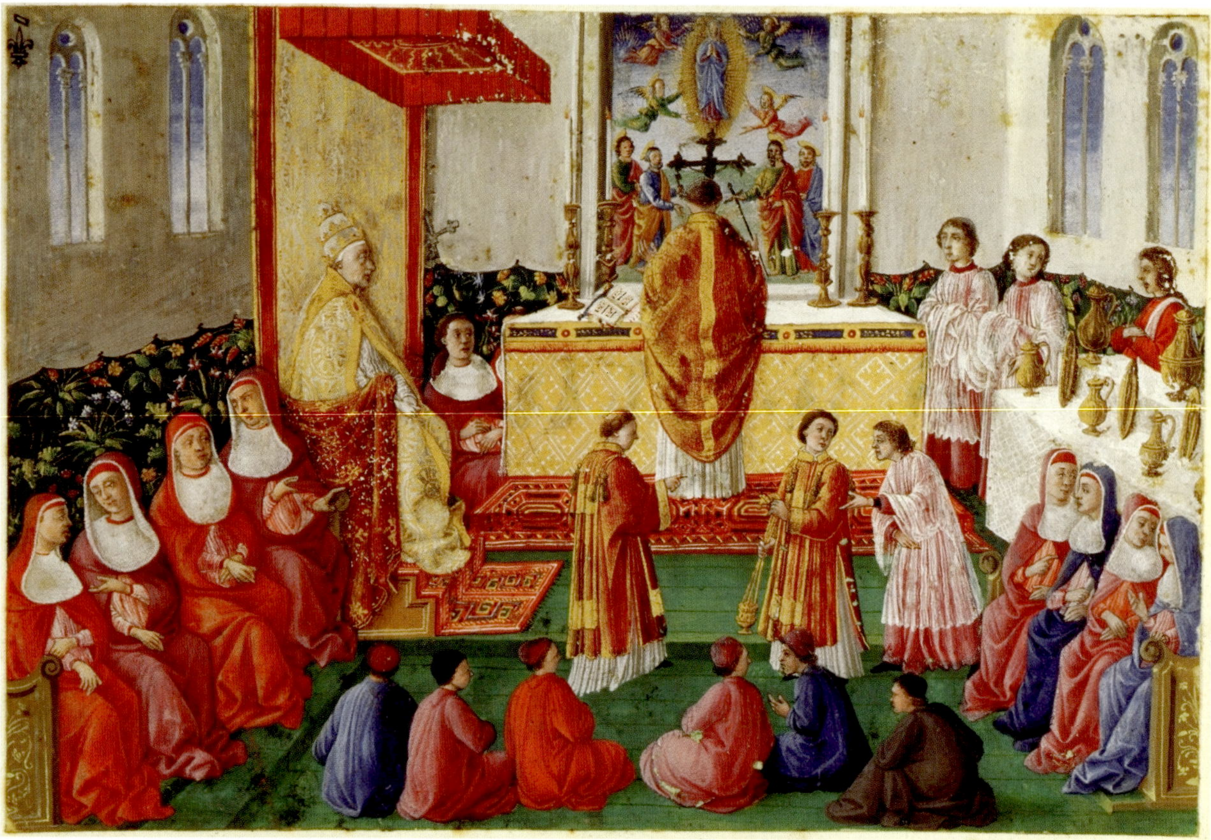

Figure 10. A Pontifical Mass, Pope Sixtus IV in the Sistine Chapel: Miniature from an Italian manuscript. Tempera and gold on parchment. Italy, 15th century. Musée Condé, Chantilly, France.

Photo: Réunion des Musées Nationaux / Art Resource, New York

Nevertheless, the medieval church would have impressed the churchgoer through the ceremony, the chants, the smell of incense, and the visual edification of art and liturgical objects.

In this way, it may be seen that liturgical practice of the medieval church required basic sacral objects, such as the chalice and paten, the missal and Gospel Book, vestments for the priest and other ministers, and copious other objects for the elaboration of the rite. As individual churches accumulated these objects, they became the foundation of church treasuries. Needless to say, churches, monasteries, and cathedrals of great wealth or with great benefactors assembled the most elaborate and costly treasuries. The greatest of these is, of course, the administrative and spiritual center of the Roman Church, the Vatican in Rome *(fig. 10)*.

CHAPTER THREE

Artistic Metalwork for the Altar

The variety of liturgical objects that were produced during the Middle Ages seems almost endless. Of those that have survived the ravages of time, we cannot help but marvel at the quality of these objects and the great skill with which they were wrought. It is apparent that the church was the greatest patron of art and artists throughout the period. The fact that ecclesiastical objects, such as monstrances, crosses, and reliquaries, were secured in church treasuries throughout the Middle Ages and after accounts for the survival of so many of these objects today. Secular objects, particularly those made of precious metals, frequently were melted down when fashions changed or when their owners needed revenue. Ecclesiastical objects in the church treasury remained functional and were less susceptible to the whims of fashion.

The great metalworking centers of Europe during the Romanesque and early Gothic periods included the Meuse Valley (the area of today's Belgium), Lower Saxony in north Germany, and the Rhine Valley. These regions distinguished themselves in the sacral arts because of the availability of the raw materials needed for the production of copper, bronze, silver, and gold, as well as the smelting technology. Also, increasing prosperity and stability in these areas, along with the presence of numerous wealthy abbeys seeking to stock or replenish their liturgical treasures, stimulated the metalworking crafts.

Beyond the Germanic territories, central and northern France and Spain provided additional important production centers. The twelfth and thirteenth centuries in particular saw the construction of new churches, including monastic or convent churches and cathedrals in large urban centers. Prosperity and the expansion of religious pilgrimage were possible factors in the demand for new church buildings. However, the result was that church construction across Europe stimulated the need for liturgical objects.

Most sacral objects in the Middle Ages were embellished in some fashion through a variety of metalworking techniques. These might include simple engraving, repoussé, filigree decoration, and the application of gemstones. Only in the most austere or impoverished situations were plain liturgical objects preferred. The reformed Cistercians, for example, elected to use unadorned liturgical vessels within an unadorned sacred space. Wealthy foundations, however, always opted for lavishly decorated chalices and patens, processional crosses, crosiers, and other objects.

The most common metalworking technique was enameling. Enamel is a vitreous material that is applied to a metal support in a powdered form. The ingredients of glass, flint or sand, and metallic colorants were prepared in advance to create this powdered enamel flux. The powder was held in place with recessions gouged into the metal surface and fused at high temperature in the kiln (about 800° C).[1] The use of enamels to

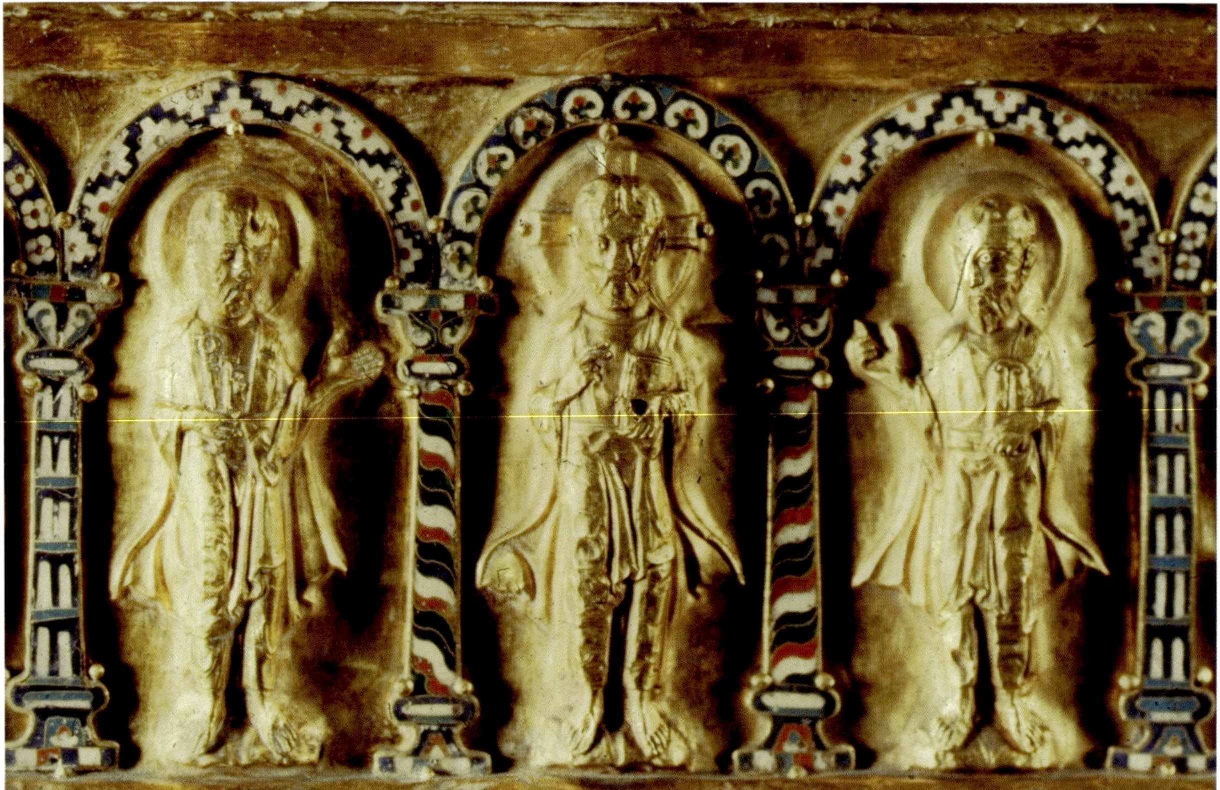

Figure 11. Portable Altar of Countess Gertrude (detail). Gold, gemstones, and cloisonné enamel. Hildesheim, Germany, ca. 1045. The Cleveland Museum of Art, Gift of the John Huntington Art and Polytechnic Trust, Acc. 1931.462.

embellish liturgical objects significantly extended the expressive range of artists, enabling them to create chromatic images on the metal's surface.

Though numerous enameling techniques were exploited by European artists during the Middle Ages, only the methods of cloisonné and champlevé were significant with respect to liturgical objects in the treasury. The earliest enameling technique, cloisonné, involved bending thin metal bands to form a design and then soldering them onto a metal object *(fig. 11)*. The resulting cells were then filled with powdered enamel of various colors, and the piece was fired. Because of the delicacy of this technique, it was most suitable on precious metals like silver and gold. Cloisonné enameling in Western Europe was profoundly influenced by the superior products of the Byzantine East during the tenth and eleventh centuries *(fig. 12)*. This was probably the result of the growing patronage of the court and the church in the Empire.

The great German centers of Mainz, Regensberg, Cologne, and Essen were among the most noteworthy producers of fine cloisonné objects found in the medieval ecclesiastical treasuries. This work readily lent itself to such objects as processional crosses, reliquaries, portable altars, and book covers. During the second half of the eleventh century, cloisonné enamel in Western Europe gradually declined. This was probably the result of the expense of working in this technique and the scarcity of gold needed for its production.

Another enameling technique, champlevé *(fig. 13)*, gradually replaced the more costly cloisonné. Champlevé enameling reached its peak in the twelfth and thirteenth centuries and used base metal, usually copper, as its

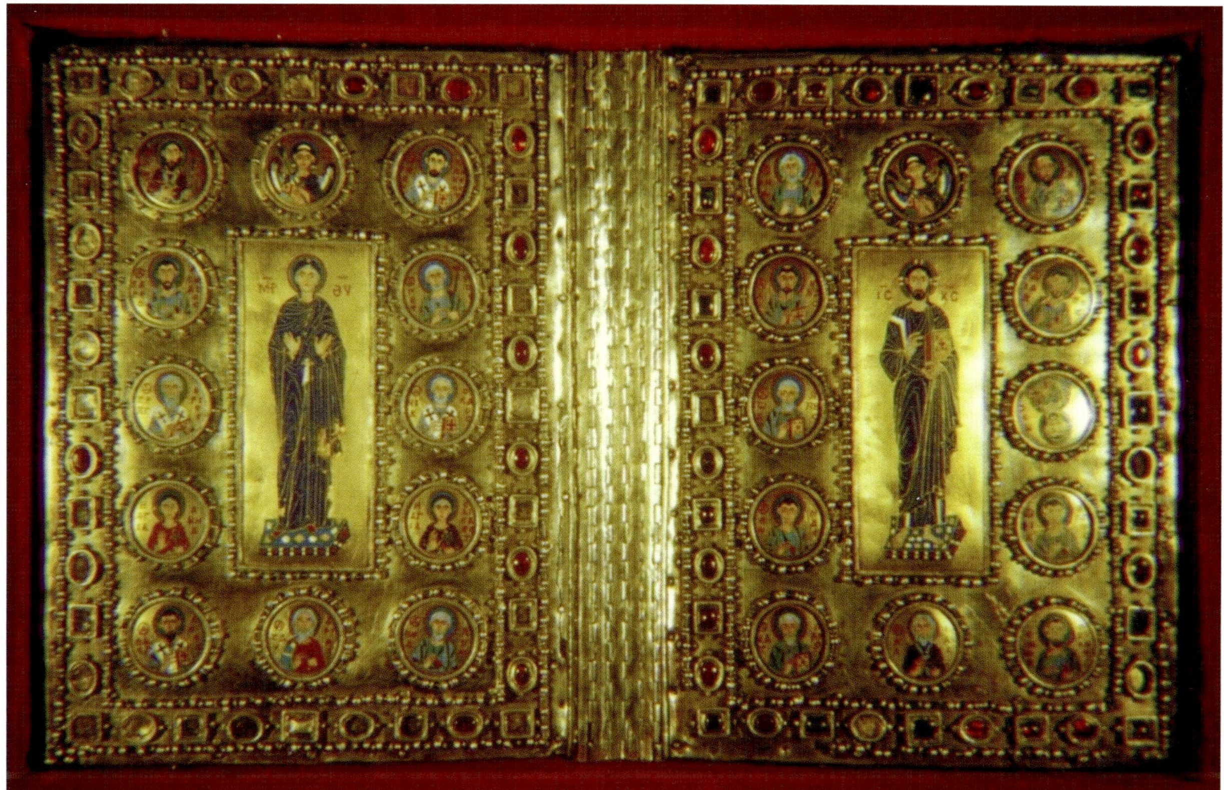

Figure 12. **Book Cover with Christ and the Virgin Orans.** Gilt-silver over wood with cloisonné enamel, gemstones, and pearls. Byzantium, 10th to early 11th century. Biblioteca Marciana, Venice, ms. Lat. Cl. I, 100.

support. Because champlevé was less expensive than cloisonné, it became widely preferred. In this method, the design was chiseled out into the copper plate using a gravure. As with cloisonné, the resulting depressions were then filled with powdered enamel and fired. The act of cutting the design left thin ridges of metal standing between the cells. Thus a skilled artist of great surety could create subtle and highly involved designs. The process, however, also required metal of a certain thickness to be successful and was therefore used on base metals like copper and bronze, whose relative cheapness allowed for the fabrication of much larger objects. The jewel-like colors and rich golden surfaces of these objects belied their fabrication from base metal.

Champlevé enameling was largely developed in the monastic institutions of the Meuse Valley *(fig. 14)*. Other important centers rapidly emerged at Hildesheim in Lower Saxony and especially in the Limousin region of France. By the 1160s the champlevé enamels produced at Limoges were the hallmark of the region and were highly prized by important ecclesiastical patrons *(figs. 13, 15)*. Appealing liturgical and devotional objects were to be found not only in Limousin and the neighboring region of Auvergne but also in Paris, in monasteries along the pilgrimage routes leading to Santiago de Compostela, at the Vatican, and as far away as the cathedrals of Scandinavia.

In examining the functionality of metallic liturgical objects in the medieval treasury, we should first consider those objects made for use on or near the altar. These include the chalice and paten, ciboria, pyxes, Eucharistic doves, altar crosses, and cruets—that is, objects used in the celebration of

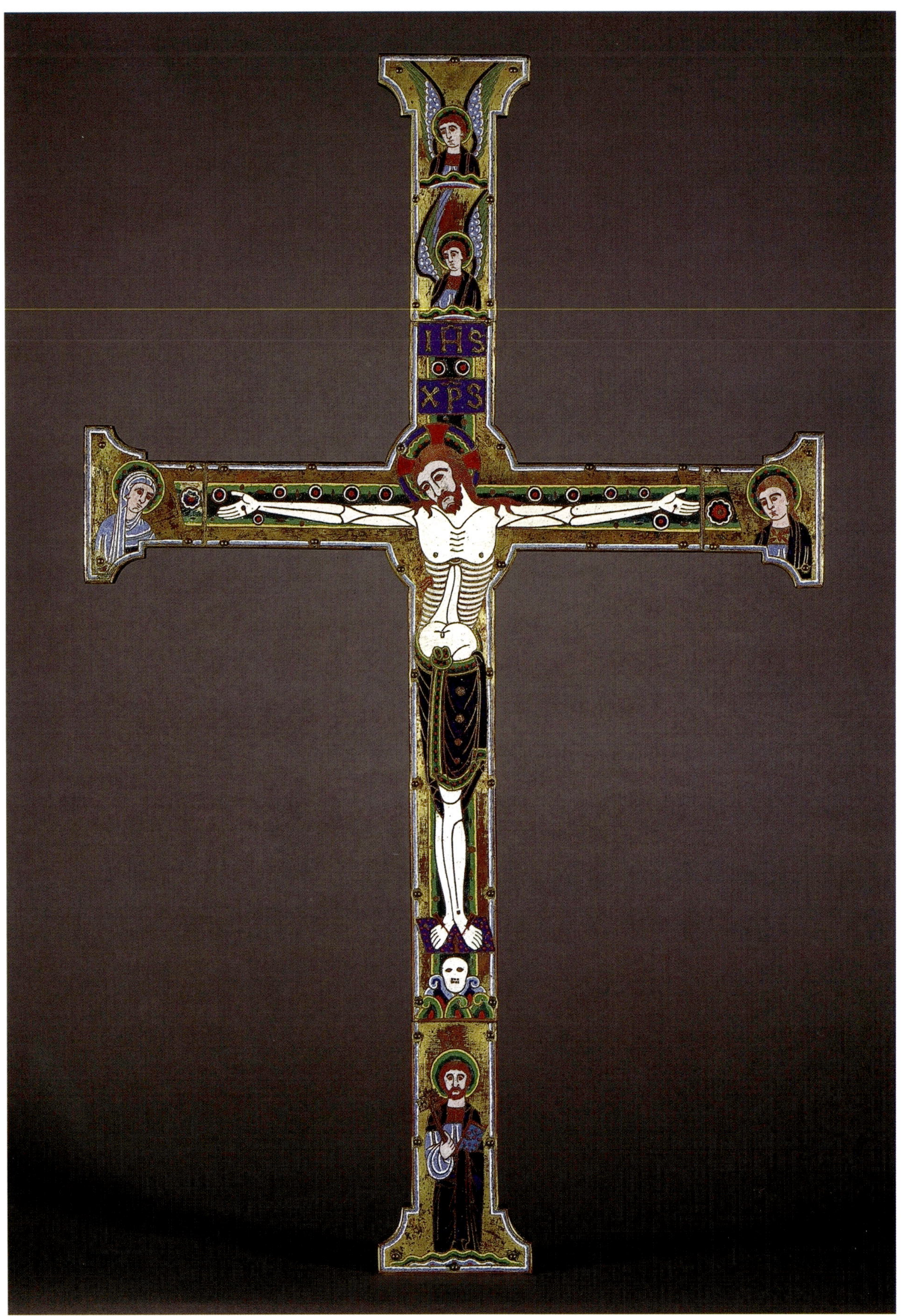
IHS
XPS

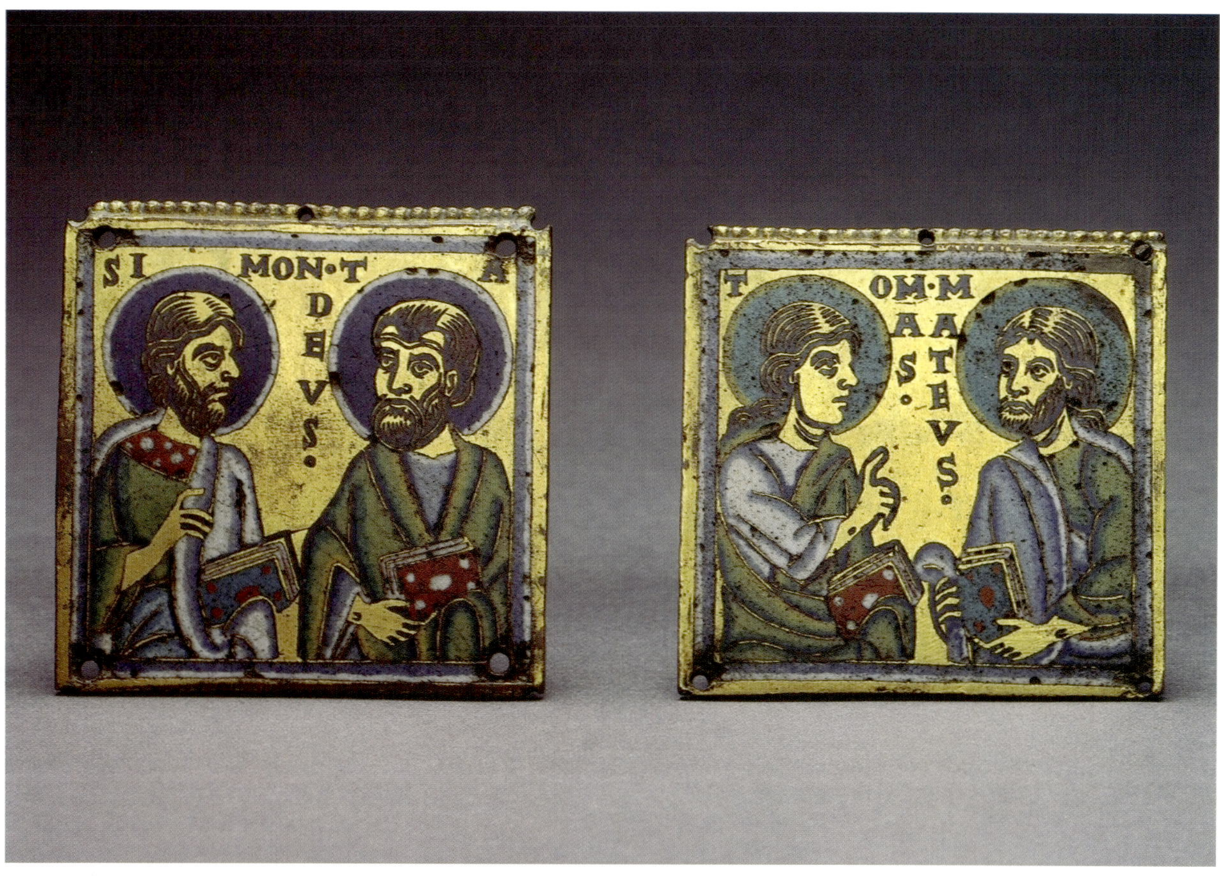

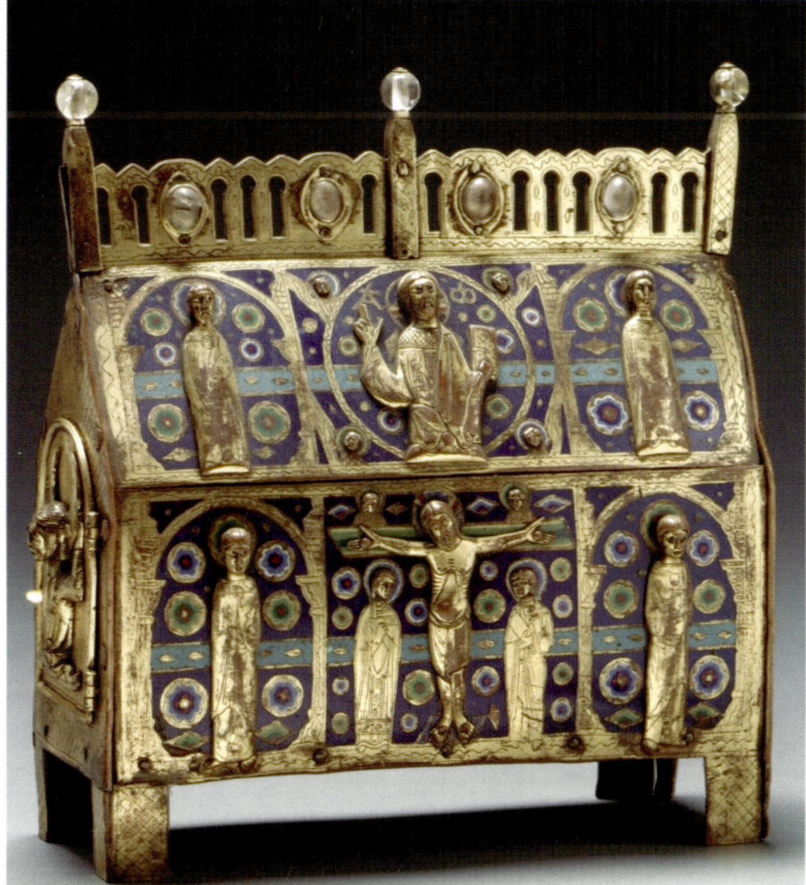

Figure 13 (facing page). Processional Cross. Champlevé enamel and gilding on copper. Master of the Royal Plantagenet Workshop. Limoges, France, ca. 1190. The Cleveland Museum of Art, Gift from J. H. Wade, Acc. 1923.1051.

Figure 14 (above). Two Plaques. From **Reliquary Châsse: Matthew and Thomas.** Champlevé enamel and gilding on copper. Meuse Valley, Belgium, ca. 1160. The Cleveland Museum of Art, Purchase from the J. H. Wade Fund, Acc. 1952.462–463.

Figure 15 (left). Châsse. Champlevé enamel and gilding on copper. Limoges, France, 13th century. The Cleveland Museum of Art, Gift of S. Livingston Mather, Constance Mather Bishop, Philip R. Mather, Katherine Hoyt Cross, and Katherine Mather McLean in accordance with the wishes of Samuel Mather, Acc. 1940.347.

the Mass or for the containment of the reserved sacrament. To these we might also include candlesticks and oil lamps, which were placed both on the altar and around it.[2]

The chalice, the cup used for the Eucharistic wine during the Mass, was the most important vessel used by the church and had profound influence on the developments of the goldsmiths' craft over the centuries. The consistent demand for chalices was the mainstay of many goldsmiths, continuously challenging their skills in design and technique. Also, many secular vessels were based on the shape of the chalice. Not all early chalices were made of precious metals, however. Early Christian examples found in the catacombs of Rome and elsewhere appear to have been simple, stemless bowls with handles on either side. There is some evidence that many of these early chalices were fashioned from glass. Even baser materials, such as ivory, wood, and earthenware, seem to have been used. Yet the predilection to use gold and silver emerged early in the church's history. Saint Augustine mentions two golden and six silver chalices at Cirta in Africa. Similarly, John Chrysostom speaks of a golden chalice set with gems.[3]

Few of these early chalices have survived, and our knowledge of them is derived from their representation in art, chiefly in mosaics, frescoes, and carved sarcophagi. From these sources we may adduce the shape of early chalices—essentially stemless bowls on a foot with two handles. By the sixth century, examples appear that more or less constitute the form of the chalice through the present day *(fig. 16)*. These vessels essentially include a bowl, a stem, a knop, and a foot. Medieval examples were usually made of precious metals, such as silver or silver-gilt, and elaborately decorated with gems, enamels, and incised or embossed designs.

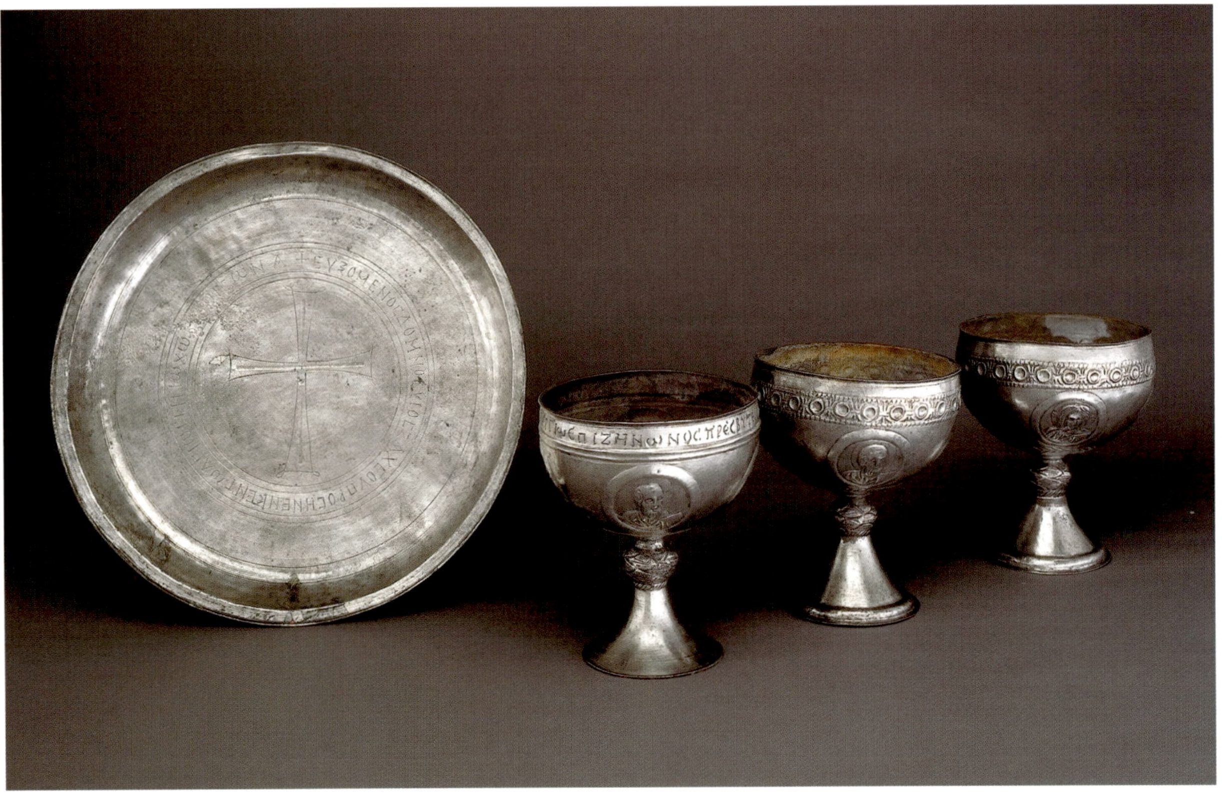

Figure 16. Paten and Three Chalices. From **The Beth Misona Treasure.** Silver. Syria, 6th to 7th centuries. The Cleveland Museum of Art, Purchase from the J. H. Wade Fund, Acc. 1950.378–381.

Such beautifully wrought chalices survive in many museums as major masterpieces of goldsmiths' art. Among these are the ninth-century Ardagh Chalice *(fig. 17)*, a spectacular example of Irish (Hiberno-Saxon) art, and the Wilten Chalice of about 1160–70 *(fig. 18)*. The latter example was presented to the Abbey of Wilten in Tirol by Count Berthold III of Andechs. It is made of silver with partial gilding and niello decoration, a

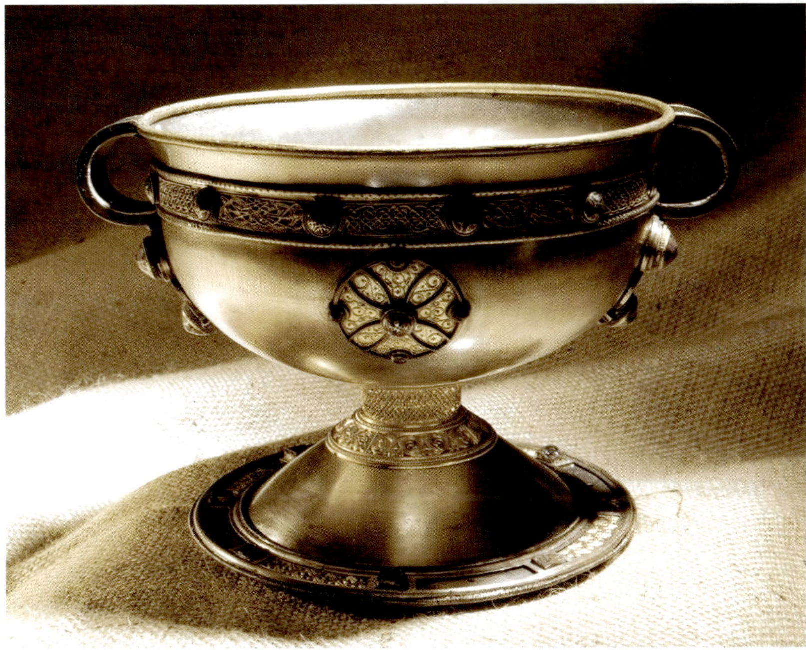

Figure 17. Ardagh Chalice. Silver, gilt-silver, bronze, and enamel. Ireland (Celtic), 9th century. National Museum of Ireland, Dublin.

Photo: Erich Lessing/Art Resource, New York

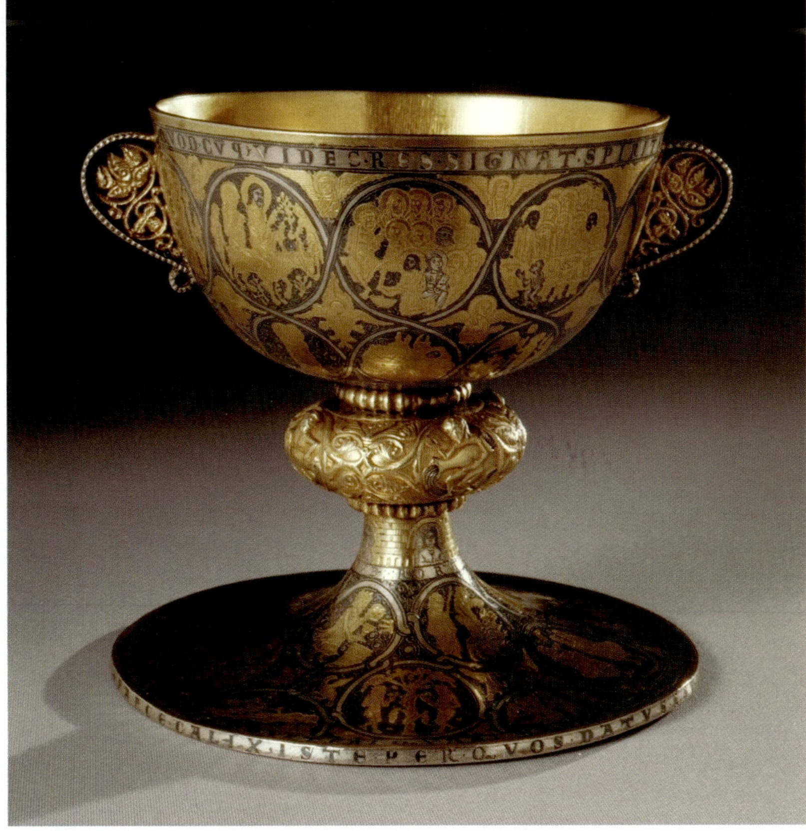

Figure 18. Wilten Chalice. Silver, partially gilt with niello. Lower Saxony, Germany, ca. 1160–70. Kunsthistorisches Museum, Vienna, Inv. KK 8924.

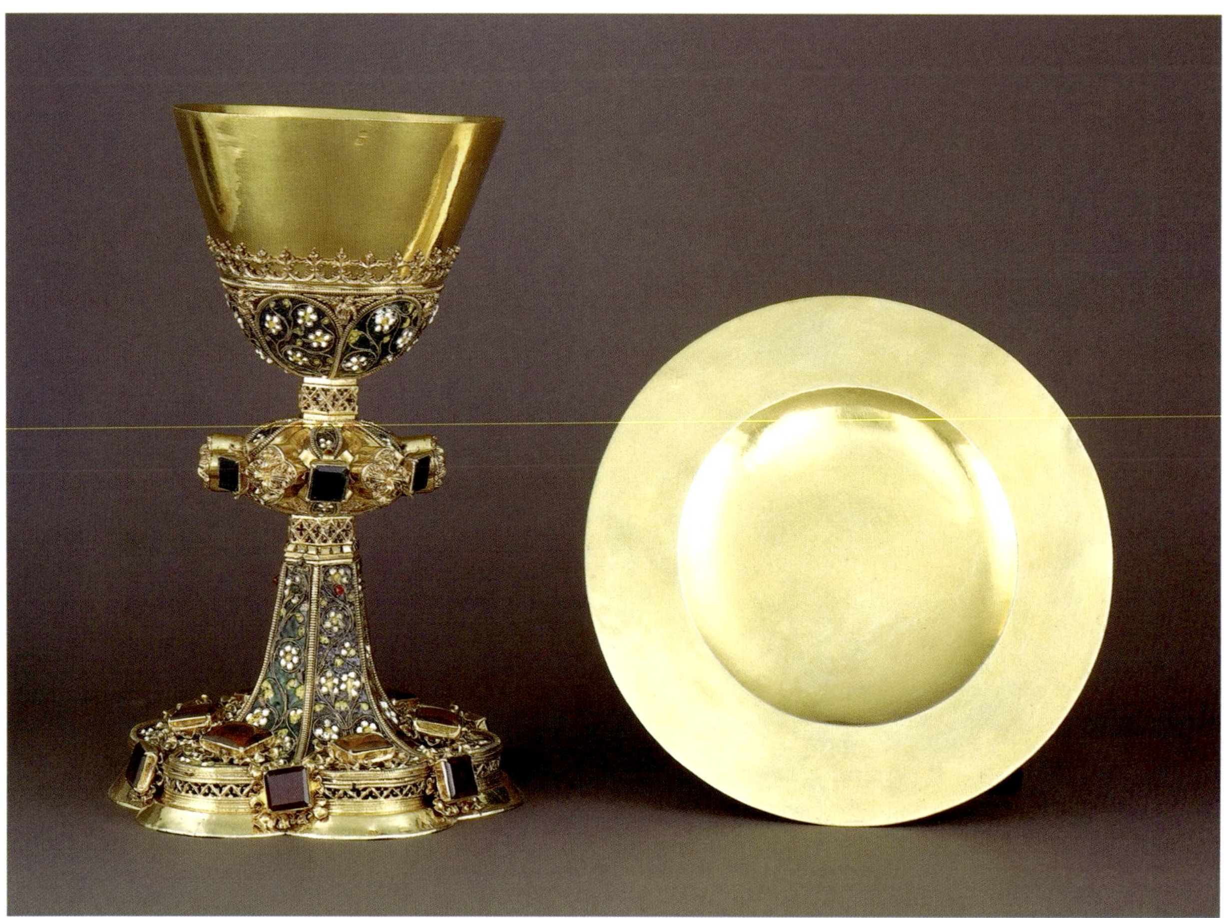

Fig. 19. **Chalice and Paten.** Gilt-silver and filigree enamel. Budapest(?), Hungary, second half of 15th century. The Cleveland Museum of Art, John L. Severance Fund, Acc. 1990.3–4.

true masterpiece of the Romanesque goldsmiths' art. These are examples of calices ministeriales, or ministerial chalices. Distinct from the sacrificial chalices used by bishops and priests in the Mass, ministerial chalices had larger bowls and broad, low, circular forms, providing a more secure means of administering communion to the faithful.

During the early Middle Ages, the laity received communion in the form of both bread and wine. There were certain practical difficulties for priests in offering communion under the species of wine. The large bowls and handles helped to some degree. However, during the Carolingian period, priests used a fistula, a tube, usually metal, through which the communicant took the Eucharistic wine. This practice was abandoned following the Cistercian reforms of the late twelfth century.[4]

Chalices used by parish priests and monks for private Masses were likely simpler in character. In the eighth and ninth centuries, various synodal decrees, particularly in England, began to require that the chalice and paten be made of "molten material." The Corpus Juris, probably the most famous decree on the subject, required "that the chalice of the Lord, together with the paten, if not gold, must be entirely made of silver. If, however, anyone is so poor, let him at least have a chalice of pewter. The chalice must not be made of brass or copper, because it generates rust, which causes nausea. And let no one presume to say Mass with a chalice of wood or glass."[5]

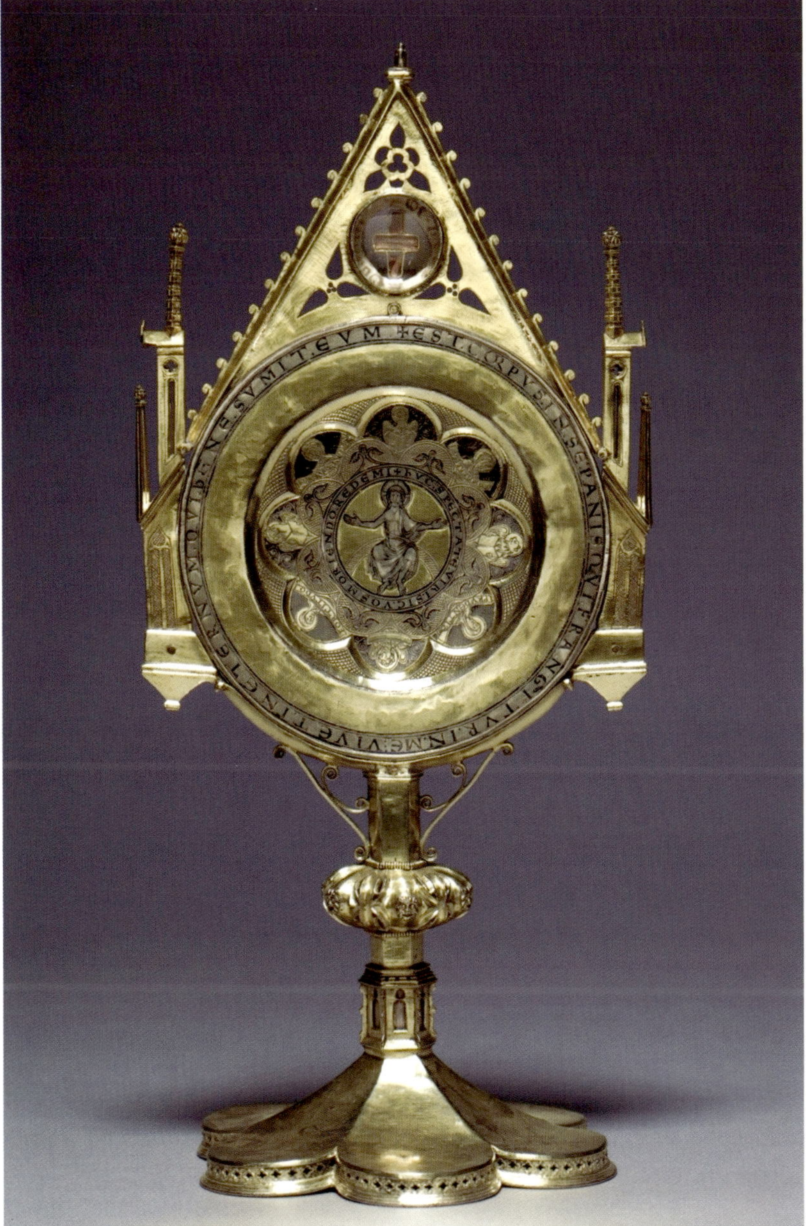

Figure 20. **Monstrance with the Paten of Saint Bernward (from the Guelph Treasure).** Gilt-silver, rock crystal, niello, with relics wrapped in silk. Paten: Hildesheim(?), Germany, ca. 1185; Monstrance: Braunschweig, Germany, late 14th century. The Cleveland Museum of Art, Purchase from the J. H. Wade Fund with additional gift from Mrs. R. Henry Norweb, Acc. 1930.505.

Such legislation was clearly motivated by an interest in encouraging a suitable reverence for the Mass and the Sacrament. It is easy to see how such requirements in the Middle Ages would encourage the opulence of materials and ornamentation that many chalices achieved. As such, they became important objects in the medieval treasury. To some degree, these strictures still survive. Current church law requires that the modern chalice used by the priest, or at least the cup of it, be made of either gold or silver. If silver, then the interior of the bowl must be gilt.[6] All chalices and patens, during the Middle Ages as now, had to be consecrated by a bishop—an ancient rite involving the use of holy chrism.

By the thirteenth century, the giving of Communion to the laity under both species, bread and wine, became more restrictive, and the chalice was gradually withheld from the laity. It was therefore necessary that the chalice only be large enough to serve the priest. One significant change that occurred to the shape of the chalice after 1300 was the gradually diminished size of its bowl. It also became taller and slimmer with a more conical bowl. Late gothic chalices also gradually developed angular or faceted knops, generally hexagonal, with lobed feet.

A splendid example of the fully developed gothic chalice is preserved today in the Cleveland Museum of Art *(fig. 19)*. Made in Hungary during the second half of the fifteenth century, this chalice survives with its original paten. It is a sublime example of decoration with filigree enamel. Twisted gold wire forms a floral design that is filled with colorful glass pastes. Gemstones are added for further ostentation.

The paten is the Eucharistic vessel that accompanies the chalice. From the later Middle Ages onward, chalices and patens were made together en suite, that is, as a set. Since they were fabricated by the same goldsmith, they tended to be similar in material, ornamentation, and style *(see fig. 19 for example)*. The paten was essentially the small plate on which the Eucharistic bread was offered to God at the Offertory of the Mass. The consecrated Host is again placed on the paten for the Communion. Until about the ninth century, patens tended to be large, flat plates made of various materials, often glass, that served to collect the faithful's offerings of bread. After the priest had broken the Eucharistic bread, he distributed the consecrated fragments to the faithful on the paten (patenae ministeriales).

Like the chalice, the paten underwent changes, particularly during the thirteenth century and later. It shrank in size, largely because the Host became smaller. Small wafers made by monks or nuns gradually replaced large loaves of bread donated by the laity. At this time, the chalice and paten were made as a matched set, sometimes with a leather carrying case. The paten fitted neatly over the bowl of the chalice so that one person could carry both securely. This became necessary since priests were now celebrating an increasing number of masses without a congregation and without assisting clergy.

It was commonplace during the early centuries of Christianity to inscribe the donor's name on costly vessels presented to churches. The so-called Beth Misona Treasure in the Cleveland Museum of Art includes a set of three chalices and a large paten made in Syria during the sixth or early seventh century *(fig. 16)*. The silver paten is almost thirteen inches in diameter and was large enough to hold a circular loaf of bread. One of the chalices is inscribed in Greek around the rim and reads, "The Priest Kyriakos, son of Domnos, [gave this chalice] to Saint Sergios, in the time of Zeno the priest." Similarly, the paten is inscribed: "Having vowed, Domnos, Son of Zacheos, has offered [this paten] to Saint Sergios of the Village of Beth Misona."[7]

A Sienese chalice now in the Victoria and Albert Museum in London bears a Latin inscription that translates as "Brother Iachomo Mondusi of Siena made me." Brother Mondusi was probably the patron who commissioned the chalice, not the craftsman who made it.[8] Some chalices or patens became associated with revered saints who were also skilled craftsmen. The Chalice of Chelles, for example, was preserved until the French

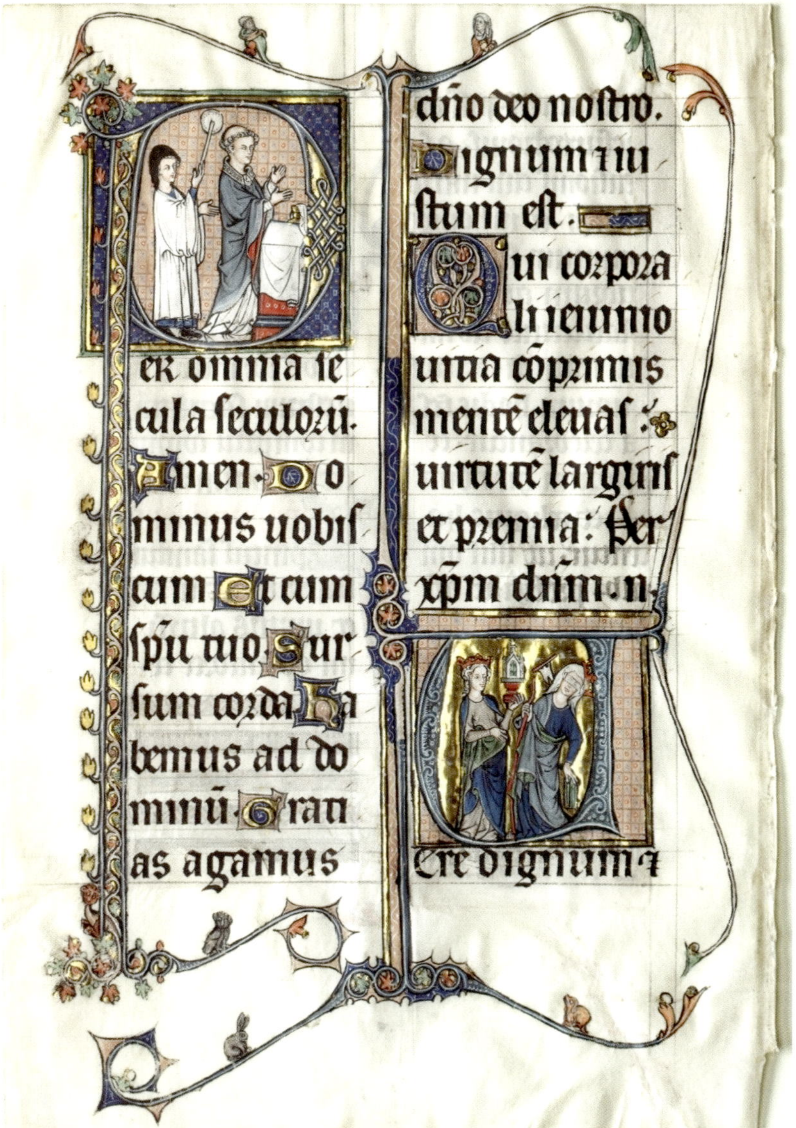

Figure 21. **Leaf.** From **A Missal with Two Historiated Initials**. Tempera and gold on parchment. Beauvais, France, ca. 1300. The Cleveland Museum of Art, Gift of Mr. and Mrs. Milton Freudenheim in memory of Otto Ege, Acc. 1982.141. The upper initial "P" shows an acolyte holding a flabellum.

Revolution in the belief that it was made by Saint Eligius of Noyon, patron saint of goldsmiths, who died in 659. The Paten of Saint Bernward, made in Hildesheim around 1185, was mounted in a monstrance during the fourteenth century as a holy relic *(fig. 20)*. Bernward, the Bishop of Hildesheim who died in 1022, was commonly regarded as having been a goldsmith, a metalworker, and a renowned patron of the arts. It was believed that he made his own paten, though this is unlikely as the paten's decoration dates to the century after his death. Nevertheless, the paten was venerated as a saintly memento and became part of the celebrated Guelph Treasure, now dispersed.[9]

Elaborate liturgical fans known as flabella were used during the Middle Ages to keep flies and other insects away from the sacred species during the Mass. The flabellum consisted of a large round fan made of leather, silk, parchment, or feathers with a handle of wood or ivory *(fig. 21)*. The Apostolic Constitutions read, "Let two of the deacons, on each side of the

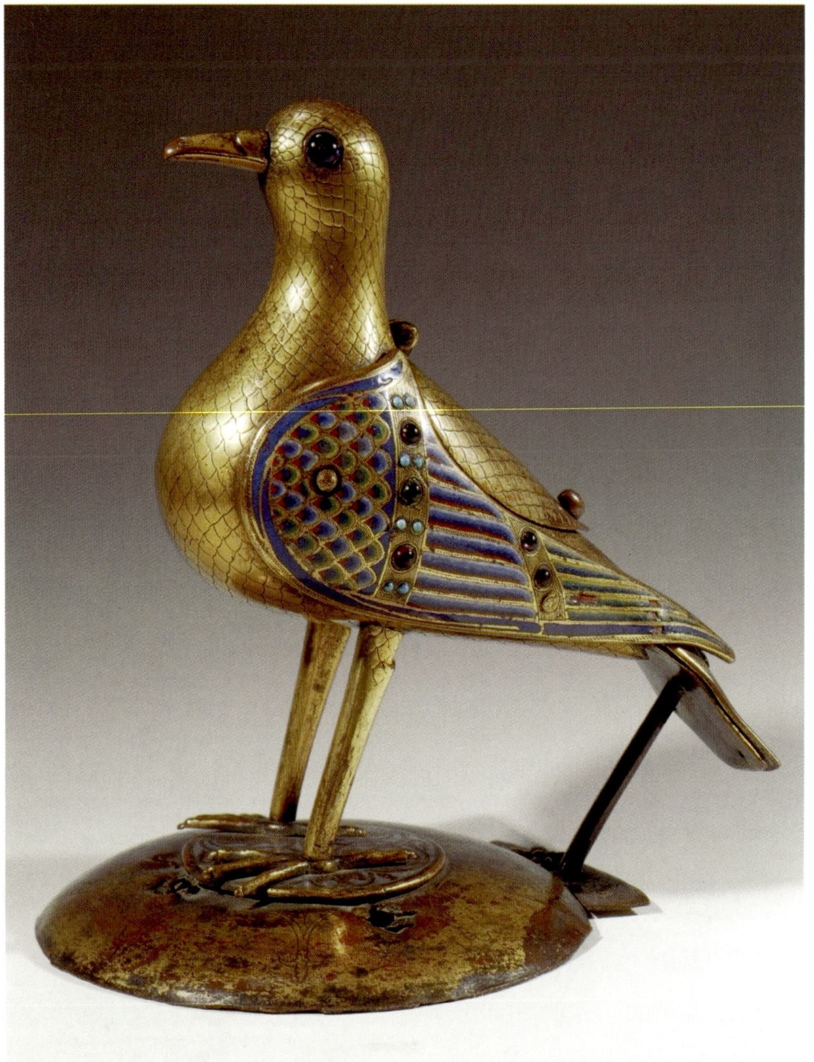

Figure 22. Eucharistic Dove. Champlevé enamel and gilding on copper. Limoges, France, ca. 1200–1225. Cathedral and Museum, Salzburg.

Photo: Erich Lessing/Art Resource, New York

altar, hold a fan, made up of thin membranes, or of the feathers *[fig. 33, upper register]* of the peacock or of fine cloth, and let them silently drive away the small animals that fly about, that they may not come near the cups."[10] Elaborate examples in silver are known from the inventory evidence, and a few of these have survived. The most elaborate is a flabellum of the thirteenth century made for the Abbey of Kremsmümster in Upper Austria. Flabella were common in medieval treasuries, though they were used only symbolically in recent times when the pope was carried in state. The symbolic use of flabella was discontinued during the pontificate of John XXIII (1958–63).

The unused, or reserved, consecrated hosts required special vessels for their containment. Eucharistic vessels in various forms met this need during the Middle Ages. Foremost among these were the Eucharistic doves, which were made in quantity during the twelfth and thirteenth centuries. Fashioned in the form of a dove, the symbol of the Holy Ghost, these vessels were generally made of copper or brass with gilded and enameled ornamentation *(fig. 22)*.

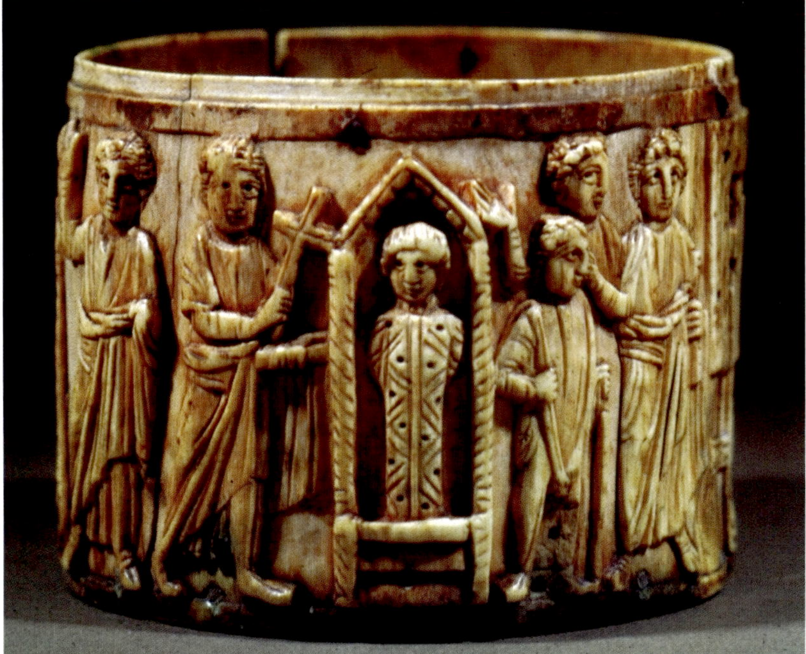

Figure 23. Pyx (missing lid). Ivory. Byzantium, 6th century. The Cleveland Museum of Art, Purchase from the J. H. Wade Fund, Acc. 1951.114, a-b.

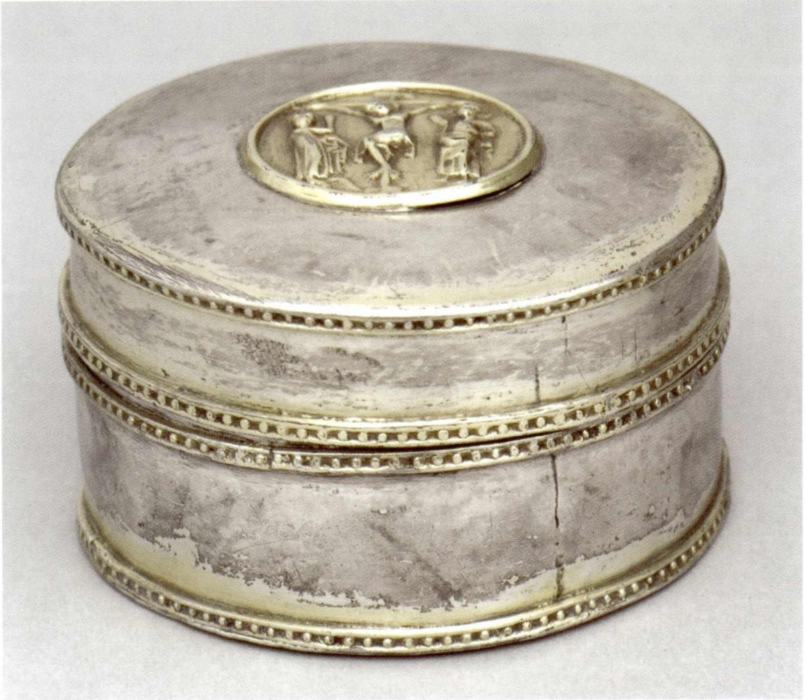

Figure 24. Pyx. Silver, gilt-silver borders, and gilt-silver medallion of Crucifixion. Salzburg(?), Austria, ca. 1300. The Cleveland Museum of Art, Gift of the John B. Putnam Foundation, Acc. 1970.125.

Doves have not been in widespread use in the West for several centuries. The use of doves in churches, though somewhat rare, still exists.[11] This is presumably because they fulfilled specific liturgical needs only for a few centuries. The principal center of their production was the French town of Limoges, which specialized in champlevé enameling. Eucharistic doves were usually suspended over an altar from the balducchino, sometimes beneath a small votive crown. The dove itself was hollow. Either a wing or the back of the dove was hinged so that the priest could open it

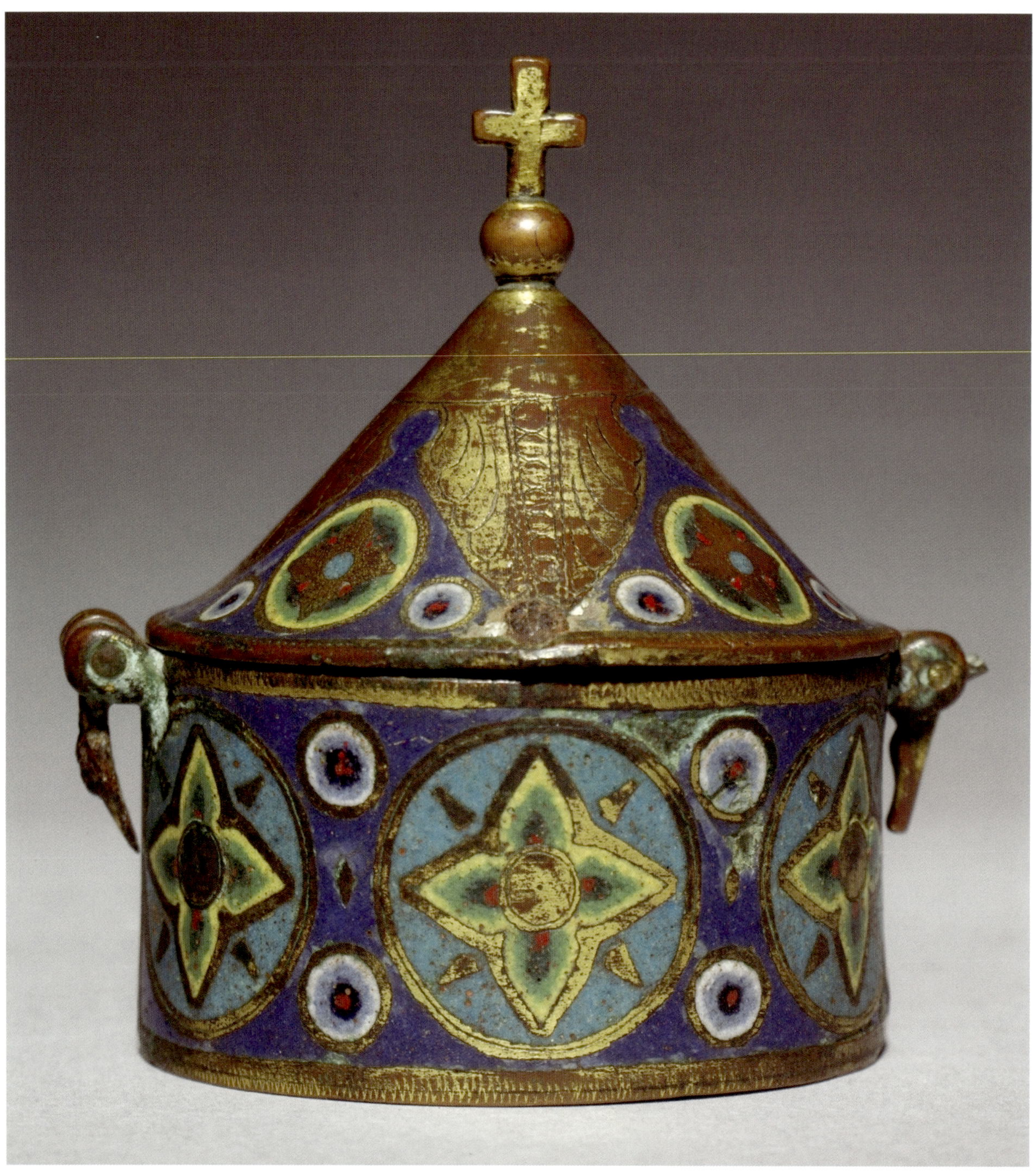

Figure 25. **Pyx.** Champlevé enamel and gilding on copper. Limoges, France, ca. 1250. The Cleveland Museum of Art, Purchase from the J. H. Wade Fund, Acc. 1952.328.

and place the consecrated Host within its interior for safekeeping. The earliest evidence of manufactured doves in the West is from the eleventh century and principally from France.[12] By the twelfth century, the practice of suspending doves above an altar had spread to Italy, England, and the Germanic countries. While inventory references indicate that Limoges was producing and exporting large numbers of enameled doves, examples in glass and various other materials are known to have existed.

The dove itself was only the outer vessel, which enshrined the pyx within. The pyx was usually a cylindrical container with a lid. After a certain number of hosts had been consecrated, they were placed within the

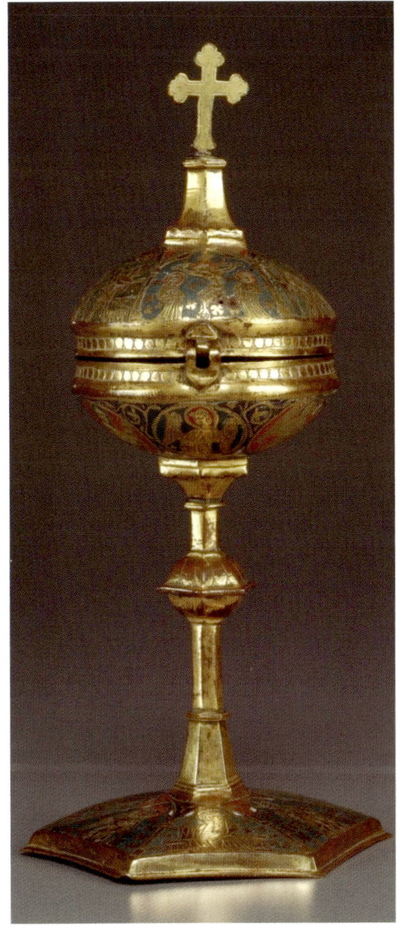

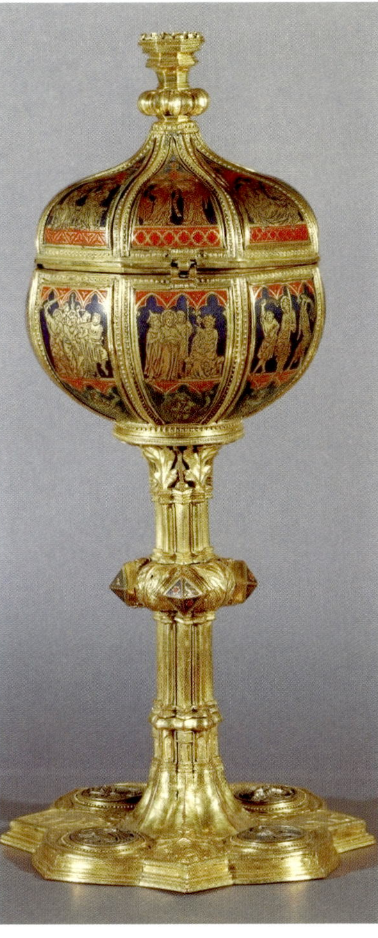

Figure 26 (left). Ciborium. Champlevé enamel and gilding on copper. Spain, 14th century. National Gallery of Art, Washington, D.C., the Widener Collection, Acc. 1942.9.279.

Figure 27 (right). Ciborium. Gilded copper and enamel. Klosterneuburg Abbey, Austria, ca. 1330. Sammlungen des Stiftes.

Photo: Erich Lessing/Art Resource, New York

pyx, which in turn was placed within the suspended dove. The eleventh-century Custumal of Cluny refers to the "deacon taking the golden pyx out of the dove which hangs permanently above the altar."[13] During the week, as hosts were needed for the services, the pyx could be removed from the dove. After removing a certain number of hosts, the pyx would then be returned. Udalric, the eleventh-century prior of the Cluniac church of Hirsau, mentions the presence of a Eucharistic dove in his church. He further reveals that sufficient hosts were consecrated at one time to serve the needs of his monastic community for a week, that the dove was never empty, and that at least two hosts were always reserved.[14]

In parish churches and cathedral chapters, where priests could celebrate Mass regularly and thereby provide the faithful with consecrated hosts as needed, doves presumably served a different function: as a storage place for reserved hosts for communing the sick and dying.[15] In the later Middle Ages, many ecclesiastics began to require that reserved hosts be kept under lock and key. Eucharistic doves gradually fell from use in favor of the locked tabernacle behind the altar. Nevertheless, some are still used in churches, a vestige of an ancient tradition. Many doves survived and are in museums as superb examples of the enameller's art.

As Eucharistic doves ceased to be used above the altar, the pyx was secured directly within the tabernacle. There is some uncertainty as to the ecclesiastical preferences for the materials from which the pyx was to

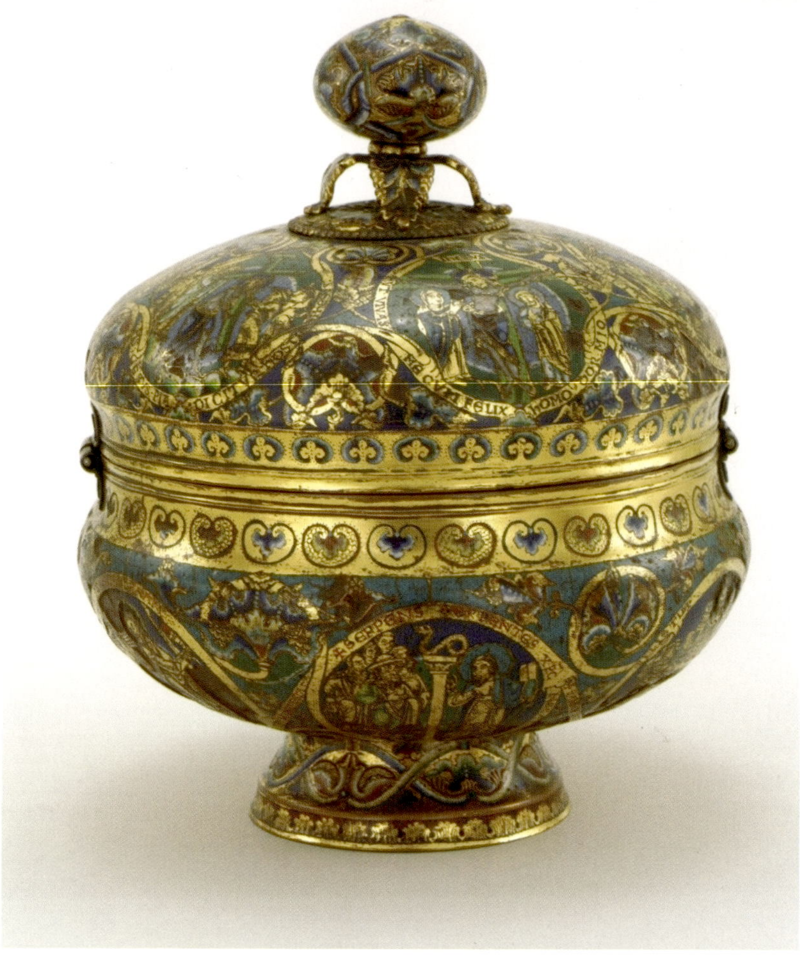

Figure 28. Footed Pyx ("The Malmsbury Ciborium"). Champlevé enamel and gilding on copper. England, ca. 1160–70. The Pierpont Morgan Library, New York.

Photo: The Pierpont Morgan Library/Art Resource, New York

be made. Early examples, particularly in the Byzantine East, were often made of ivory *(fig. 23)*. However, inventories and documents show that in the West, pyxes were made in a variety of materials, including cork, ivory, wood, onyx, tin, silver, gold, and, of course, copper, which was commonly decorated with champlevé enamels *(figs. 25, 28)*.

More recently, the reserved host is placed within the ciborium, a chalice-like vessel with a round bowl and conical cover. This receptacle contains the reserved species for distributing Holy Communion within churches. In Early Christian times, the ciborium was the canopy that surmounted the altar. Notwithstanding this ambiguity, the ciborium as a Eucharistic vessel appears to have emerged during the later Middle Ages *(figs. 26, 27)* but not before the fourteenth century. Earlier versions of this vessel are more properly referred to as a footed pyx *(fig. 28)*, and usage of the term "ciborium" corresponding to today's usage emerged only during the sixteenth century. In today's Roman Catholic Church, the pyx is exclusively the viatic pyx, which is used for carrying communion to the sick.

Other objects found in the medieval treasury that relate to the altar and the sacrifice of the Mass are the cruets, a pair of small vessels that contained the water and wine used during the ritual. Unfortunately, their destruction during the Reformation has left few medieval liturgical cruets

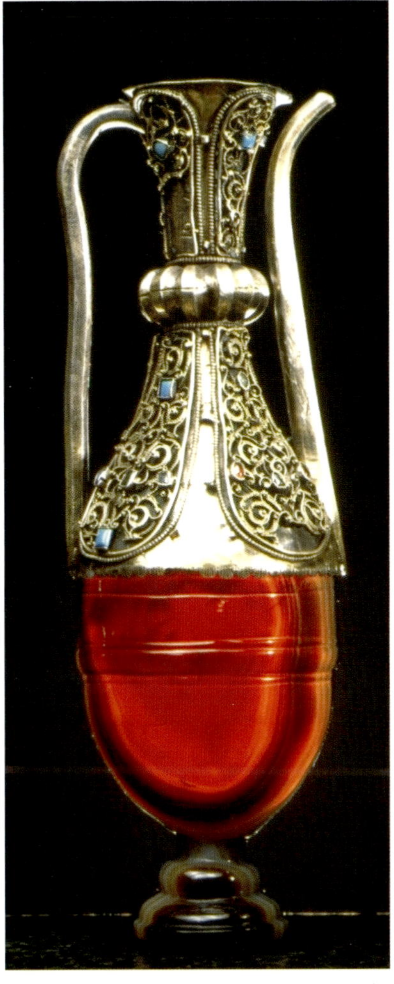

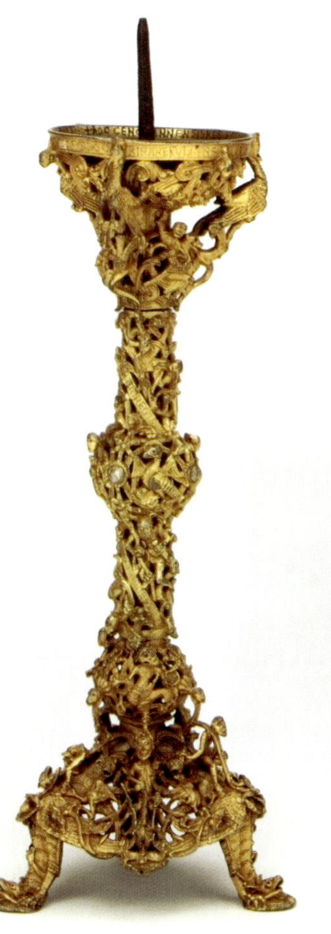

Figure 29. Cruet. Sardonyx body (3rd century) and metal mount. Venice, ca. 1250–1300. Treasury of San Marco, Venice, Inv. 81.

Figure 30. The Gloucester Candlestick. Gilded base metal. England, early 12th century. The Victoria and Albert Museum, London, Inv. 7649–1861.

Photo: Victoria and Albert Museum/Art Resource, New York

intact. Cruets were often stored in a niche in the wall to the right of the altar, as depicted in panel paintings and manuscript miniatures. Liturgical cruets resembled their secular counterparts, table ewers, used for serving wine. During the Gothic era, silver and gilt-silver were favored materials, while base metals, such as bronze and pewter, were known but less commonly used. During the early Middle Ages, glass was highly favored because its transparency prevented the celebrant from confusing the water with the wine. That problem was resolved on metal cruets by stamping each with an A for aqua or with a W for vinum.

The wealth of some medieval churches facilitated the use of exotic materials, such as carved hard stones and rock crystal. A liturgical ewer in the Treasury of San Marco in Venice features a third-century hollowed sardonyx that was fitted in the thirteenth century with a gilt-silver and filigree mount *(fig. 29)*. In the early Middle Ages, the altar cruets were not always a matched set. More frequently, the celebrant used a brass or bronze aquamanilia, or water vessel, for the ritual washing of hands. In that instance, a single, unmatched cruet was used for the wine.

Candlesticks, often made of gilded bronze, were usually placed on the altar during the Middle Ages and lighted during the celebration of the Mass. Although there is little evidence that candlesticks were used on altars before

Figure 31. Altar Cross. Gilt-bronze. Hildesheim, Lower Saxony, Germany, ca. 1175–90. The Cleveland Museum of Art, Purchase from the J. H. Wade Fund, Acc. 1944.320.

Figure 32 (facing page). Altar or Processional Cross. Gilt-copper, champlevé enamel, gemstones. Constance, Upper Rhine, Germany, ca. 1300–1310. The Cleveland Museum of Art, Purchase from the J. H. Wade Fund, Acc. 1942.1091.

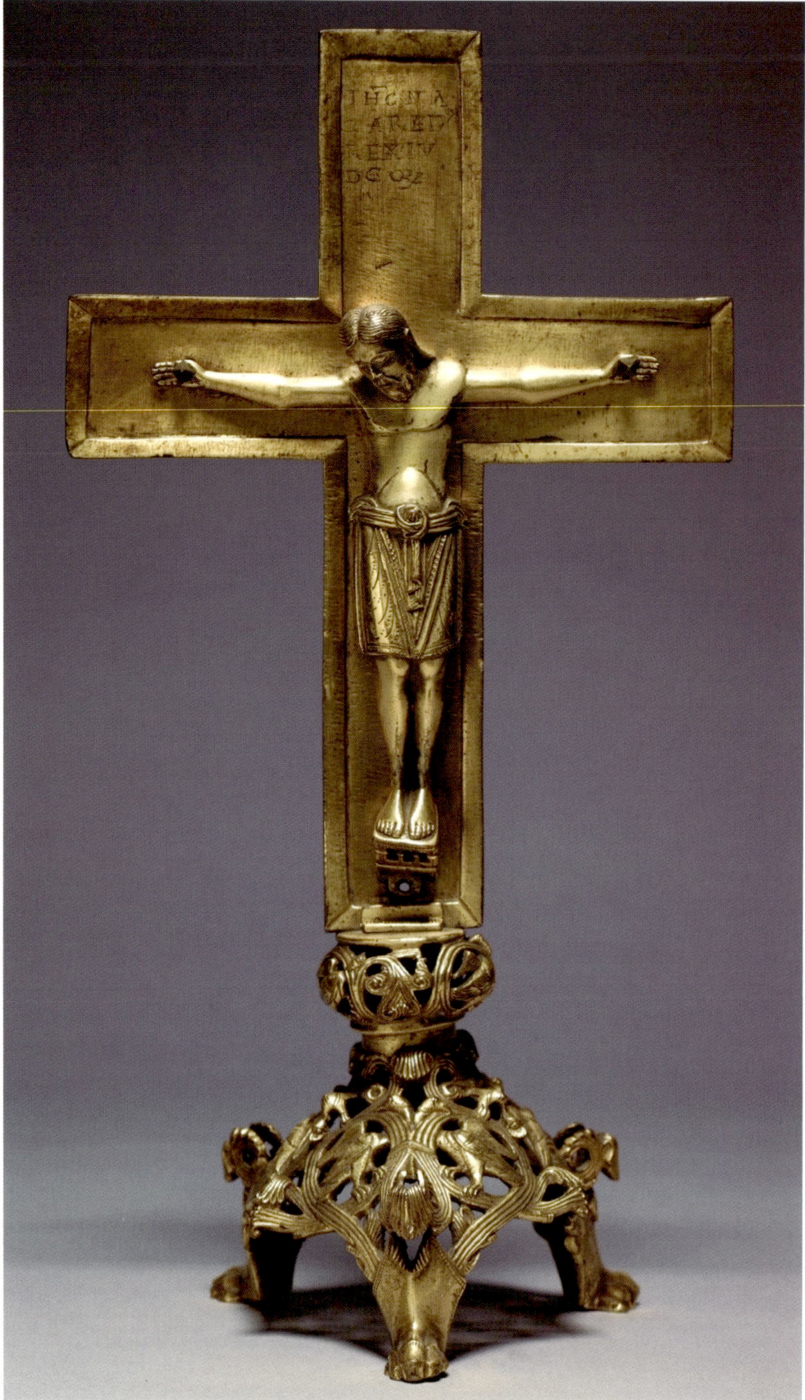

the tenth century, candles and oil lamps were used within church interiors for much-needed light. Before the tenth century, acolytes held or carried candlesticks near the altar or placed them on the floor of the sanctuary or at the corners of the altar. The placement of candlesticks or suspended oil lamps around the altar is well established prior to the tenth century. Chandeliers were also suspended above altars to provide light. After the tenth century, however, candlesticks became an important furnishing for the altar. While they were seldom made of precious materials, they became highly ornamental and should rightfully be considered part of the medieval treasury.

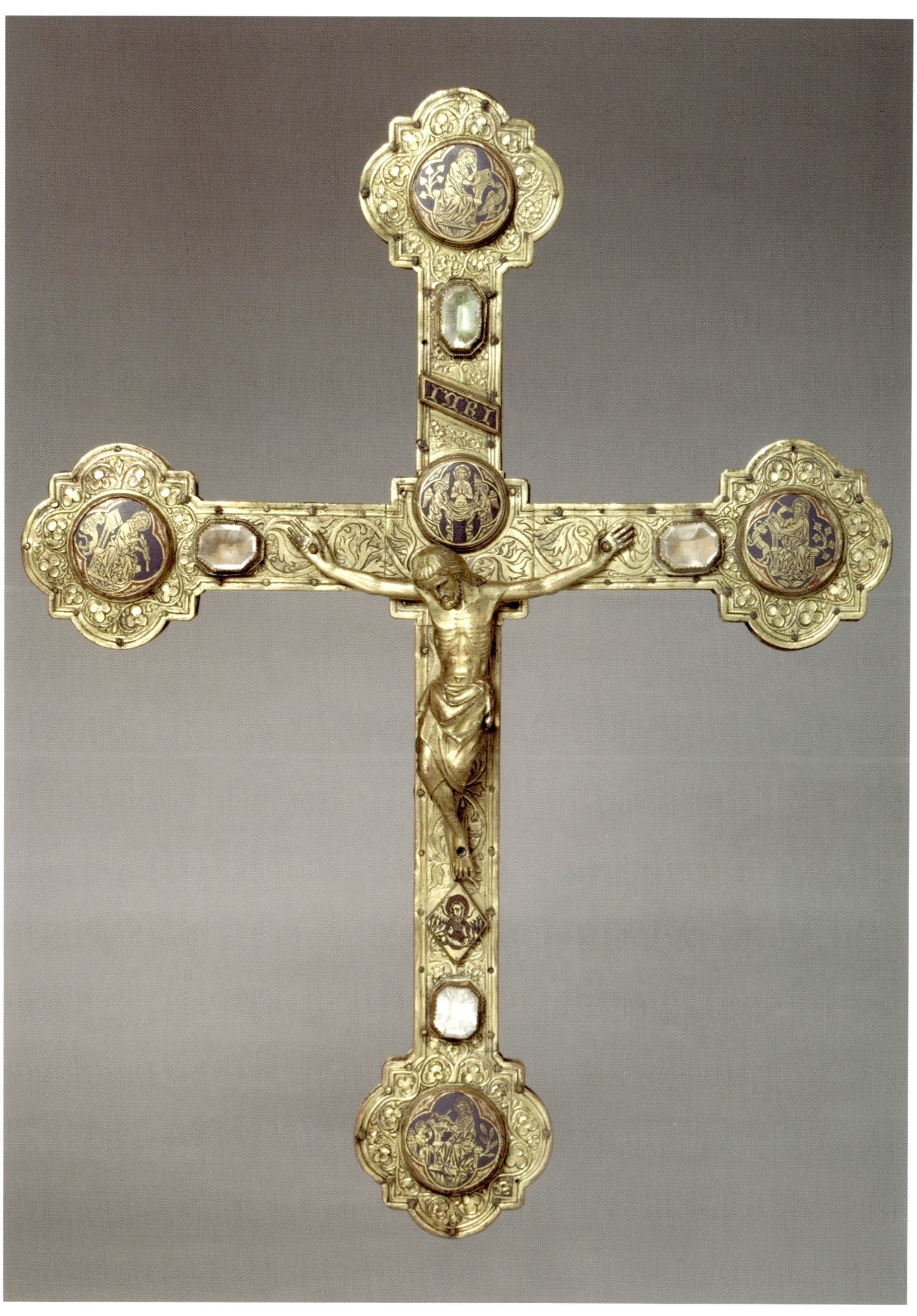
I.N.R.I.

A celebrated example from the twelfth century, the Gloucester Candlestick (now in the Victoria and Albert Museum) is one of a pair made between 1104 and 1113 for the church of Saint Peter's at Gloucester *(fig. 30)*. Its design is a profusion of inhabited vine scrolls with human and animal figures climbing through the vines toward the light of the candle. The symbolism is obvious: man, captured by the chaos of the world, strives toward the "true light." The Gloucester Candlestick is an extraordinary example of Romanesque metalworking and is among the more elaborate candlesticks to survive from the Middle Ages.

The placement of candles and candlesticks on the altar became general practice during the sixteenth century. Before that time, only two were used on the altar. Afterward four to six were used for solemn High Mass *(see fig. 10)*.

The altar furnishings during the Middle Ages also included an altar cross, although the presence of a cross on the altar cannot be traced back with certainty before the thirteenth century. While altar crosses and crucifixes (those bearing the additional corpus of Christ) are known before this time *(fig. 31)*, a mandate for their use is attributed to Innocent III, who, in his treatise on the Mass, states, "A cross is set upon the altar, in the middle between two candlesticks."[16] Before Innocent's time, crosses were placed over the ciborium and the rood loft, rendered as mosaics within the apse of the church, or suspended over the altar, a tradition that remained in Italian churches of the Renaissance. Thus, the cross in various forms historically had a presence above or near the altar—a visible symbol of Christ's sacrifice repeated on the altar during the Mass *(see figs. 1, 10)*.

With the prevalence of altar crosses in Western churches during the later Middle Ages, they became objects of extraordinary artistic conception and precious materials. Historically, altar crosses were cast in bronze and then gilded, rendered in champlevé enamel, or, when a church or cathedral chapter could afford, altar crosses were commissioned in silver or silver-gilt. These often included the additional embellishment of applied gemstones, filigree, and cloisonné enamels *(fig. 32)*. Many such crosses have survived from the Middle Ages and were often the most prized possessions of ecclesiastical treasuries.

CHAPTER FOUR

Objects for Procession and the Vesting of the Priest

A modern observer transported back to the Middle Ages would notice the frequent, rhythmic, almost continuous peal of bells. This is the one sound, above all others, that pierced the relative silence of their world and, on certain occasions, elicited deep emotions. Bells gave structure to medieval life. Small villages had a parish church, which would have had a small bell tower to summon the faithful to mass, and grander cities had cathedrals and convents *(fig. 33)*. All of these sounded their bells to announce feast days or major events, such as the birth or death of royalty, or disasters, such as floods and pestilence.

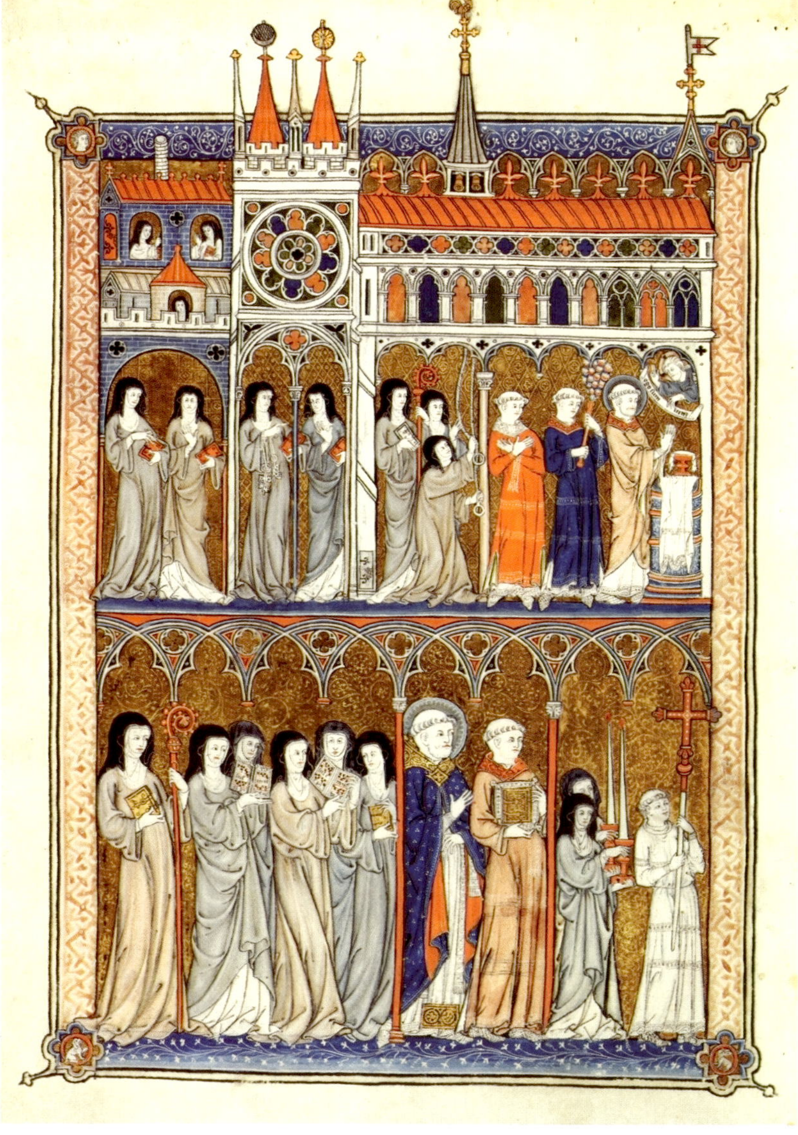

Figure 33. Pierre de Blois, La Sainte Abbaye. Fol. 6v., Cistercian Nuns attending Mass (above) and in procession (below). Tempera and gold on parchment. Central (Paris or Maubuisson?) or Northeastern Lorraine, France, ca. 1290. The British Library, London, Yates Thompson, MS 11.

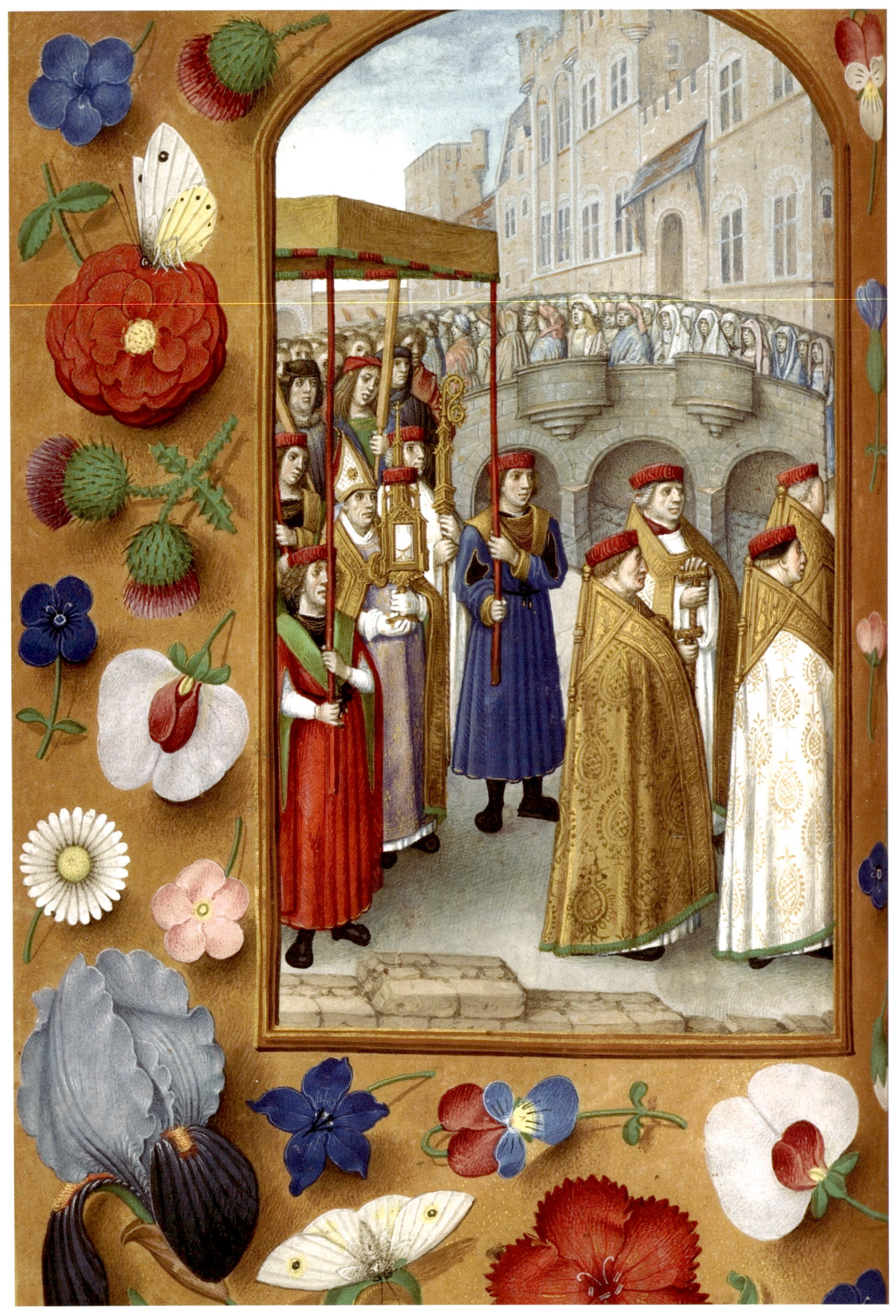

The modern observer would also note the prevalence of religious processions only glimpsed at in our own times. Religious processions occurred not only within most churches but also throughout the winding streets of large cities and towns *(fig. 34)*. On these occasions, the Holy Sacrament or great relics moved in procession before the faithful, as did devotional sculptures of Christ, the Virgin, and a virtually unlimited hierarchy of patron saints. The clergy, with their colorful and ostentatious vestments, would have been particularly conspicuous. Bishops carried their crosiers, and attending clergy carried processional crosses, monstrances, and occasionally elaborate reliquary shrines.

Figure 34 (facing page). Procession of the Blessed Sacrament. Fol. 43v. From the **Book of Hours of Queen Isabella the Catholic.** Tempera and gold on parchment. Flanders, Ghent, or Bruges, ca. 1497–1500. The Cleveland Museum of Art, Purchase, Leonard C. Hanna Jr. Bequest, 1963.256.

The medieval treasury would have included numerous processional objects, such as the monstrance and processional cross, which were safeguarded in the sanctuary when not in use. When required, these objects would have been removed for ritual procession. On other occasions, some of these objects served dual functions and were also displayed on the altar.

As in the Middle Ages, all liturgical processions today are led by a processional cross *(see fig. 33, lower register, for example)*. This tradition of great antiquity extends back to the early centuries of the medieval period and speaks to all Christians as followers of Christ. In following the processional cross, the clergy and the faithful symbolically follow Christ. All medieval churches had at least one processional cross, and many examples from the Middle Ages survive today in museums and church treasuries. The earlier crosses did not include the figure, or corpus, of Christ and thus were not true crucifixes *(fig. 2)*. Generally made of expensive materials, the crosses often had a wooden core and were covered with gilt-copper or gilt-silver. This was further embellished with filigree, niello, gemstones, or another decorative technique.

In some instances, processional crosses included relics sealed behind a rock crystal, making them true votive objects. In the early Middle Ages, processional crosses seem to have been placed in a stand near the altar when not in use. By the thirteenth and fourteenth centuries, the crosses began to include the figure of Christ, rendering them crucifixes. Typically the cross was permanently affixed to a long shaft so that it could be carried in procession. Eventually, in the eleventh or twelfth century, the shaft was designed to be removable. This enabled the upper portion, the cross itself, to be placed in a stand on the altar when not required for procession. Particularly opulent crosses or those containing relics were thus able to serve as both processional and altar crosses. An example of this cross is the Ceremonial Cross of Countess Gertrude in the Cleveland Museum of Art *(fig. 35)*. An inscription on the reverse of the cross indicates that it was made to house relics of Saints Peter, Liutrudis, and Gertrude.[1] During the Gothic period, processional crosses evolved into wondrous sculptural objects with multiple figures to complement the Corpus of Christ at center. Visually, they would have presented a stunning focus to liturgical processions *(figs. 36, 36a)*.

Other objects in liturgical procession included the monstrance and its related vessel, the ostensorium. The word monstrance was used generally in the Middle Ages to signify a container with a crystal or glass cylinder that was designed to expose a relic or the consecrated Host for veneration

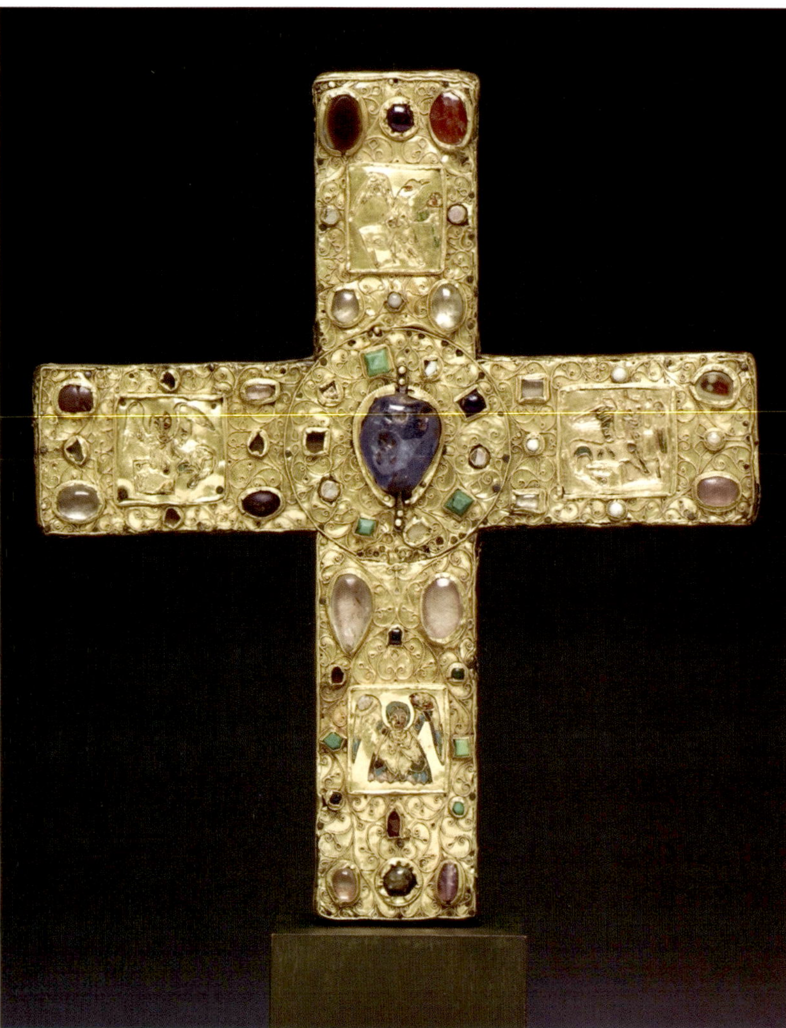

Figure 35 (left). Ceremonial Cross of Countess Gertrude (from the Guelph Treasure). Gold, cloisonné enamel, and mother of pearl over an oak core. Hildesheim, Germany, ca. 1040. The Cleveland Museum of Art, Purchase from the J. H. Wade Fund with addition of Gift from Mrs. E. B. Greene, Acc. 1931.55.

Figure 36 (below left). Processional Cross (obverse). Silver, gilt-silver, and repoussé over wood core, ca. 1440–50. Circle of Pietro Vannini, Italy, The Marches, died 1495 or 1496. The Cleveland Museum of Art, Purchase from the J. H. Wade Fund, Acc. 1926.243.

Figure 36a (below right). Reverse of Fig. 36 showing **Christ in Majesty surrounded by Evangelists.**

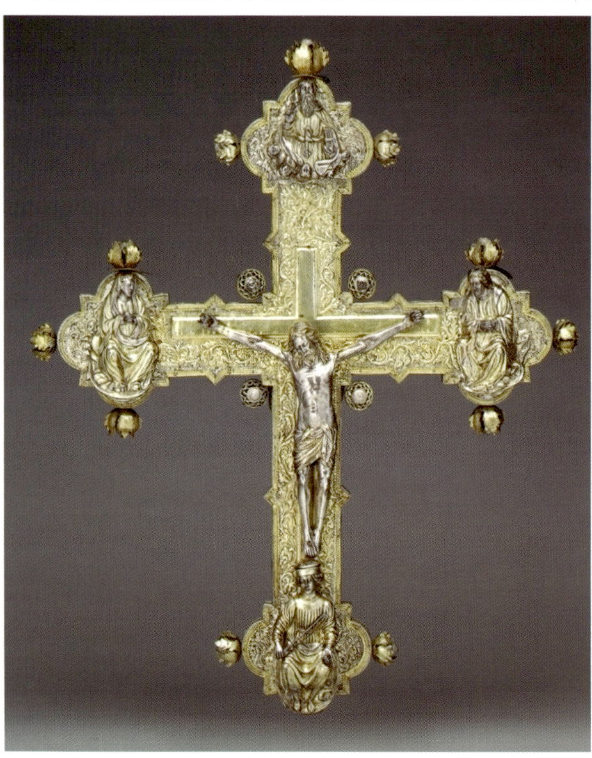

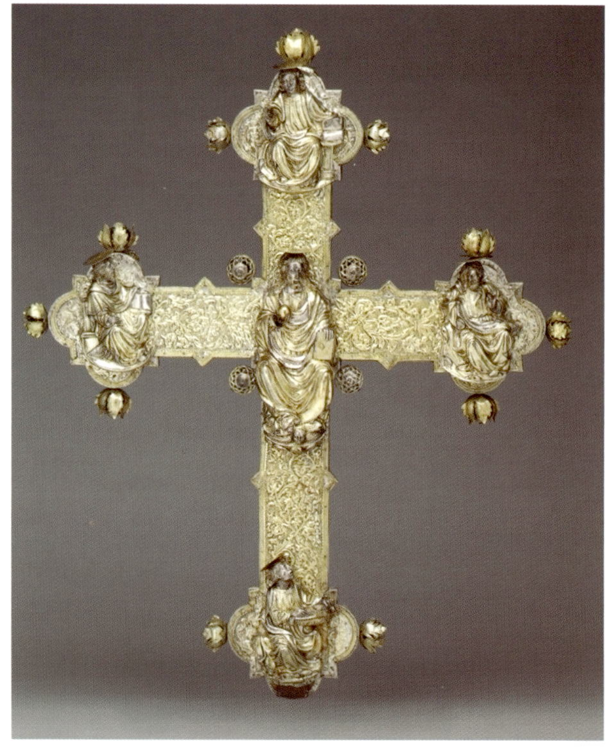

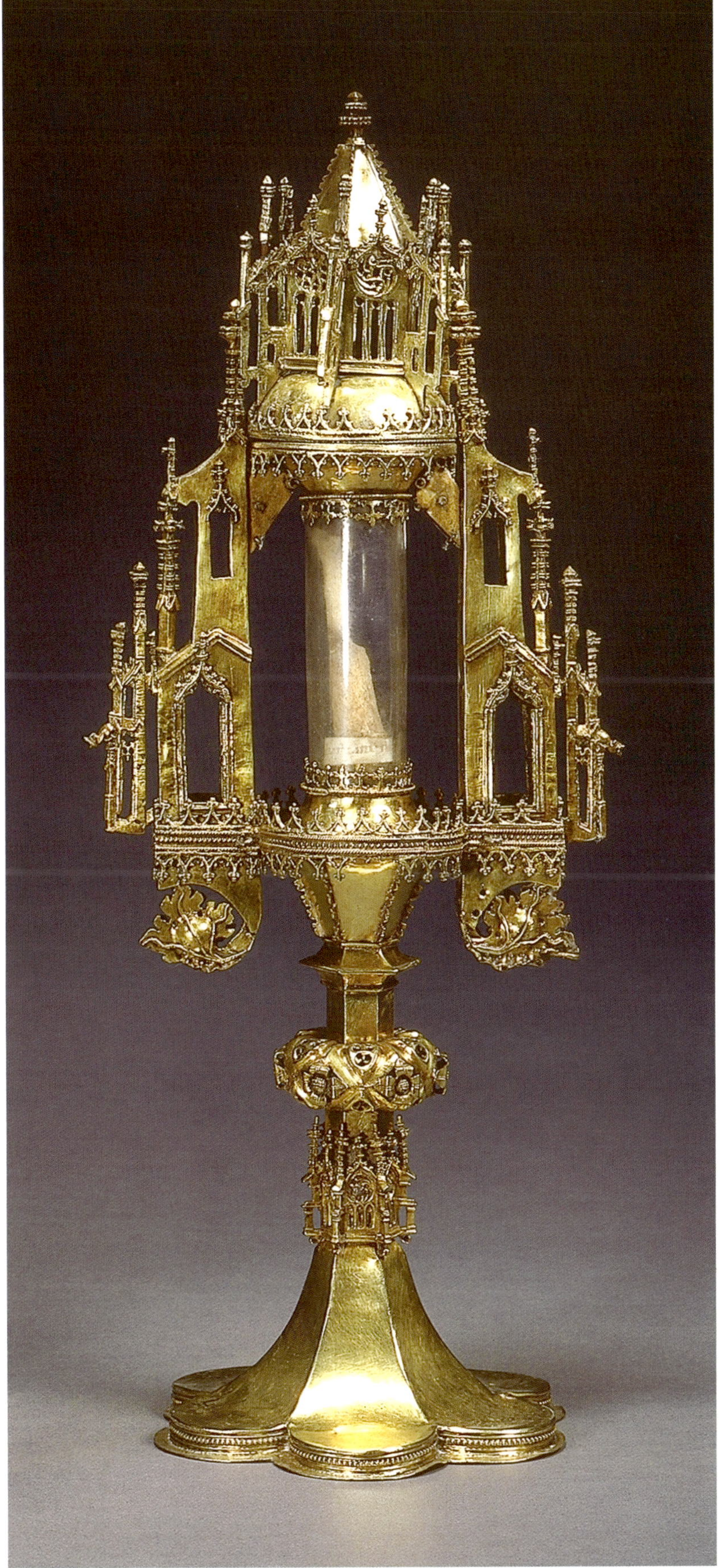

Figure 37. Monstrance with a Relic of Saint Sebastian (from the Guelph Treasure). Gilt-silver and crystal. Braunschweig, Lower Saxony, Germany, ca. 1475. The Cleveland Museum of Art, Gift of Julius F. Goldschmidt, Z. M. Hackenbroch, and J. Rosenbaum in memory of the exhibition of the Guelph Treasure held in the Cleveland Museum of Art in 1931, Acc. 1931.65.

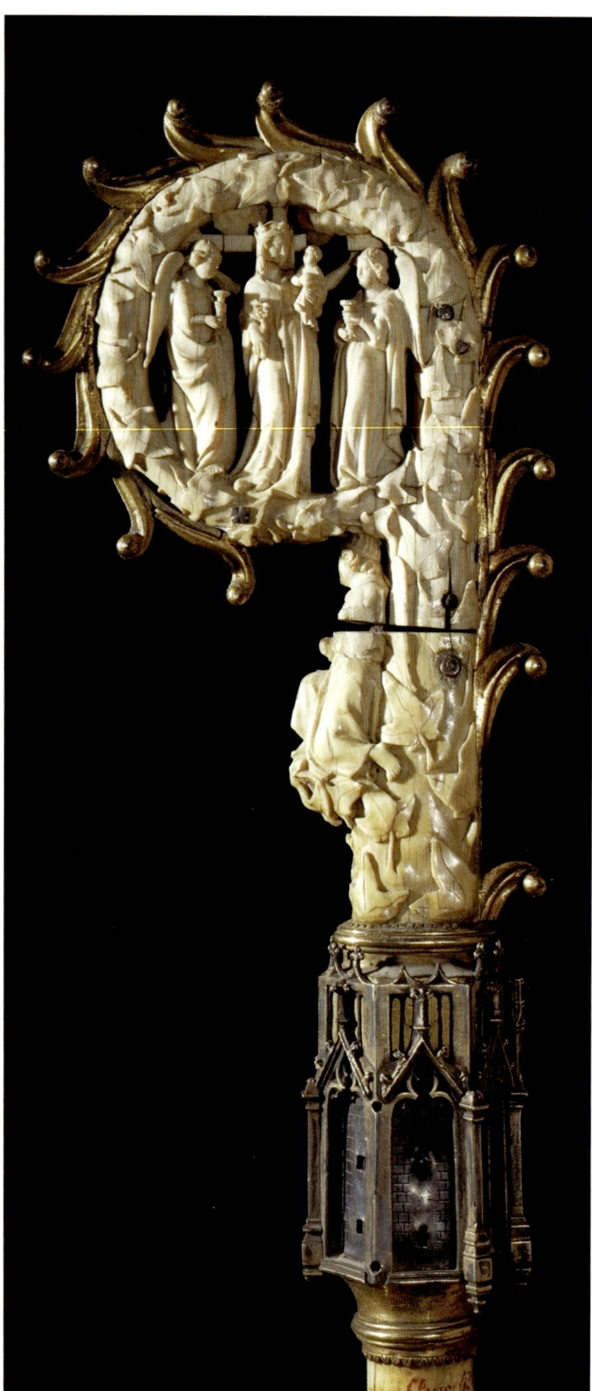

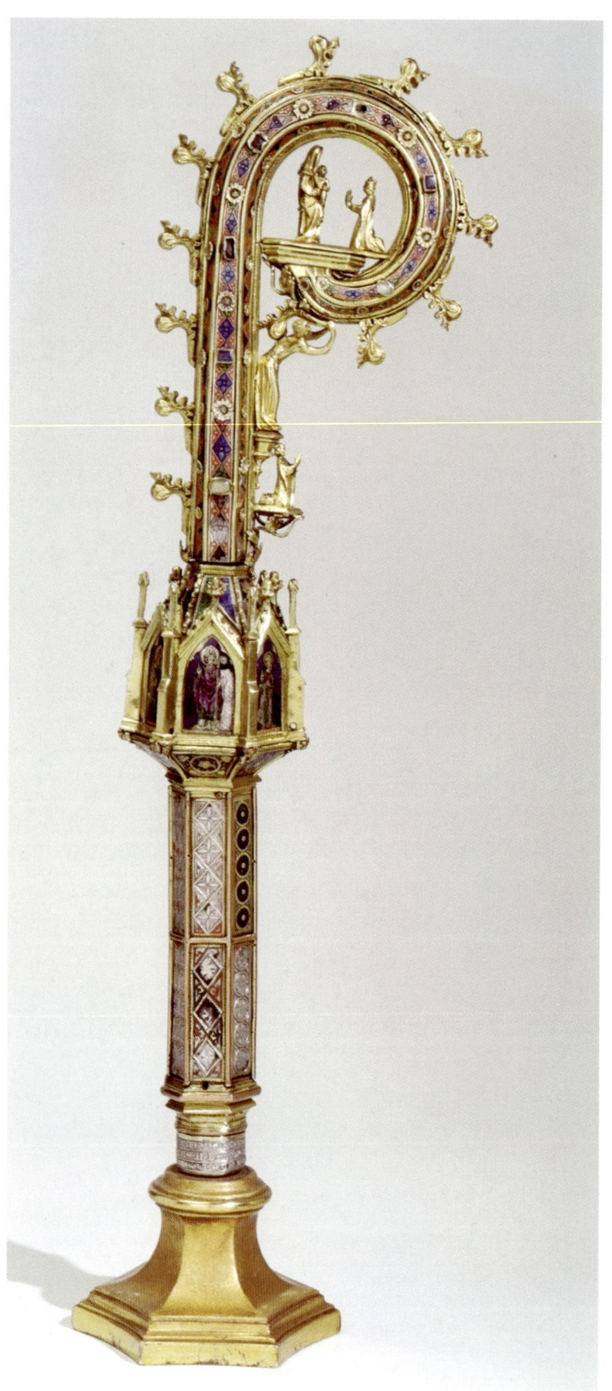

(*fig. 37*). The term ostensorium was used more widely during the sixteenth century and later for vessels intended to expose the sacred Host.

Through the late twelfth century, heated disputes and controversies within the church were rampant concerning the true nature of the Host and the moment of consecration. The final position of the church on the doctrine of transubstantiation was promulgated in 1215 at the Fourth Lateran Council. It stated that the bread and wine are at the moment of consecration changed into the substance of the body and blood of Christ, who is then truly present under the appearance of the bread and wine. As a result, the reserved Host became an object of cult outside of the Mass. Impulses from the laity increasingly expressed the need to look at the Host and, through the petitions of Saint Juliana of Mont Cornillon in Belgium, the Feast of Corpus Christi was eventually sanctioned by the church after 1246.

From this time forward, monstrances began to proliferate in the inventories of medieval treasuries. Some were designed exclusively to expose the Host *(fig. 34)*, always protected behind a crystal lens, while others were intended for relics only. They generally developed independently of reliquaries, which assumed a variety of forms. A fourteenth-century monstrance is now mounted with a paten attributed to Saint Bernward, Bishop of Hildesheim *(fig. 20)*. The paten is treated as a holy relic in this context. Monstrances were always fashioned of precious metals, or at least of brass or copper, which was then gilded or silvered. Their form included a foot, a stem, and an ornate upper body with a crystal repository. Some achieved truly elaborate levels of ornamentation with architectural forms highly favored throughout the Middle Ages. Monstrances could be carried by the clergy in ritual procession and afterward temporarily placed on the altar for veneration *(see fig. 34)*.

Crosiers, or pastoral staffs, were ecclesiastical ornaments conferred on bishops and mitered abbots at investiture to symbolize authority and jurisdiction. Crosiers had a large shaft with a volute curve resembling a shepherd's crook and were carried in procession. Generally, an abbot's crosier was smaller than a bishop's during the Middle Ages. Both could be very ornate, and most of the ornamentation was conferred on the volute. Crosier heads were made of various materials, including precious metals, ivory *(fig. 38)*, and champlevé enamel *(fig. 39)*. Extraordinary examples have survived, many with architectural decoration, others with a wealth of allegorical ornamentation. Crosiers were specific to particular prelates and would have been found in the treasuries of cathedrals and wealthy abbeys throughout medieval Europe.

Other objects used near the altar, but also in procession, were the holy water bucket, or situla, and the aspergillium, a metal rod with a brush or sponge at one end for sprinkling the altar and the congregation. Early examples of the situla dating to the Carolingian and Ottonian periods are very ornate and often in ivory and lined in metal *(fig. 40)*. Censers, more commonly known today as thuribles, survive in large numbers from the Middle Ages. Usually they are made of bronze, sometimes in architectural form, and suspended by chains. Medieval examples in silver and gilt-silver do exist and often have elaborate ornamental details *(fig. 41)*. Small perforations permitted the smoke from the burning incense to escape. Censers were used at solemn High Mass, funerals, Vespers, benediction, processions, and other important offices of the church.

No discussion of medieval treasuries can take place without the inclusion of relics and reliquaries. So fundamental were relics to the medieval view of the cosmos that they were critical to faith and salvation. British historian R. W. Southern wrote: "Relics were the main channel through which supernatural power was available for the needs of ordinary life. Ordinary men could see and handle them, yet they belonged not to this transitory

Figure 38 (facing page, left). Crosier Volute decorated with Mary and Angels. Ivory and gold. France, 14th century. Musée du Moyen Âge (Cluny Museum), Paris.

Photo: Erich Lessing/Art Resource, New York

Figure 39 (facing page, right). The Reichenau Crosier. Enamelled silver with mounts of gilt-copper. South Germany, 1351. The Victoria and Albert Museum, London.

Photo: Victoria and Albert Museum/Art Resource, New York

Figure 40. Situla (Bucket for Holy Water). Ivory with copper alloy and inlays. Carolingian, ca. 860–880. The Metropolitan Museum of Art, New York, Gift of J. Pierpont Morgan, Acc. 1917, 17.190.45.

Figure 41 (facing page). The Ramsey Abbey Censer and Incense Boat. Gilt-silver. England, ca. 1375. The Victoria and Albert Museum, London, Inv. M.268–1923.

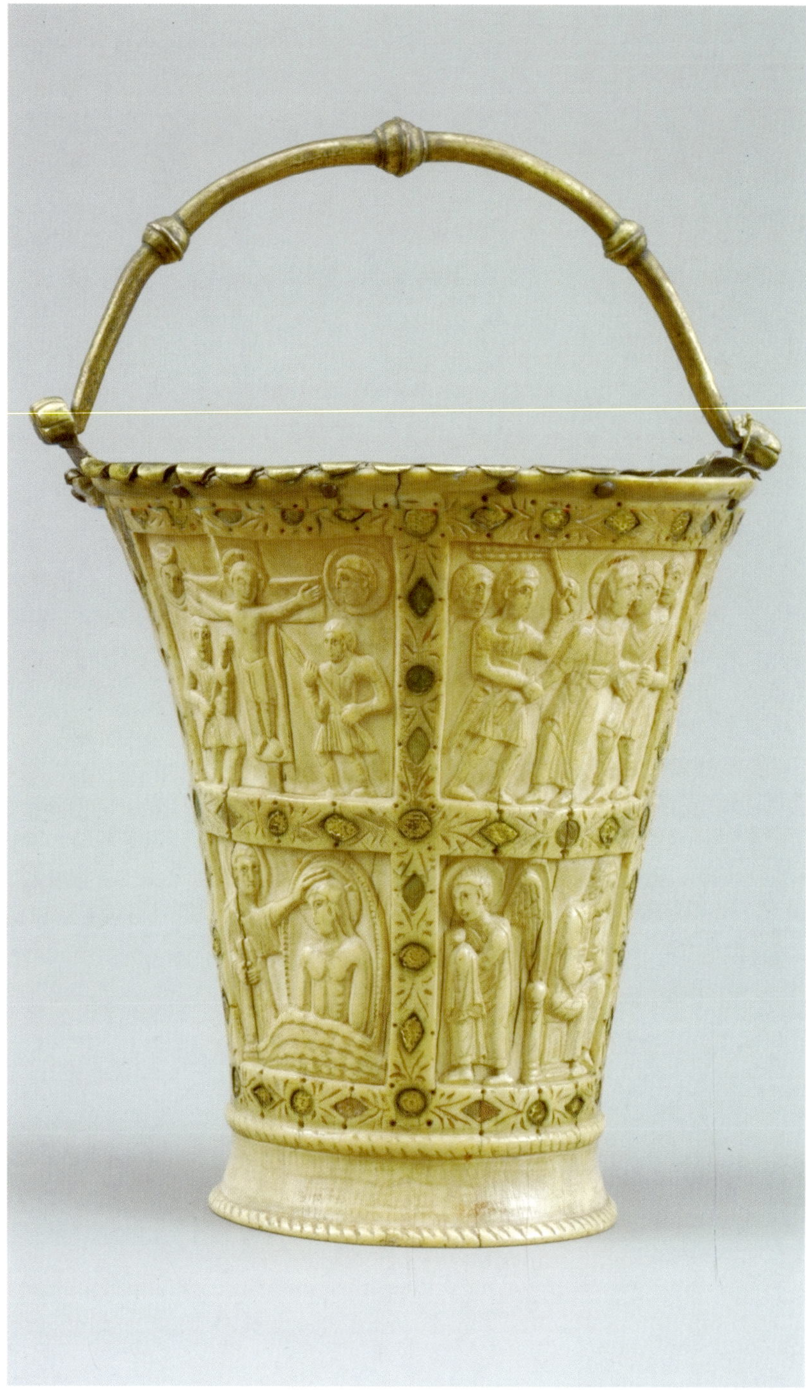

world but to eternity. On the Last Day they would be claimed by the saints and become an integral part of the kingdom of Heaven. Among all the objects of the visible, malign, unintelligible world, relics alone were both visible and full of beneficent intelligence."[2]

Relics also served as a physical link between the natural and supernatural worlds. The saints were, of course, the holy dead who, through the meritorious actions of their lives, had earned salvation and a place in heaven near God, the angels, and the Virgin. The saints were thus natural and obvious intercessors for mankind. Relics were the physical remains of the saints, chiefly their bodies, and also, by extension, objects that were owned or

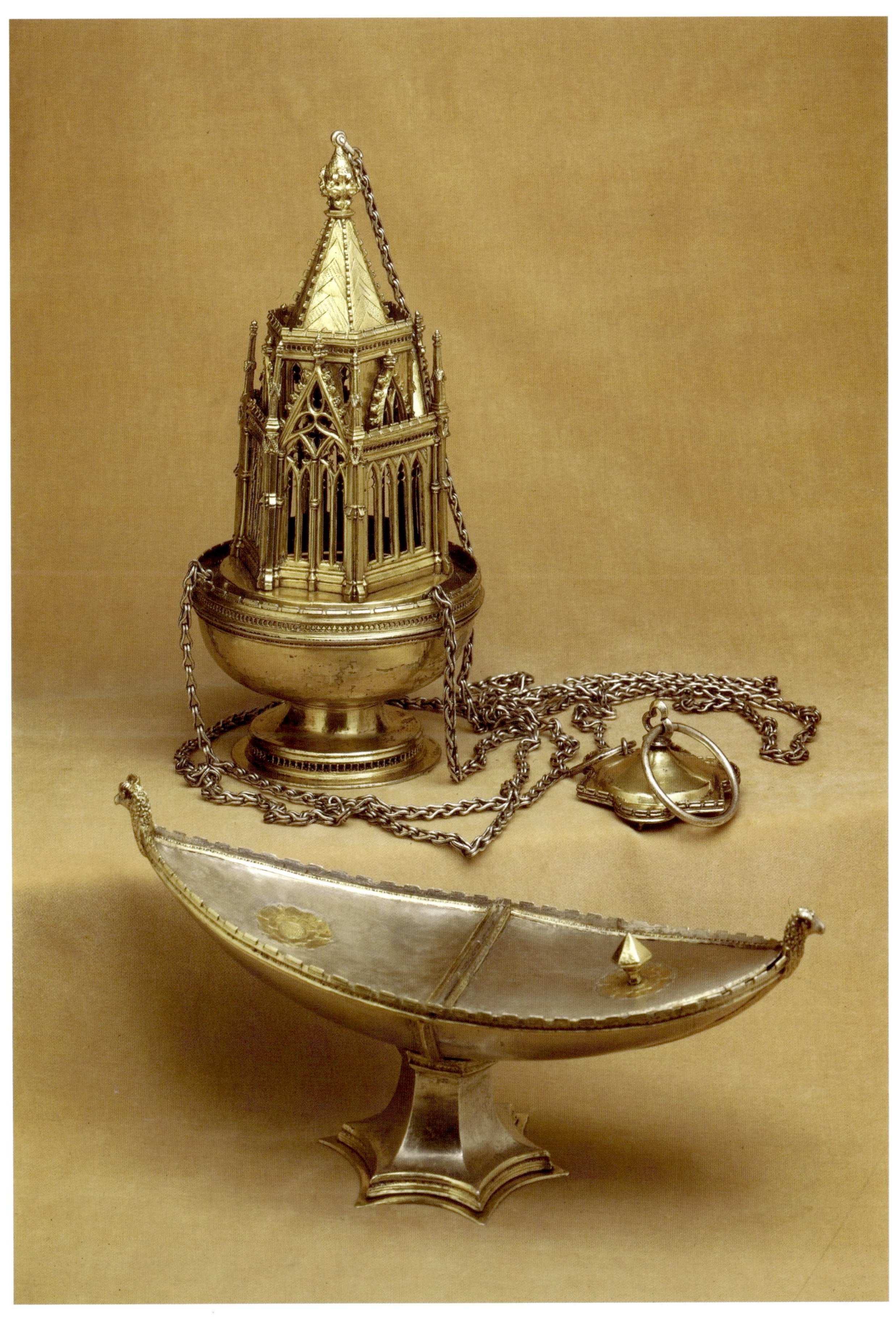

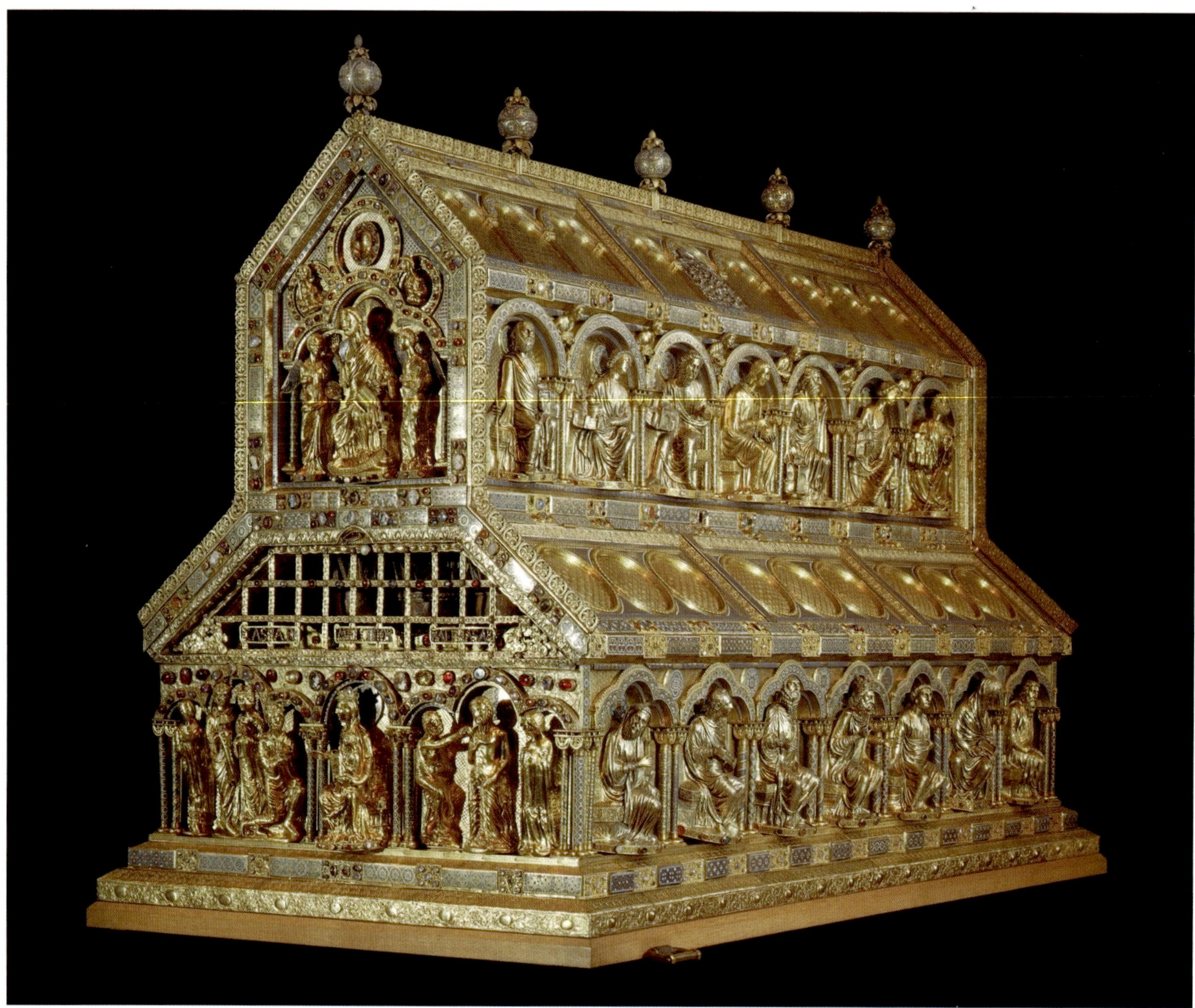

Figure 42. Shrine of the Three Kings. Gold, gilt-silver, gilt-bronze, gems, pearls, antique cameos. Nicolas of Verdun, French, ca. 1130–1205, Cologne Cathedral.

Photo: Erich Lessing/Art Resource, New York

Figure 42a (facing page). Detail of the Shrine of the Three Kings.

Photo: Erich Lessing/Art Resource, New York

touched by these holy men and women. The power of the saints was therefore manifest by and through their relics. The living, instilled with medieval concepts of justice, venerated the relics of the saints in order to seek their patronage, which in turn provided a proximate link to the divine ruler.

It was popularly believed during the Middle Ages that saintly patronage was made manifest through miracles, such as the cure of disease or protection from natural calamities. It is no wonder that medieval pilgrims, in a world fraught with peril, sought close physical contact with relics. Such contact protected both the spiritual and temporal welfare of laypeople and religious communities who honored saints through the veneration of their relics. So powerful was this belief that pilgrims sometimes placed pieces of cloth or other objects, known as brandea, in close physical contact with relics in order to transmit and contain their power. There existed a direct appeal for the possession of relics, not only by ecclesiastical institutions but also by powerful laypersons who could procure them through trade or purchase. The veneration of relics came to rival the sacraments in the daily life of medieval Christians.

Not all relics consisted of the remains of saints' bodies. Some important relics were associated with Christ or the Virgin, and these were consid-

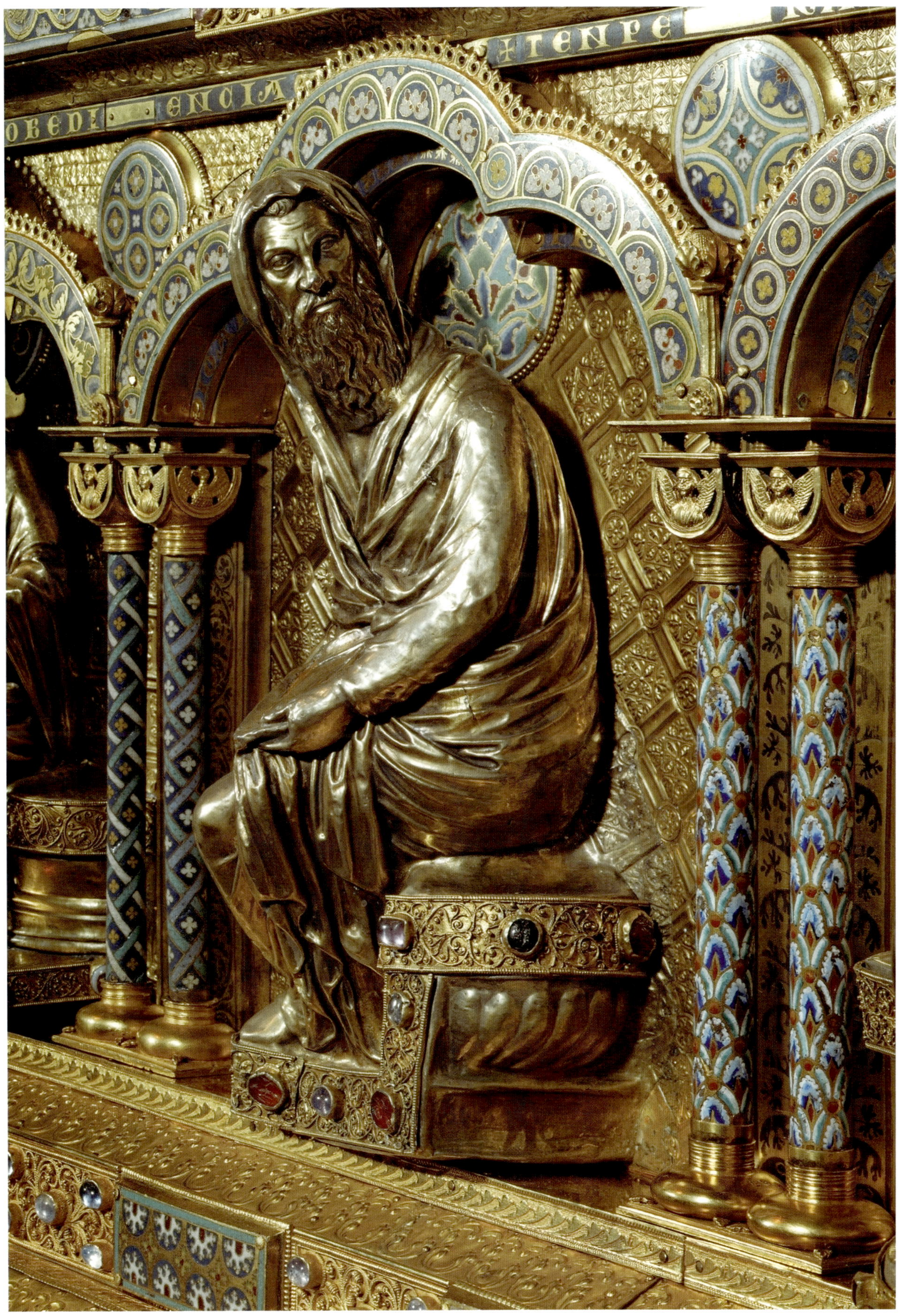

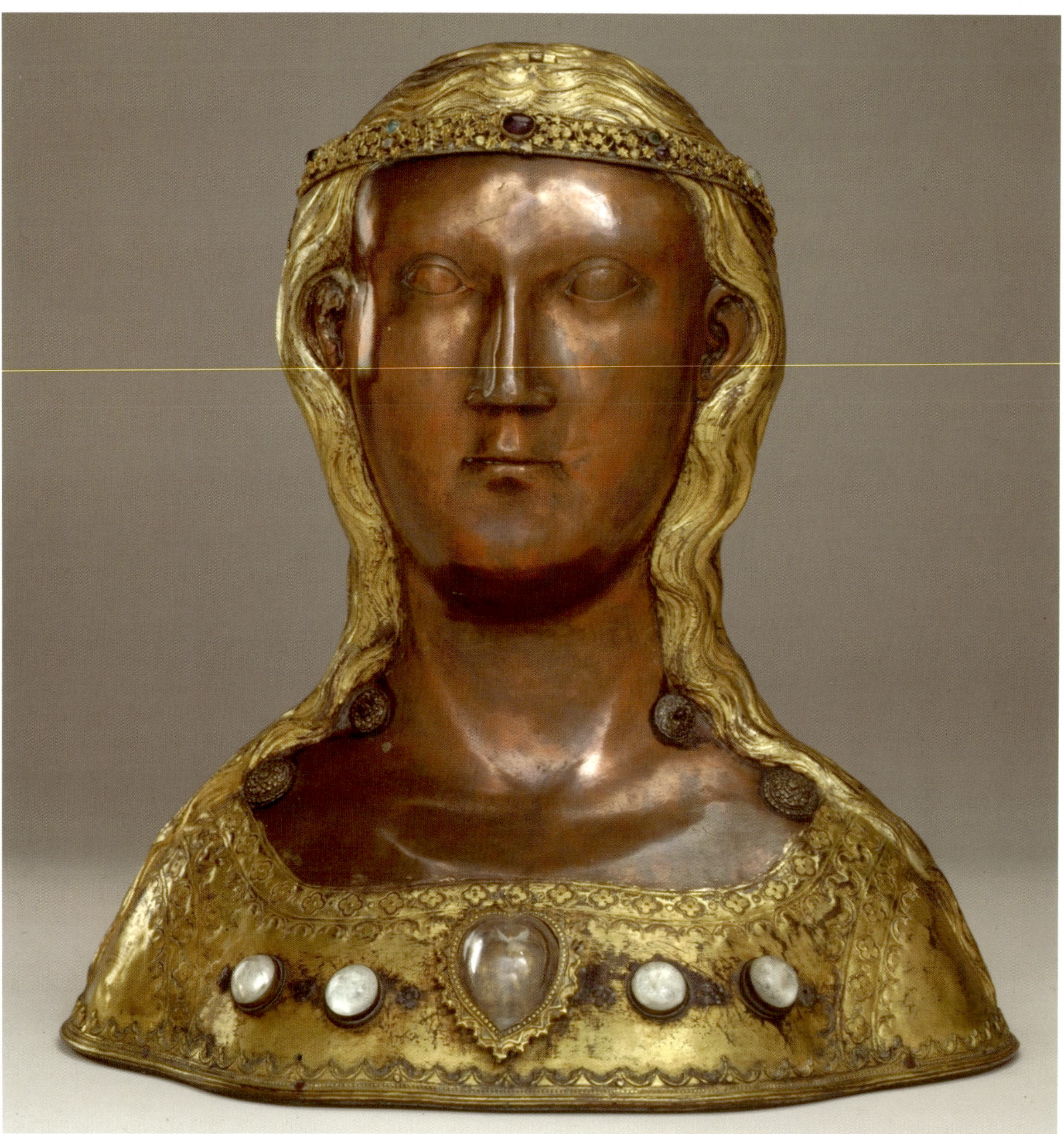

Figure 43. Head Reliquary of a Female Saint (Ursula?). Gilt-copper and semi-precious stones. Franco-Flemish or Cologne(?), Germany, 15th century. The John and Mable Ringling Museum of Art, Sarasota, Bequest of John Ringling, Inv. 1936, SN 1099.

ered to be the holiest in Christendom. One of the most valued relics was the Crown of Thorns, which French King Louis IX (1226–70) acquired in the Holy Land while on Crusade. Louis ordered the construction of the exquisite royal chapel on the Ile-de-la-Cité in Paris as a repository for this important relic *(see fig. 4)*. Relics were sometimes placed in secular objects, such as the throne of Charlemagne. Even the mythical sword of Roland was said to contain a relic in its hilt.

Relics were also used for the swearing of oaths. The special role of relics during the Middle Ages had a direct impact on the lives of men and women in a way that cannot be imagined today. Every town, guild, confraternity, and church had its patron saint. Each individual also had his or her patron saint. Relics were so fundamental to the economic as well as the spiritual well-being of religious communities that such communities often spared no effort in obtaining them.

By the eighth century, relics were included in all altars throughout the Christian West as part of their dedication.[3] Major relics, usually housed in glittering reliquaries made expressly for that purpose, were considered the most important possessions of medieval churches. Relics bestowed honor and privilege upon the possessor, and monasteries and cathedrals across Europe vied with one another to hold the most prestigious reliquaries *(fig. 37)*. Such relics attracted pilgrims, often from all over Europe. Candles were lit before the holy remains. They were censed. Pilgrims made offerings in the name of the saint, who was honored and cherished in a very direct way. There emerged a rationale of gift exchange between the devout and the saint whose relics were being venerated. The living earned the patronage of the saints by rendering to them their service and devotion. The saints, in reciprocity, also had obligations to those who served and honored them.

Given this intensity of devotion, pilgrims traveled across Europe to pray before important shrines and earn indulgences or favors. With the acquisition of the relics of the Three Magi in 1164, the city of Cologne transformed itself into one of Europe's most important pilgrimage centers and, not coincidentally, one of medieval Europe's most prosperous cities. These relics are still contained within their exquisite reliquary shrine *(figs. 42, 42a)* behind the high altar of Cologne Cathedral.

The medieval faithful would have known through word of mouth where they might venerate the remains of important saints. English worshippers who traveled to Westminster could pray before the remains of Saint Edward the Confessor or those of Thomas Becket at Canterbury. By traveling to Bari in Italy, pilgrims could venerate the remains of Saint Nicholas; in Padua, Saint Anthony; or in Venice, the evangelist Mark. The monastery of Santiago de Compostela in distant Spain emerged as the most important center of pilgrimage in northern Europe by virtue of its possession of the remains of the apostle James.

Those who had relics in their possession were obliged to display them prominently and to construct elaborate reliquaries and shrines to house them. Given their perceived value and importance, reliquaries were lavishly adorned with precious metals, enamels, ivory, and gemstones. These became core objects in the medieval treasury and a major form of artistic production in medieval Europe and Byzantium. Reliquaries were central to any ecclesiastical treasury, and the precious relics that they contained became linked to the identity of a church or even a city that possessed them. Suger, the venerable abbot of the royal monastery of Saint-Denis (1122–51), presided over an old Carolingian building that housed numerous important relics and the tombs of the kings of France. The pilgrims who sought to venerate the relics in his church caused such congestion that Suger concluded the church must be renovated and expanded:

> Through a fortunate circumstance attending the singular smallness — the number of faithful growing and frequently gathering to seek the intercession of the Saints — the aforesaid basilica had come to

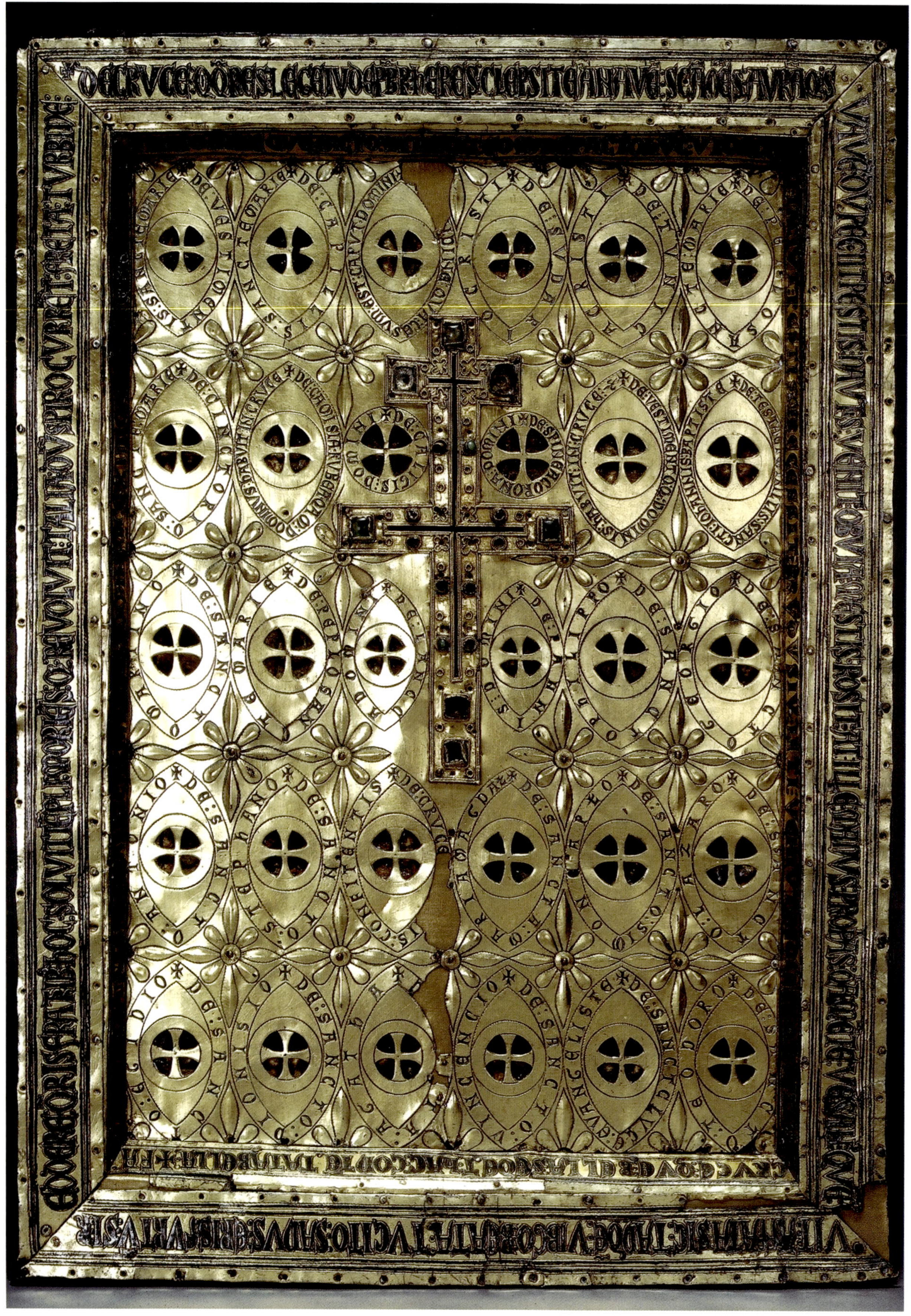

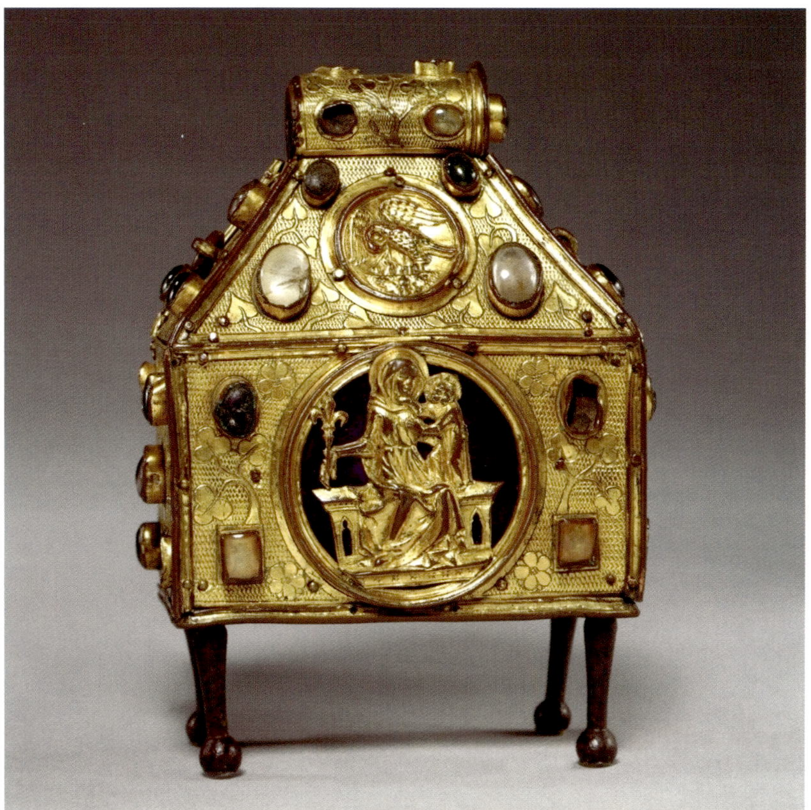

Figure 44 (facing page). **Reliquary of the True Cross (Staurothek).** Gilt-silver and niello over wood. Germany or South Italy(?), dated 1214. The Cleveland Museum of Art, Purchase from the J. H. Wade Fund, Acc. 1952.89.

Figure 45. **Reliquary in Purse Form.** Copper chased and gilded with cabochons and glass inlay. Vienna, Austria, ca. 1330. The Cleveland Museum of Art, Purchase from the J. H. Wade Fund, Acc. 1932.422.

> suffer grave inconveniences. Often on feast days, completely filled, it disgorged through all its doors the excess of the crowds as they moved in opposite directions, and the outward pressure of the foremost ones not only prevented those attempting to enter from entering but also expelled those who had already entered. At times you could see, a marvel to behold, that the crowded multitude offered so much resistance to those who strove to flock in to worship and kiss the holy relics, the Nail and Crown of the Lord, that no one...could move a foot; that no one, because of their very congestion, could do anything but stand like a marble statue, stay benumbed or, as a last resort, scream.[4]

Reliquaries throughout the Middle Ages assumed varied forms ranging from caskets, bookcovers, and crosses *(see fig. 35)* to figural reliquaries and those that were more sculptural and complex. Some mimicked parts of the human body *(fig. 43)*. Several distinct forms emerged during the early centuries of the church. Perhaps the oldest of these is known as the staurotheca, which held a relic of the True Cross. These were usually distinguished by the symbol of the double-armed cross, often rendered in openwork to make visible the precious relic enclosed behind it. Staurotheca were often flat rectangular objects, sometimes in triptych form, that Europeans copied from Byzantine examples *(fig. 44)*.

In early medieval Europe, pilgrims returning from their travels sometimes carried cloth purses that contained relics acquired in distant lands. These relics were the most precious possessions of Christian travelers. So emblematic were their reliquary purses that they were later reproduced

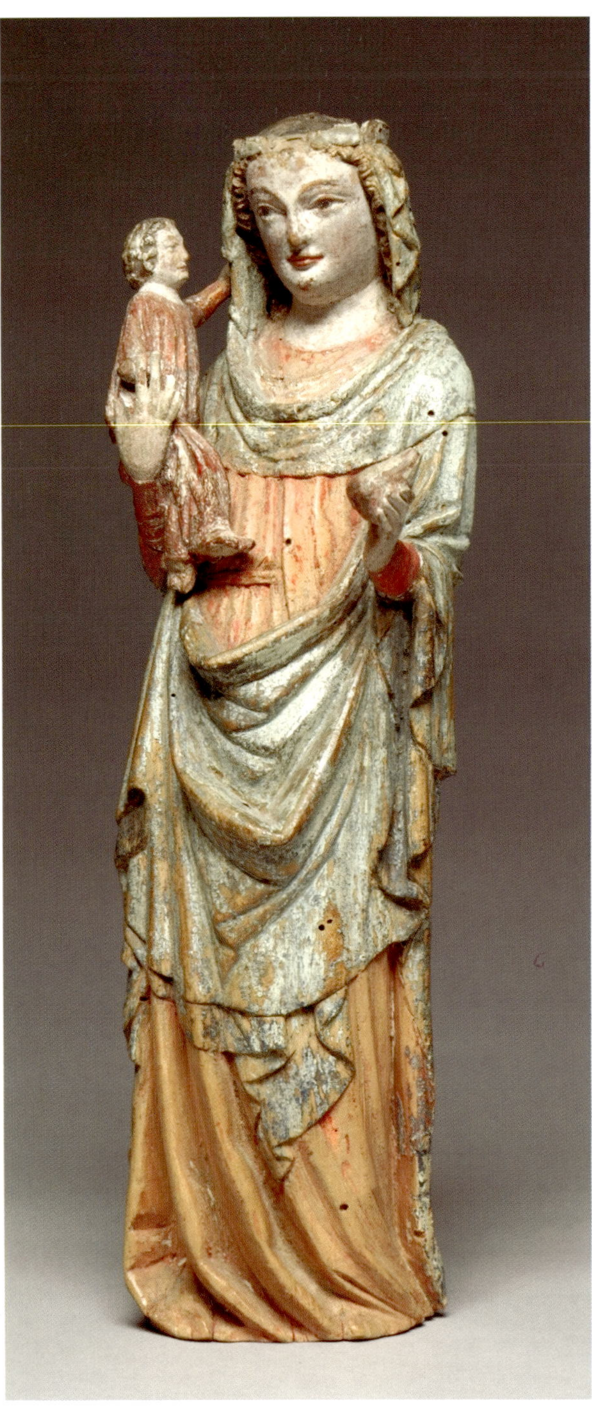
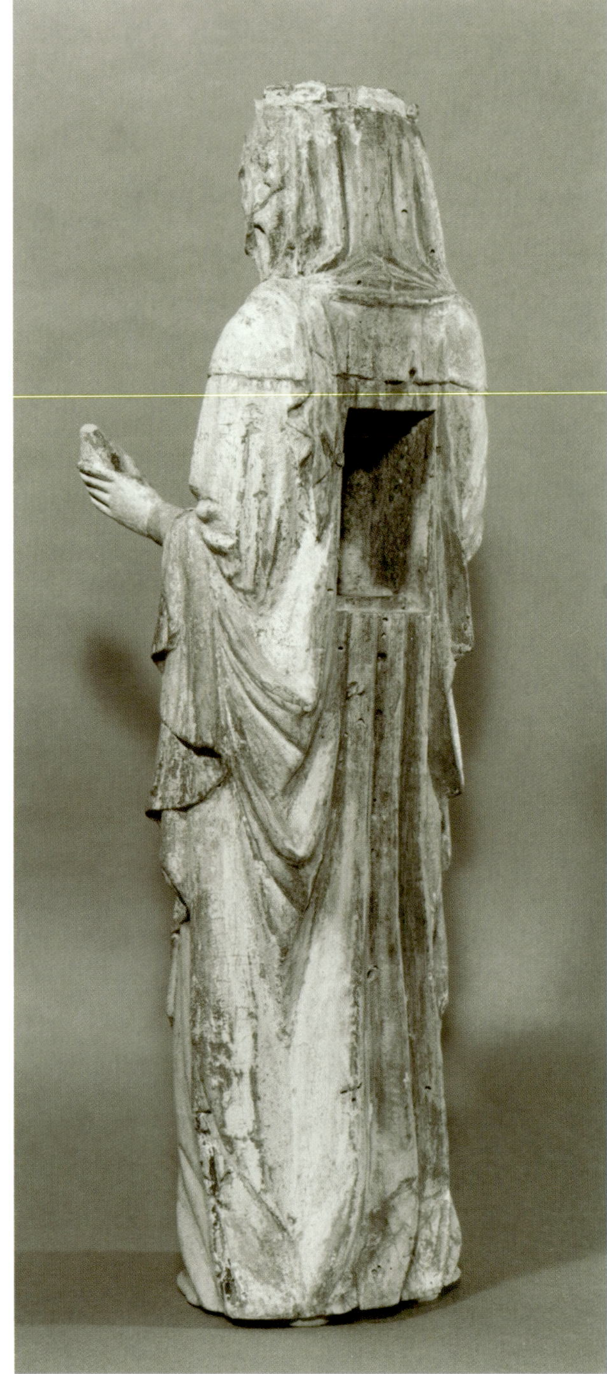

in the more permanent and costly materials of gold, copper, gemstones, and enamel. They were constructed over a hollow wooden core that could store a relic. Instead of being carried on the person, as was their original function, these purse reliquaries could be placed directly on the altar for display, or, as in the case of one now in the Cleveland Museum of Art, suspended above the altar *(fig. 45)*.

Figural reliquaries, particularly those in the form of the standing Virgin with Child, emerged in popularity during the thirteenth century in keeping with the rise of veneration to the mother of God. These standing figural reliquaries straddled the arts of sculpture, goldsmithing, and even architecture. They could be simple wood carvings of the Virgin, which were painted and had a cavity in the back to hold the relic *(figs. 46, 46a)*, or more elaborate versions, which were wrought from gilt-silver and embellished with enamel or gemstones. These elaborate reliquaries were in vogue during the thirteenth and fourteenth centuries and were often donated to churches by aristocratic patrons.

Some of the grandest reliquaries of the Middle Ages were the large reliquary shrines that housed the relics of important saints. Often measuring over three feet in length, such shrines were architectural in form with a pitched roof and gables and often included figural ornamentation along the sides. Among the largest and most ostentatious of these medieval reliquaries are the Shrine of the Three Kings in Cologne Cathedral *(figs. 42, 42a)* and the Shrine of Saint Servatius in Maastricht, each with glittering gilt surfaces of gemstones and rock crystal. They occupied a conspicuous place in the ecclesiastical treasury.

During the late Romanesque and early Gothic era, particularly venerated relics were frequently housed within receptacles that espoused the form of the holy memento. In this way, a fragment of bone from a saint's arm was placed within an arm reliquary that sculpturally represented the object it contained but ad vivum *(fig. 47)*. According to this tradition, the Middle Ages also knew foot reliquaries, hand reliquaries, and head reliquaries *(see fig. 43)*, all depicting the saintly memento that was concealed within. In this way, the receptacle itself became a tangible representation of the saintly relic that could be processed or placed on an altar and made visible to the faithful. This tradition would eventually be superseded by an impulse to place relics in monstrances or to otherwise display them behind a piece of crystal so that worshippers could view the actual relics.

The specific design of the monstrance, a footed vessel with a crystal or glass display window, was to facilitate the display of something sacred, either the Sacred Host itself or, frequently during the Middle Ages, a relic. Such reliquary monstrances became fashionable in Europe during the late fourteenth century and throughout the fifteenth century. Many have survived in treasuries and museums and are typically circular or architectural in form. One architectural monstrance containing a relic of Saint Sebastian was originally part of the Guelph Treasure, the former ecclesiastical treasure of Braunschweig Cathedral. It now survives in the Cleveland Museum of Art *(see fig. 37)*. This monstrance is highly decorative and is structured as a church with an involved series of buttresses and a lantern tower. A crystal cylinder contains a fragment of bone identified by a strip of parchment as that of Saint Sebastian. It is known from inventory evidence that this relic of the saintly healer had been acquired by Duke Henry the Peaceful in 1473, probably to ward off the plague, which was then active in Lower Saxony.

Around 1400, aristocratic French laymen commissioned elaborate constructions for their private chapels *(fig. 48)*. Such reliquaries exuded the look of great luxury with a new enameling technique called email-surronde-bosse or "enameling in the round." This technique involved the

Figure 46 (facing page, left). Reliquary Statuette of the Virgin and Child. Polychromed lindenwood. Salzburg, ca. 1330. The Cleveland Museum of Art, the Mary Spedding Milliken Memorial Collection, Gift of William Mathewson Milliken, Acc. 1973.143. This statuette has a rectangular opening in the back that once held a relic. Reliquaries made of wood were less common than those made of more precious materials. The Virgin's crown is now missing.

Figure 46a (facing page, right). Reverse of the Reliquary Statuette of the Virgin and Child (previous illustration) showing cavity for relic.

Figure 47. Arm Reliquary of the Apostles (from the Guelph Treasure). Silver, gilt-silver, and champlevé enamel on a core of oak. Hildesheim(?), Lower Saxony, Germany, ca. 1190–1200. The Cleveland Museum of Art, Gift of the John Huntington Art and Polytechnic Trust, Acc. 1930.739.

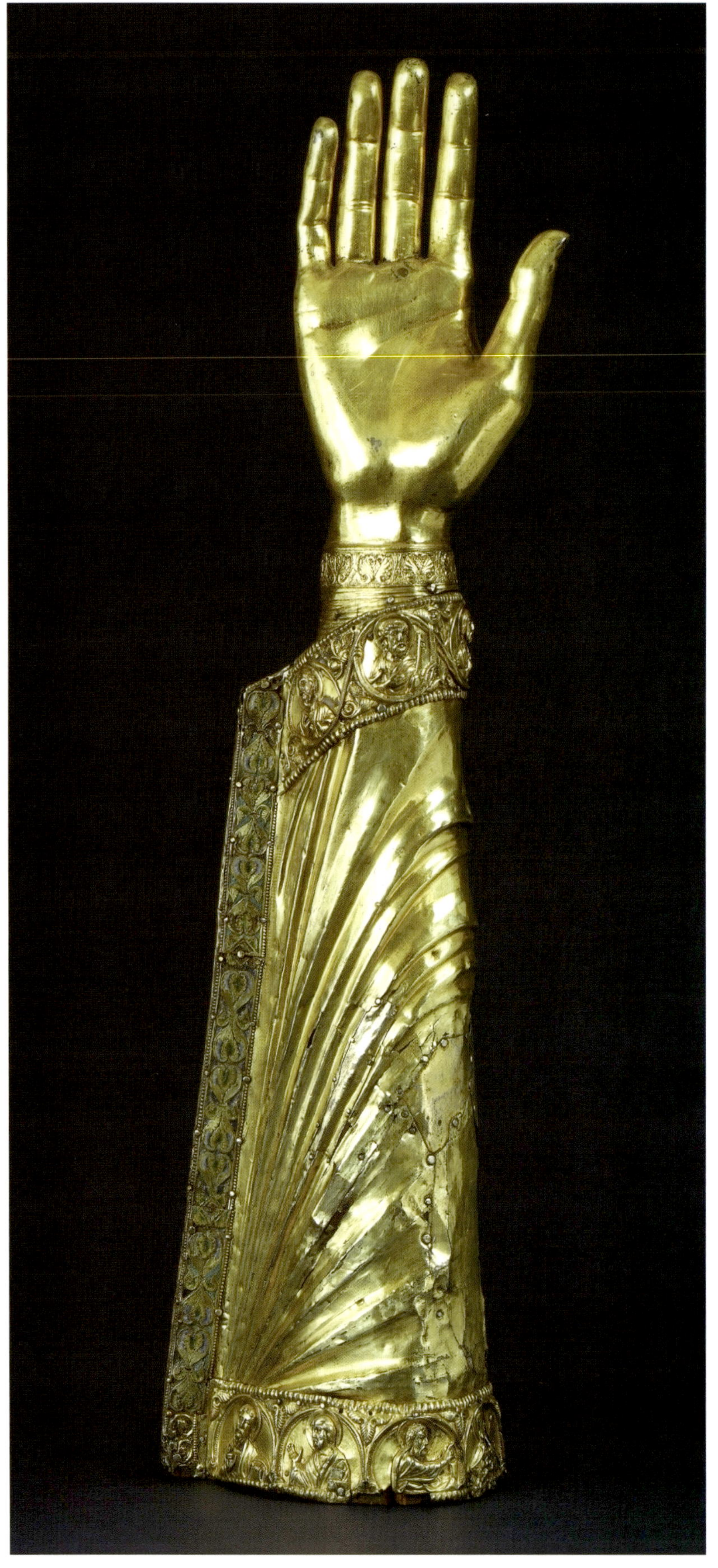

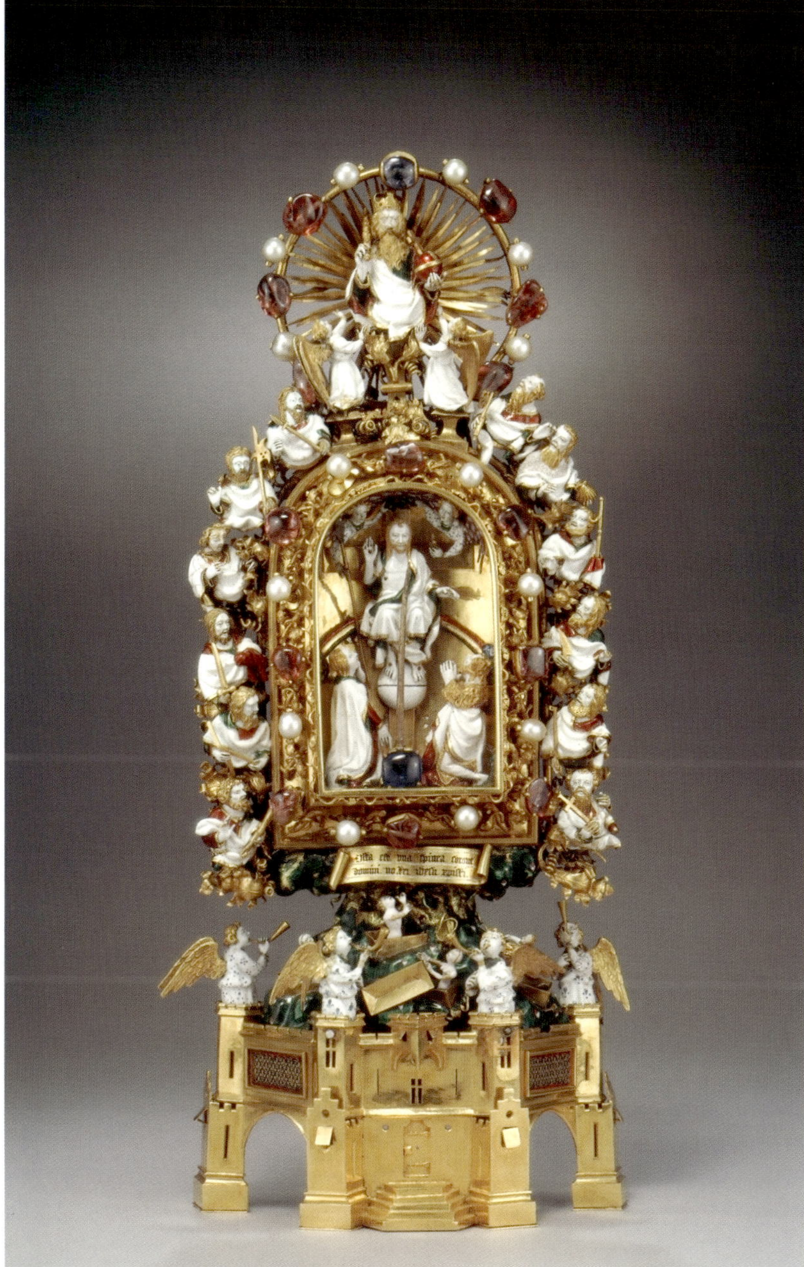

Figure 48. Holy Thorn Reliquary of Jean, duc de Berry. Enamel, pearls, and precious stones on gold. Paris, ca. 1400–1410. The British Museum, London, Waddesdon Bequest.

Photo: HIP/Art Resource, New York

encrustation, or coating, of irregular surfaces with multiple figures in high relief. These sculptural compositions were invariably of gold or silver with roughened surfaces to hold the enamel coating in place. One such opulent reliquary was commissioned by the Valois prince, Duke Jean de Berry, around 1400–1410, to house a relic of the Crown of Thorns. A single thorn is displayed behind a crystal window and identified by the Latin inscription: "Ista est una spinea corone / Domine nostri ihesu cristi" (This is a thorn from the crown of Our Lord Jesus Christ). The Reliquary of the Holy Thorn, with its composite materials and exquisite enamels on gold, is among the most spectacular reliquaries from the late Middle Ages.

Gemstones and Lapidaries in Medieval Ecclesiastical Art

Gemstones, pearls, and cut glass were often used to embellish objects in the medieval treasury. Clerics who commissioned liturgical objects believed that gemstones contained supernatural or magical properties and hence had amuletic as well as aesthetic value. This was a tradition inherited from pagan antiquity. In many instances, gemstones carved as cameos or intaglios with mythological images were readapted for use in a Christian context. Though not officially sanctioned by the church, this practice was nevertheless tolerated for the most part. Indeed, most of the treatises on lapidaries produced in the Middle Ages were written by clerics.

Clergy as well as pious lay rulers often used carved antique gemstones for their signet rings. Artists incorporated the gemstones into the book covers of liturgical manuscripts *(fig. 49)*, processional crosses *(see figs. 2, 35)*, and reliquaries *(see figs. 42, 45)*. Many of these gemstones had entered the medieval West during the period of the Crusades when Western armies or pilgrims brought back looted goods. Numerous Roman cameos and intaglios from this period are preserved in ecclesiastical treasuries. Medieval Christians were fascinated by the perceived magical properties of these ancient gemstones, both carved and uncarved, and sought to incorpo-

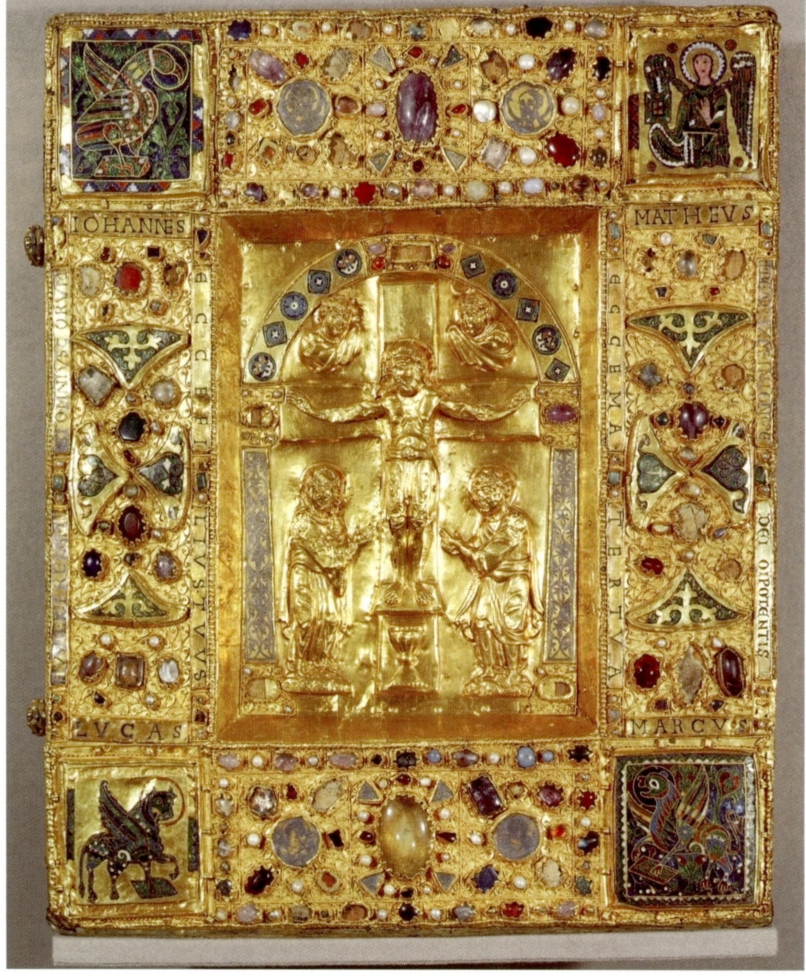

Figure 49. Book Cover with the Crucifixion and Evangelists (from the Treasury of Maastricht Cathedral). Gold, cloisonné enamel, gemstones. Regensburg(?), Germany, early 11th century. The Louvre, Paris, Inv. MR349.

Photo: Erich Lessing/Art Resource, New York

rate this "power" for Christian use as charms and amulets. Archbishop Guillaume de Champagne of Sens, for example, sealed his papers with a seal featuring a bust of Venus (1176) and Deacon André of Soisson with Leda and the Swan (1189). Other examples of this practice abound.[5]

Pagan mythological images on ecclesiastical signet rings and liturgical objects were not without controversy. From time to time, strong objections against the practice were raised. In his *Cohortatio ad gentes,* Clement of Alexandria objected to the use of "immoral" subjects as classical figures in ecclesiastical settings. Similarly, the Synod of Milan in the seventh century ruled against the use of classical figurative designs on Episcopal rings.[6] Nonetheless, these widespread objections suggest such images enjoyed a certain popularity.

Gemstones were believed to provide specific benefits to the user. Chalcedony, for example, was popularly believed to bring victory. Chrysolite, when hung on the bristle of a donkey, was thought to protect the owner from demons. Amethyst protected against intoxication. It was believed that engraved gems had similar properties. A cameo engraved with Perseus holding the Gorgon's head was thought to provide protection from lightning, storms, and demons. A stone carved with the figure of Mercury rendered the owner wise and persuasive; that with Andromeda could conciliate between a man and a woman.[7] There are numerous similar examples to document the medieval belief, even among some church officials, that such gemstones were vested with magical properties.

To counter the criticism of impropriety, the custom emerged of interpreting mythological figures in Christian terms. Venus holding a looking glass was reinvented as an image of the Virgin; Hercules with the lion became Daniel in the lion's den; and Perseus with Medusa's head became David with the head of Goliath. A gem preserved in the Cathedral of Troyes and engraved with the figure of Mercury was inscribed during the Middle Ages to suggest Saint Michael the Archangel. These examples illustrate the compelling nature of gems for medieval men and women and for many church officials of the time.

The application of gems to all kinds of ecclesiastical objects suggests that their appeal was widespread and that these superstitions persisted long after late antiquity *(see fig. 19).* The tradition of decorating precious vessels with gemstones started in the ancient world with the Byzantines, who presumably transmitted the custom and taste to the West. The translucence of gems and precious hard stones was often associated with "clarity" and the emanation of the divine nature. This belief, derived from Neo-Platonic philosophy, was often cited as a justification for their use on ecclesiastical objects.

Gemstones were thus thought to bring the worshipper closer to God, and they acquired a Christian mystical association during the Middle Ages. Crystal was associated with the Virgin due to its purity and translucency. The star sapphire was associated with the Star of Bethlehem. The red veining in the bloodstone was regarded as symbolizing the blood of the Redeemer. Also, some Christian thinkers interpreted the application of pagan gems to Christian objects as the triumph of the church over paganism *(fig. 2).*

Figure 50 (facing page). Chalice of Abbot Suger of Saint-Denis. Bowl of agate (sardonyx), Alexandria, Egypt, ca. 200 B.C.; foot and mounts of gold, gilt-silver, filigree, cabochons, pearls, and glass. Abbey of Saint-Denis, France, before 1137–40. National Gallery of Art, Washington, D.C., Widener Collection, Inv. 1942.9.277.

Gems were also thought to reveal the miraculous nature of God because of the superhuman quality. They were regarded as mysterious manifestations of nature, not man, and in this way reflect the hand of God. For these reasons, gemstones, carved and uncarved, were avidly chosen to embellish medieval ecclesiastical objects. They demonstrated the transcendental mystery of the liturgy and the relics. Undoubtedly, they were given some form of sanctification prior to their use. The famous abbot of the royal monastery of Saint-Denis writes of the miraculous power of ecclesiastical objects embellished with gemstones and how such gems disposed him to a higher mood of contemplation, helping him transcend toward heaven:

> Often we contemplate, out of sheer affection for the church our mother, these different ornaments both new and old; and when we behold how that wonderful cross of Saint Eloy—together with the smaller ones—and that incomparable ornament commonly called "the crest" are placed upon the golden altar, then I say, sighing deeply in my heart: "Every precious stone was thy covering, the sardius, the topaz, and the jasper, the chrysolite, and the onyx, and the beryl, the sapphire, and the carbuncle, and the emerald." To those who know the properties of precious stones it becomes evident, to their utter astonishment, that none is absent from the number of these (with the only exception of the carbuncle), but that they abound most copiously. Thus... the many colored gems called me away from external cares, and worthy meditation has induced me to reflect, transferring that which is material to that which is immaterial, on the diversity of the sacred virtues; then it seems to be that I see myself dwelling, as it were, in some strange region of the universe which neither exists entirely in the slime of the earth, nor entirely in the purity of Heaven, and that, by the grace of God, I can be transported from this inferior to that higher world in a anagogical manner.[8]

No other object expresses Suger's deep fascination with precious and semiprecious stones more than his celebrated chalice commissioned for his abbey (*fig. 50*). The chalice is the fusion of an ancient Egyptian agate bowl to the Parisian mounts he had expressly made for it. While Suger does not mention how the ancient vessel was transformed into a footed liturgical chalice, he does marvel at the resulting beauty: "We also procured for the services at the aforesaid altar a precious chalice out of one solid sardonyx, which [word] derives from 'sardius' and 'onyx'; in which one [stone] the sard's red hue, by varying its property, so keenly vies with the blackness of the onyx that one property seems to be bent on trespassing upon the other."[9]

For Abbot Suger, the diffused light emanating from gemstones and stained glass windows provided the church interior with a visual correspondence to the heavenly Jerusalem. The experience of the medieval spectator was a reflection of the celestial city. The colored light from sparkling gemstones was an important element in medieval aesthetics and symbolism. From Old Testament sources, such light implied the goodness, the wisdom, and the power and protection of God, while in the

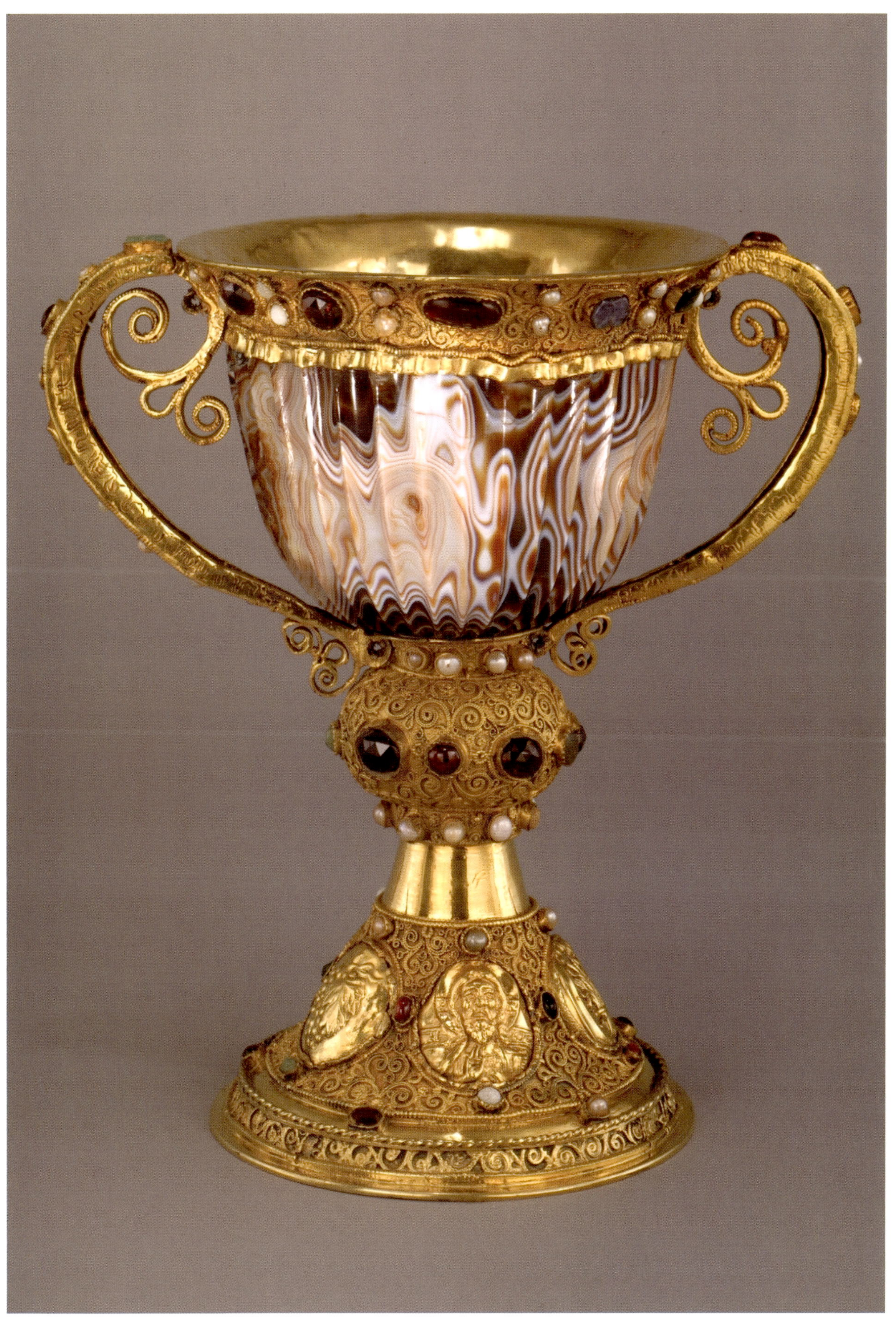

New Testament, such colored light became associated with the nature of Christ and the means of spiritual awakening. Thus, for many medieval thinkers like Suger, the radiant beauty of sparkling stones became an intimation of the nature of God.

Liturgical Vestments

In addition to the many liturgical vessels and reliquaries acquired by the great churches, there is another category of object that would have been essential to the vesting and dignity of the priest. Such objects became an essential part of the medieval treasury. These are the vestments and a group of smaller objects worn by the priest, and especially higher prelates, while celebrating the Mass or for ceremonial processions. The Middle Ages was an age of great ceremony, both ecclesiastical and secular, in which costume indicated rank and purpose within society. Ecclesiastical dress distinguished the members of the clergy from the laity, and within the church the various ranks, religious orders, and liturgical roles were each distinguished by sanctioned dress and vesting. Only those vestments used by priests and monks in the ceremony would have found their way into the treasury *(see figs. 1, 9, 10)*. The everyday garments, such as cassocks and habits, would not have been stored in the treasury and were not, strictly speaking, considered liturgical.

Distinctive liturgical vestments were not the case in the early Christian Church, however. During these early centuries there was little, if any, distinction between ecclesiastical and civil dress.[10] Instead, early liturgical dress is thought to have derived from late Roman dress, the forms of which were retained out of conservatism. It was only during the early Middle Ages that popes and councils began to make distinctions between the dress of the priest at the altar and that away from it.

By the ninth and tenth centuries, vesting prayers intended for the priest prior to liturgical functions were introduced and contained allegorical or mystical meanings. It was during this same period that particular meanings were attached to the colors used for liturgical vestments. A variety of liturgical undergarments had evolved by the twelfth and thirteenth centuries. These included the amice, the fanon, the alb, the cincture, and the surplice, all usually made of linen. While it is not possible to pursue a comprehensive discussion of these items here, we should consider in some detail the liturgical outer garments that would have been visible to the faithful.

The Tunicle and the Dalmatic

The tunicle and dalmatic were worn respectively by the subdeacon and deacon and were also worn by bishops. The tunicle probably evolved from the Roman tunic with short sleeves. It eventually developed into a narrow, long-sleeved tunic extending to the feet, though other variants were known during the Middle Ages. As the vestment of the subdeacon, par excellence, it was conferred on him at ordination. Nevertheless, other ecclesiastical functionaries, like acolytes, crucifers, and thurifers *(see fig. 33)*, might wear it.

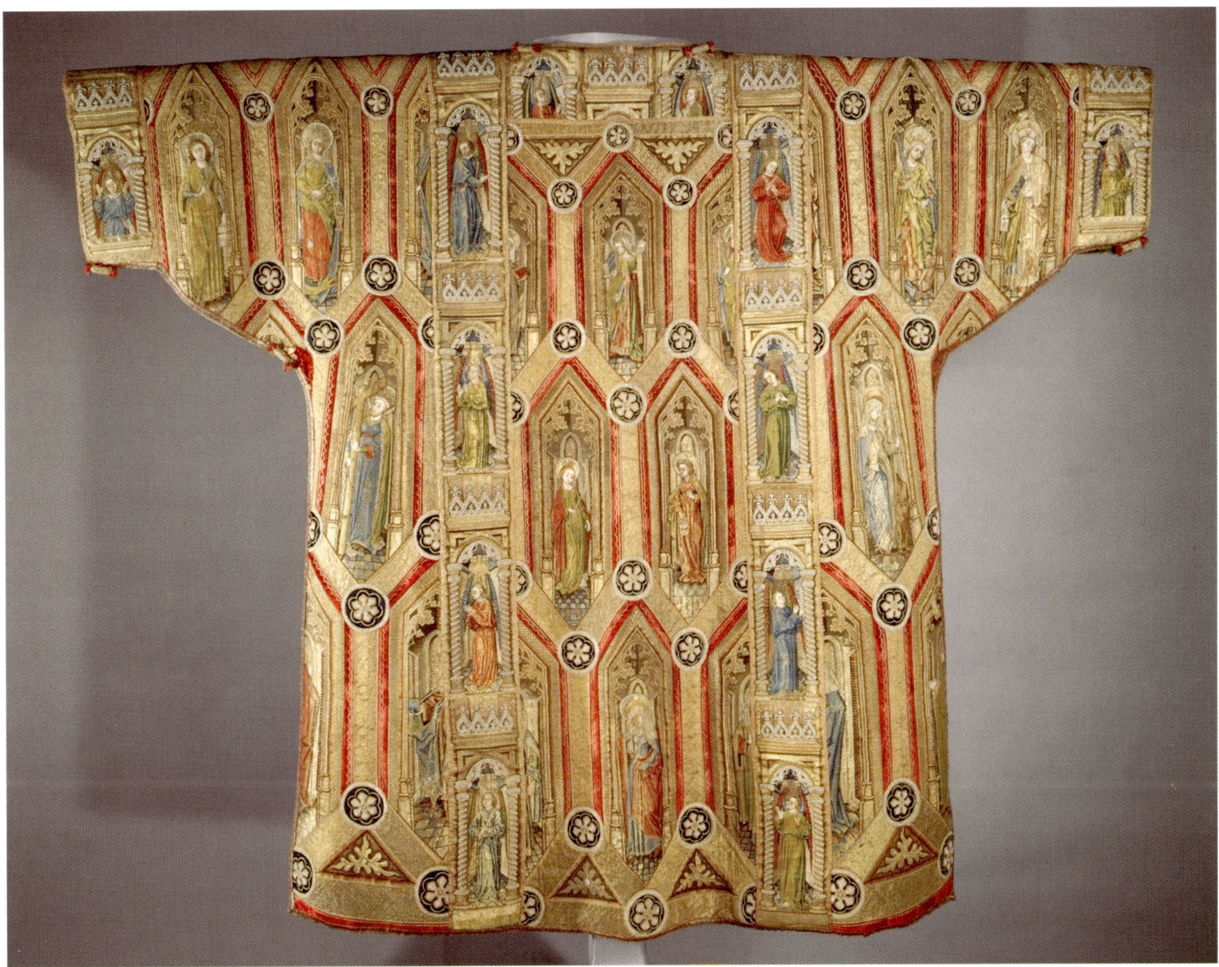

Figure 51. Dalmatic for the Chapel of the Order of the Golden Fleece. Red velvet, embroidery in gold thread, pearls, topazes, and sapphires. Netherlands, ca. 1450–80. Kunsthistorisches Museum, Schatzkammer, Vienna.

Similarly, dalmatics were special vestments of the deacon *(fig. 51)*. By the eighth century the dalmatic was given to the deacon in Rome as a symbol of his office. Outside of Rome, this practice was not universal until the thirteenth or fourteenth century. In its earliest form, the dalmatic was a long, wide tunic extending to the feet with wide sleeves. Eventually, it became shorter with narrowed sleeves and a slit down each side *(figs. 10, 52)*. Originally made of linen or wool, the dalmatic was eventually made of silk. Before the tenth century, the garment was nearly always white. Afterward, they were colored. By the thirteenth century, they were made of a color to match the priest's chasuble. Early dalmatics were ornamented with clavi, a pair of vertical bands, one over each shoulder, and a narrow band on the sleeves.

The Chasuble

The chasuble is the main sleeveless outer garment worn by priests while officiating at Mass *(figs. 53, 54)*. Originally, the chasuble was worn by all clerics. The deacon and subdeacon, for example, wore a chasuble during the penitential season. By the end of the thirteenth century, the practice had fallen into disuse, and the chasuble was reserved for priests and bishops alone.[11] The chasuble is undoubtedly the most recognizable vestment in the Roman Church due to its prominence and visibility.

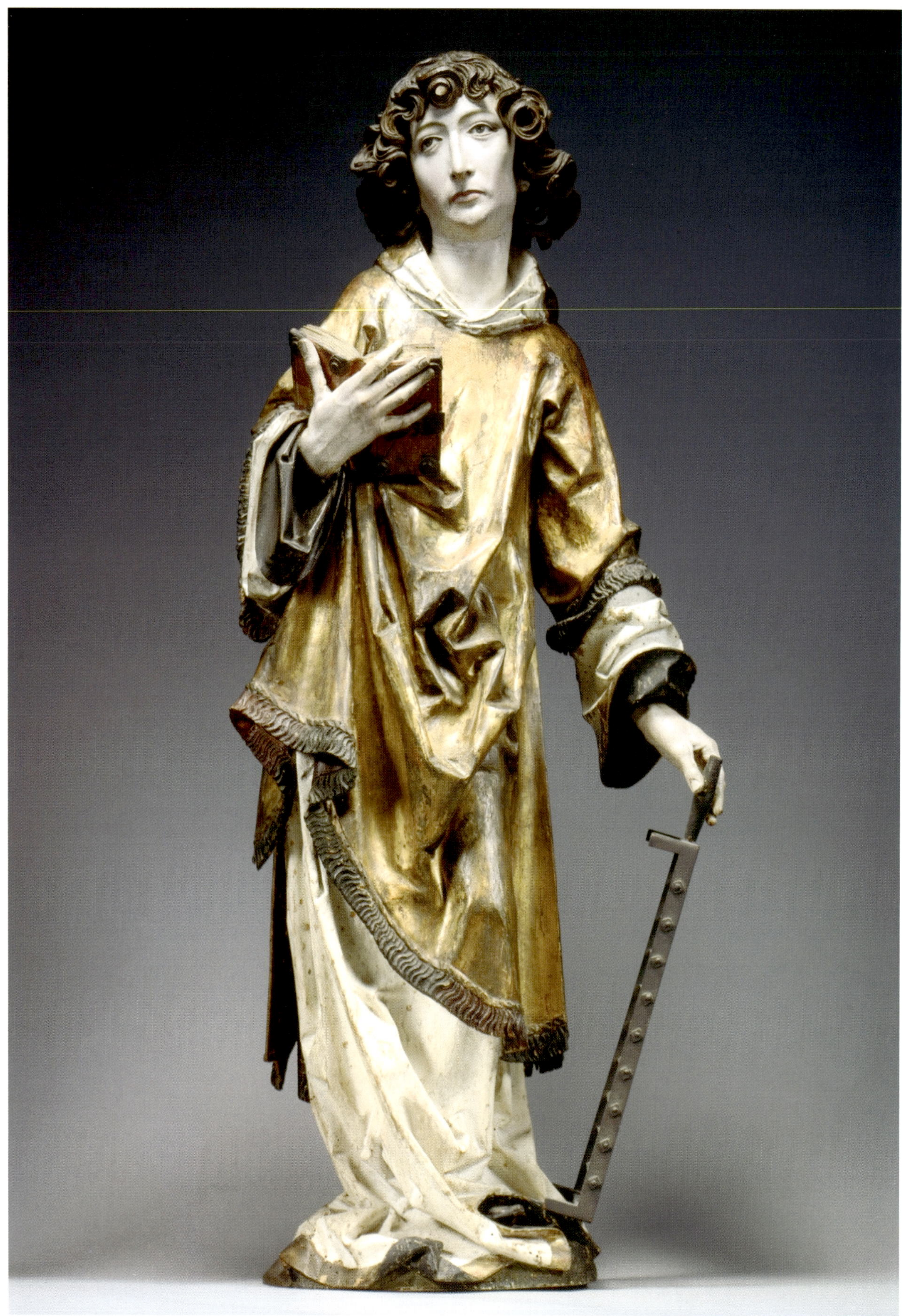

Under the chasuble or dalmatic, the priest or deacon wore an alb, a long white linen garment that symbolized the purity of the priest's ceremonial function *(see figs. 1, 10)*. In its earliest form the chasuble was a round or square piece of material with a hole in the center for the head. By the early Middle Ages, it had assumed a conical form, made with two semicircular pieces of fabric sewn together and covered in an embroidered textile known as an orphrey. After the thirteenth century the chasuble became excessively ornamented with embroideries and decorative orphreys sometimes made in the form of a cross or a crucifix. The fabric was generally made of wool or silk, but the embroideries—with gold thread, gems, pearls, enamels, and semiprecious stones—became the visual focus of the vestment.

Figure 52 (facing page). Saint Lawrence. Polychromed lindenwood. Tilmann Riemenschneider, Germany, ca. 1502–10. The Cleveland Museum of Art, Leonard C. Hanna Jr. Fund, Acc. 1959.42. Saint Lawrence was considered one of the deacons of the Roman Church. As such, artists typically depict him wearing the dalmatic.

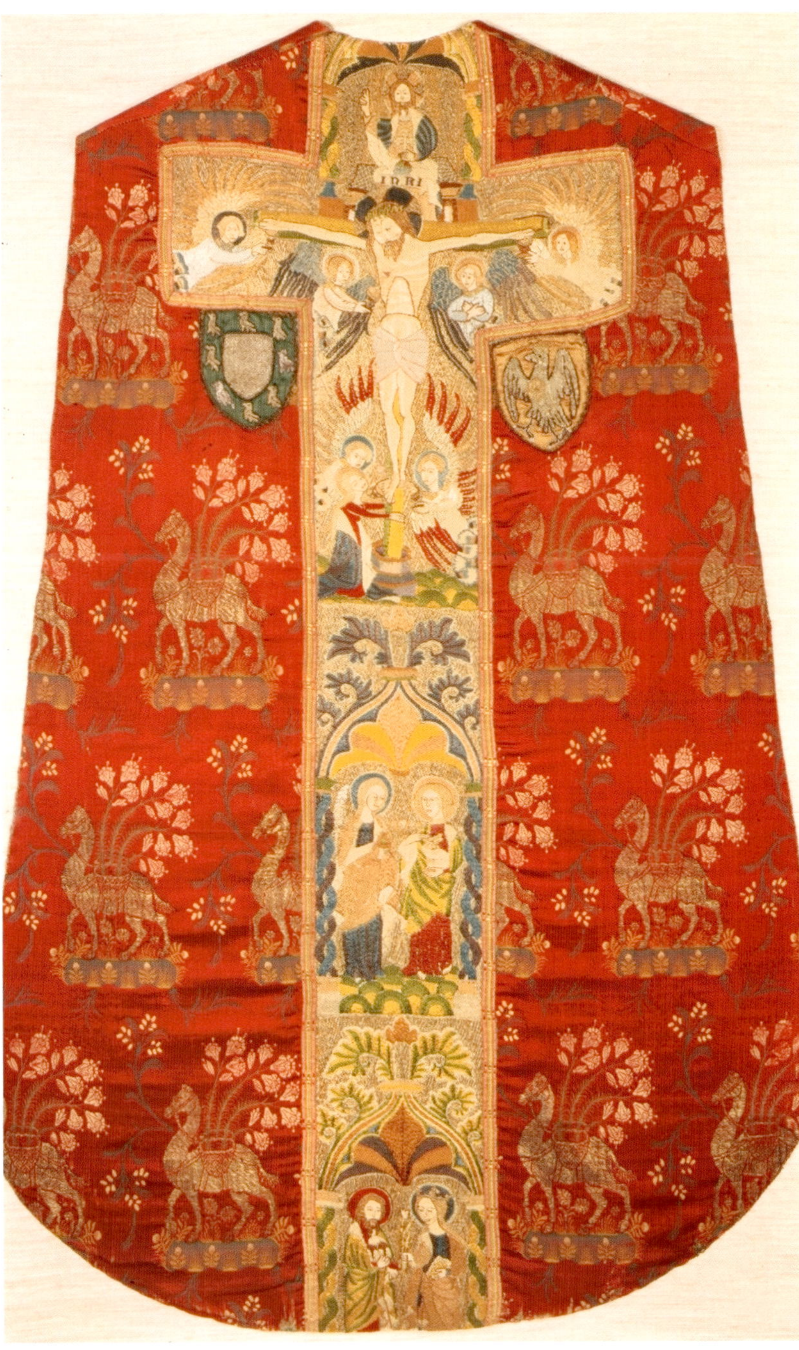

Figure 53. The Erpingham Chasuble with Crucifixion. Brocaded silk lampas woven in Italy; orphrey embroidered in England, ca. 1400–1430. The Victoria and Albert Museum, London.

Photo: Victoria and Albert Museum/Art Resource, New York

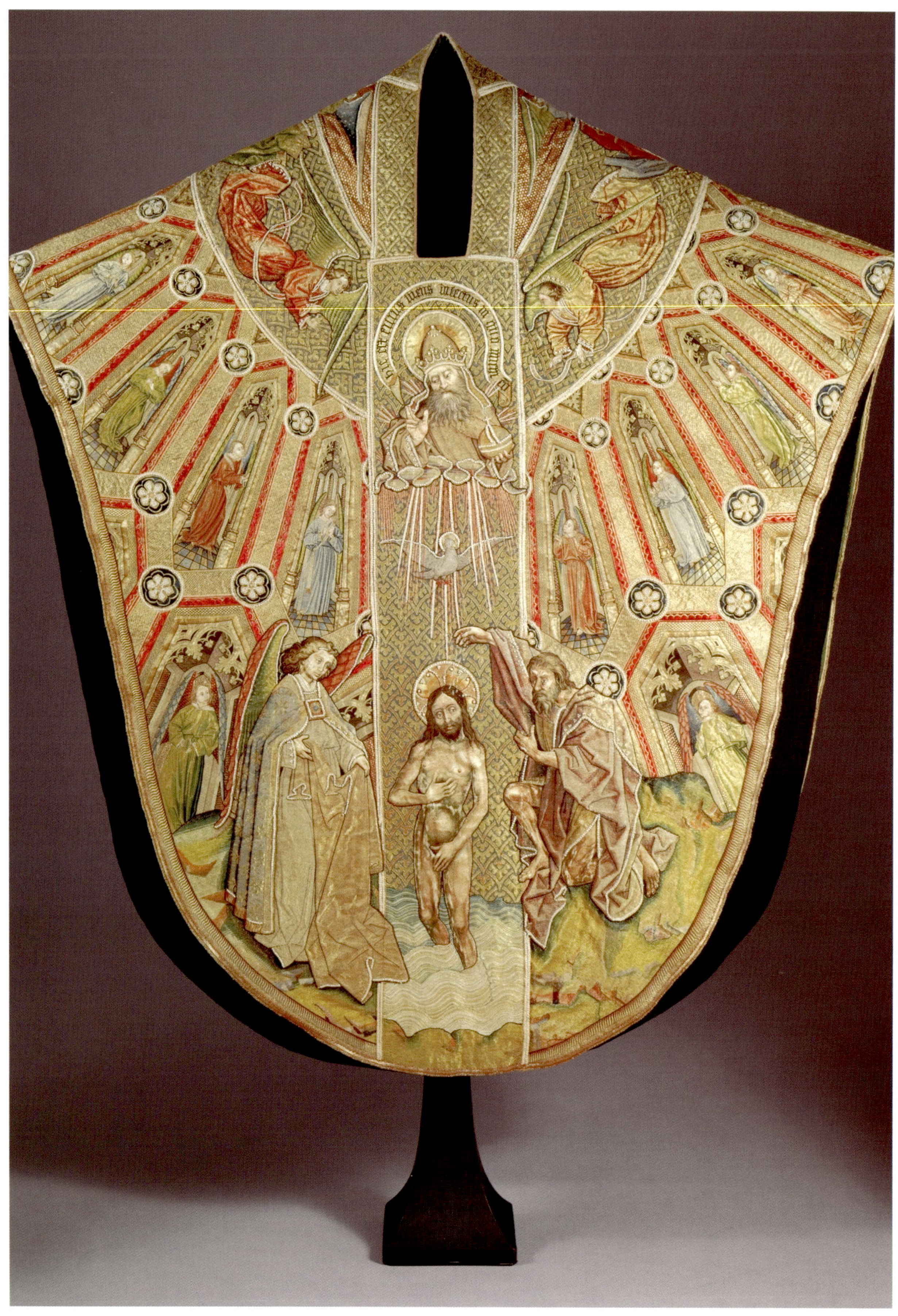

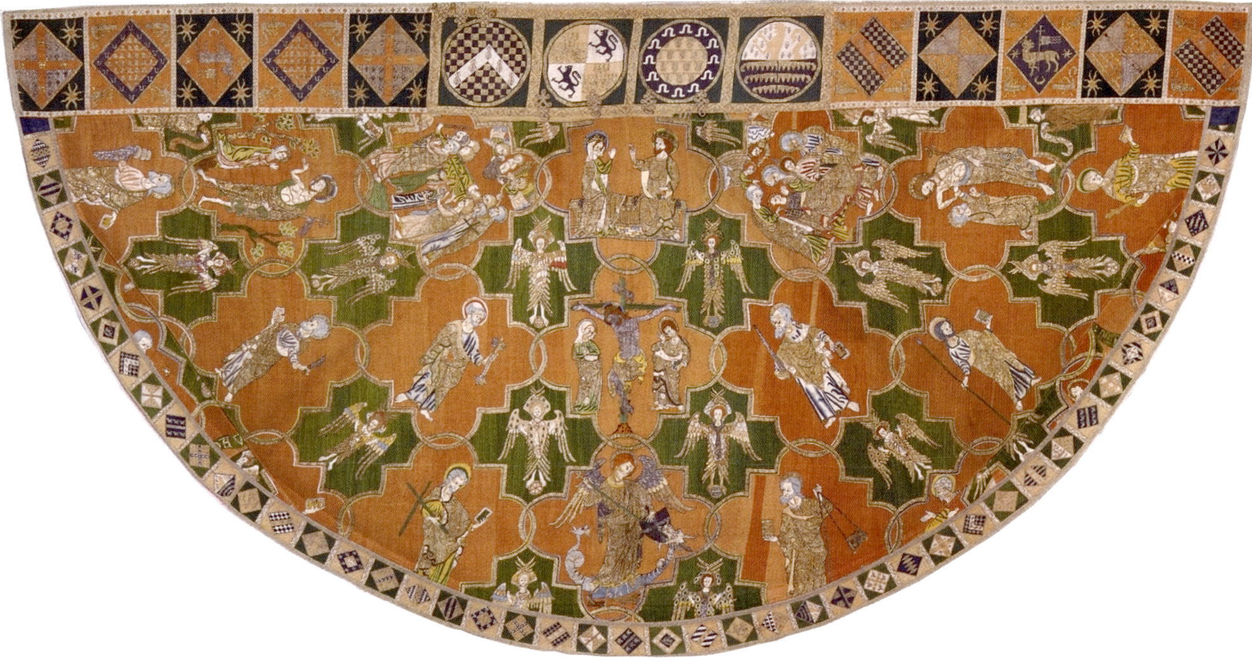

The Cope

A cope, the principal vestment of the church, is the heavy semicircular cape worn by the priest over other vestments for processions and solemn occasions *(fig. 55)*. The cope was essentially a large cape or cloak originally worn by clergy to keep themselves warm in cold churches. It was not until the thirteenth century that copes were worn for liturgical use. Priests wore copes when presiding at the office in the choir, when incensing the altar at Lauds, and during processions *(fig. 34)*, benedictions, burials, and at solemn High Mass.

By liturgical law, the church directed that the vestments worn by its priests and the draperies or hangings used in the decoration of the altar should correspond to the office of the day or the season of the year. In this way, the symbolism of violet, white, green, red, gold, black, rose, and other colors was sanctioned by the church to reinforce the mood appropriate to a liturgical season or Mass. Like chasubles, copes followed these rules when the church could afford the expense. The cope's large folded front was not sewn together (like the chasuble) but was left open. Like the chasuble, copes were often splendidly decorated with the best materials and embroidery available. The cope was fastened together with a special brooch called a morse, which was often decorated with enamels, gems, or pearls *(fig. 56)*. The fabrics would be as elaborate as the donors could afford, but the orphreys contained the most valuable decoration. The morse would also be of great expense and beauty.

Figure 54 (facing page). Chasuble of the Chapel of the Order of the Golden Fleece. Red velvet, embroidery in gold thread, pearls, topazes, and sapphires. Netherlands, 15th century. Kunsthistorisches Museum, Schatzkammer, Vienna.

Figure 55 (above). The Syon Cope. Velvet embroidered in colored silk and gilt-silver threads. England, 14th century. The Victoria and Albert Museum, London.

Photo: Victoria and Albert Museum/Art Resource, New York

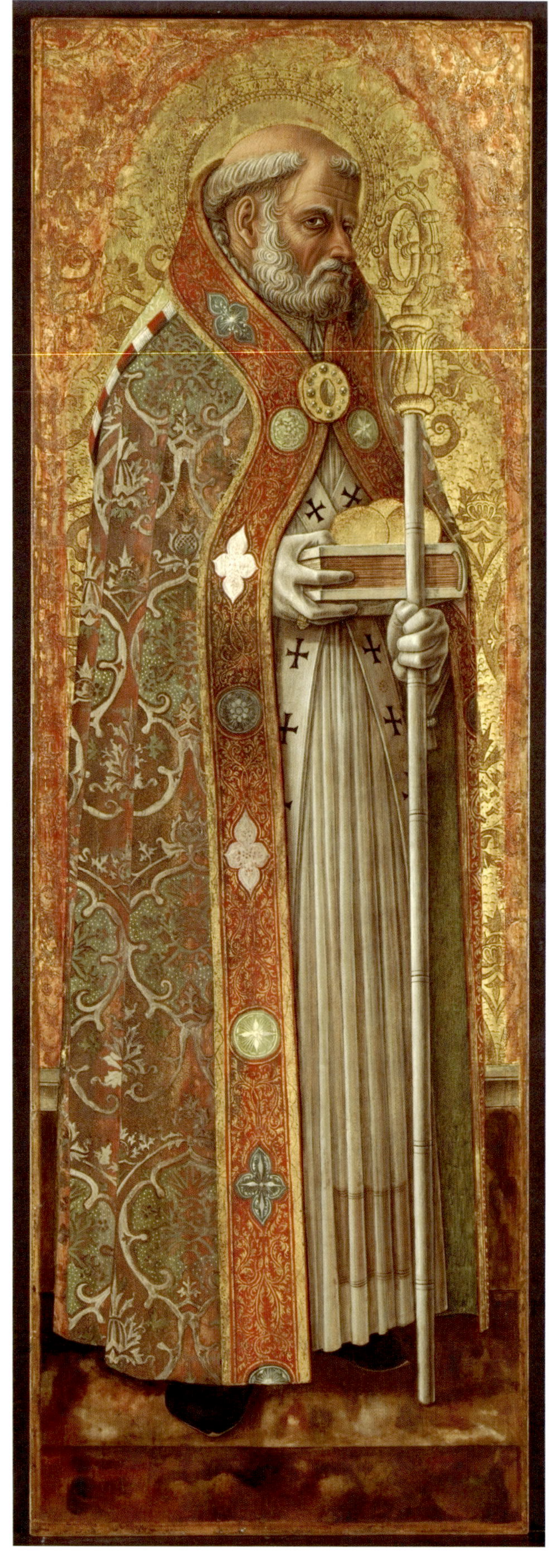

Figure 56. Saint Nicholas of Bari. Oil on panel. Carlo Crivelli, Venice, Italy, 1472. The Cleveland Museum of Art, Gift of the Hanna Fund, Acc. 1952.111.

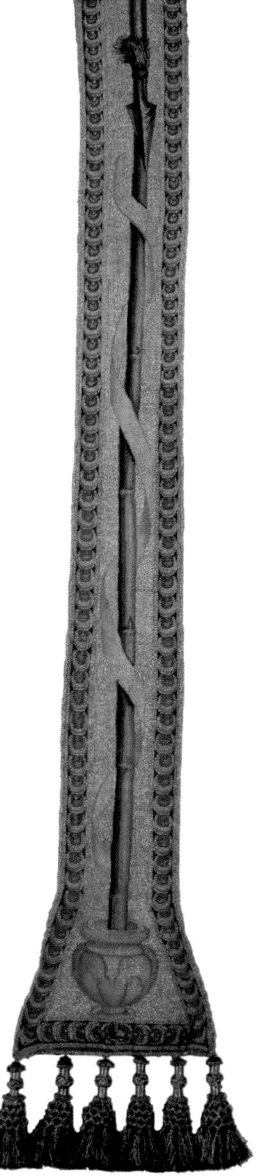

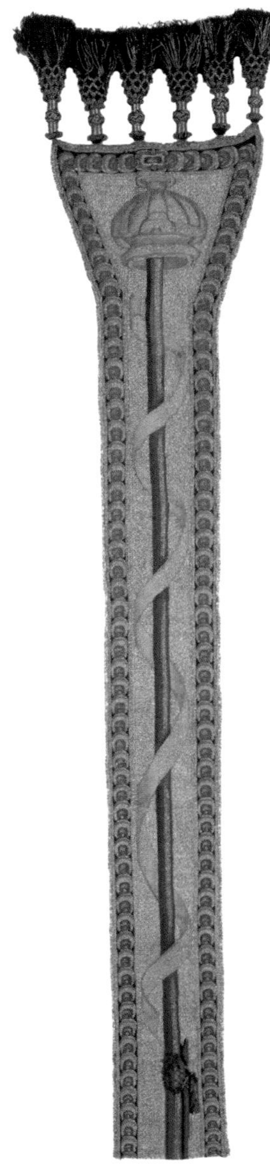

Figure 57. Stole of Pope Clement VIII (1592–1605). Embroidery in silk with gilt-silver threads. Guasparri di Bartolomeo Papini, Italy, died 1621. Biblioteca Apostolica Vaticana, Museo Sacro, Inv. 2776 A-B.

The Stole and Maniple

In addition to the major vestments, priests during the Middle Ages adopted smaller vestments that formed a genre known as insignia. These items served a strictly symbolic function and were not in the broadest sense garments. Among these were the stole and the maniple. Stoles were worn underneath dalmatics and chasubles and were essentially long slender cloths that the priest wore around his neck and that suspended nearly to the ankles *(fig. 57)*. During the vesting of the priest before the Mass, he would kiss a representation of a cross at the center of the stole before placing it around his neck. In this way, the stole symbolized the yoke of the Lord, the priest's vocation as the servant of God. The stole was typically a narrow band made of valuable fabric, decorated with orphreys and finished with fringe, tassels, or occasionally bells. Like the maniple, the stole usually contrasted in color with the chief vestments worn.

Figure 58 (facing page). Bishop's Miter. Painted silk with scenes of the Resurrection and saints. France, 14th century. Musée du Moyen-Âge (Cluny Museum), Paris.

Photo: Erich Lessing/Art Resource, New York

The maniple was a short strip of cloth worn on the priest's left arm during Mass. Some believe it symbolized the ropes binding Christ's hands during his trial before Pontius Pilate. The maniple, first used by clergy in Rome and Ravenna during the sixth and seventh centuries, had been universally adopted throughout the church by the ninth century. Primarily worn by the higher orders of subdeacon, deacon, presbyter, and bishop, the maniple was occasionally worn by acolytes. Even the lay brothers at Cluny were permitted to wear the maniple until the eleventh century. Originally a functional piece of cloth, the maniple became highly decorative after the tenth century and was often fashioned from valuable fabric with gold and silver threads. Many superb examples have survived and are in museums and church treasuries.[12]

Other Sacerdotal Objects

An assortment of smaller garments and jeweled accessories for the clergy evolved during the Middle Ages. These items, for the hand, head, and foot, might be categorized as ephemera since they were not considered valuable enough to make their way into the medieval treasury. Clerical clothing items, such as shoes, stockings, and simple skullcaps, were generally not fabricated of costly materials. In exceptional circumstances, these items may have been preserved in the treasury if they belonged to a cleric who was venerated and subsequently beatified and canonized. In these cases, they survived as saintly mementoes or relics.

Items that were preserved in the treasury because of their costly and luxurious materials were pontifical gloves, miters, and tiaras. Pontifical gloves were first used to adorn the bishop's hands and not for any practical purpose. The first recorded use of such gloves is in eighth-century France from which the practice went to Rome in the tenth century. By the eleventh century, abbots were adopting the use of gloves with special permission. Pontifical gloves were typically worn at solemn pontifical masses following communion, at solemn offices, and in processions. Surviving examples from the Middle Ages are of woven material with a cuff terminating in a long point and tassel. The backs were often ornamented with pearls, gems, or even enamel roundels.

Documentary and pictorial sources show that the tiara and early versions of the Episcopal miter were used in liturgical ceremonies early in the Christian era, at least as far back as patristic times. The earliest example of Episcopal headdress in illuminated manuscripts is a conical tiara-miter. Indeed, there may have been little distinction during the early history of the church between the tiara and miter. Numerous illustrations survive of early medieval bishops wearing tiaras. Precisely when the church adopted the miter in its present form as part of the vesting of bishops is difficult to know. Only the pope, cardinals, and bishops are allowed to wear miters. Miters that resemble today's headdress first appeared during the eleventh century and consisted of a simple cap emerging into a point and with two lappets (strips of cloth) suspended from behind *(fig. 58)*. Over the centuries, miters were elongated and greatly embellished with deluxe materials, such as gold thread, pearls, and gemstones.

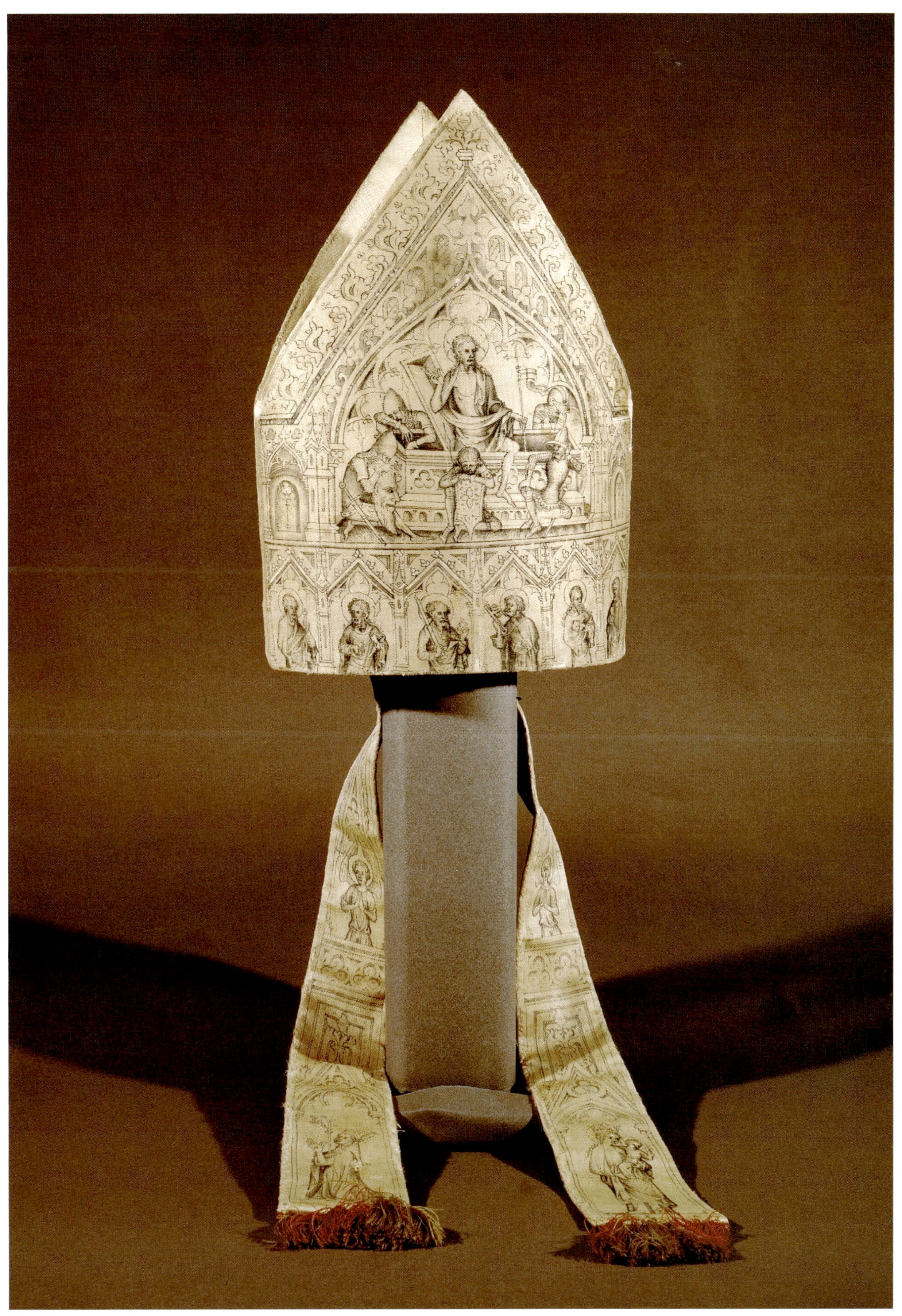

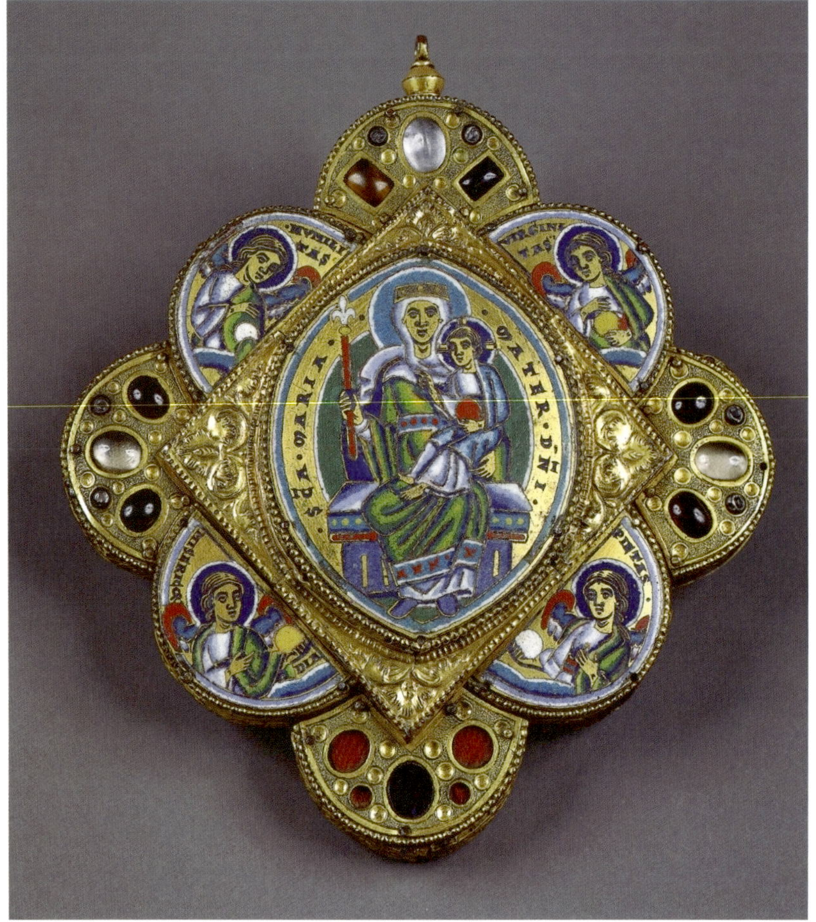

Figure 59. Disk Reliquary or Phylactery: The Virgin and Child Surrounded by the Four Cardinal Virtues. Champlevé enamel on gilt-copper with vernis brun (on reverse). Circle of Godefroid de Huy, Meuse Valley, Belgium, ca. 1160. The Cleveland Museum of Art, Purchase from the J. H. Wade Fund, Acc. 1926.428.

Other sacerdotal objects worn by clergy included signet or Episcopal rings, morses (for fastening the cope), pectoral crosses, and phylacteries. The latter, which were small devotional amulets often containing personal relics, were worn on the person by clerics *(fig. 59)*. Some of these objects achieved high levels of craftsmanship and were made of precious materials, such as gold, silver, enamel, and gemstones.

Embroidery

The most common technique used in the production and decoration of liturgical vestments was embroidery. Silk was the most commonly used material for vestments and came in a variety of forms. So-called cloth of gold was made from silk and interwoven with threads of gold. Embroidery was a decorative technique that involved stitching, cutting, withdrawing threads, and applying beads or other materials to a fabric. During the fourteenth century, plain velvet began to be used as a ground. Initially the embroidery was worked through fine silk or linen laid on the surface of the velvet. At the same time, fine silk embroideries, skillfully shaded in the needle-painting technique, were made in the Italian city-states, notably Florence and Venice, and also in Central Europe.

A technique called opus teutonicum was produced in the German-speaking lands of Europe, principally in Switzerland, Hessen, Lower

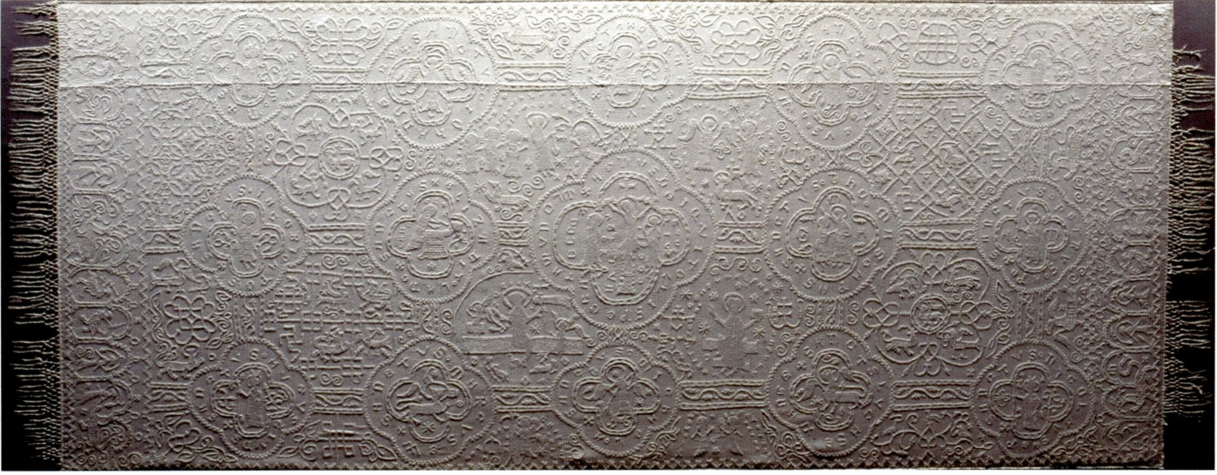

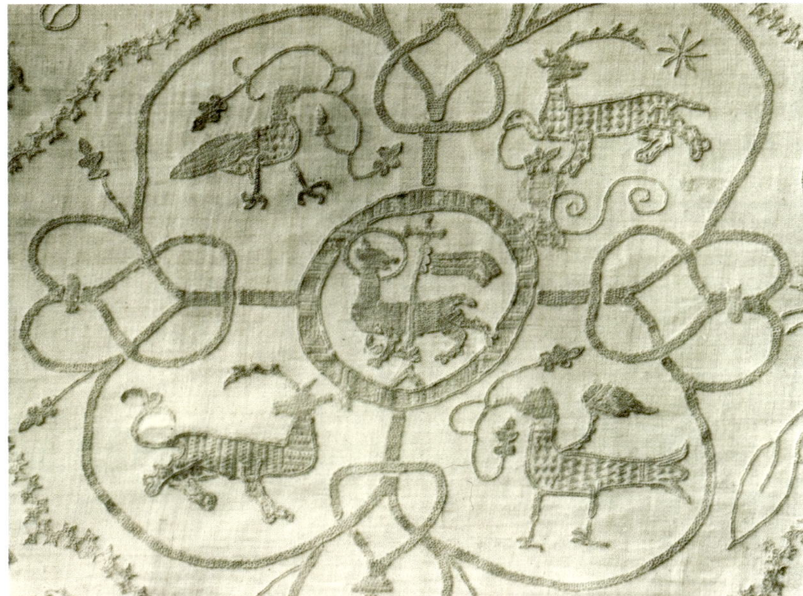

Figure 60. Lenten Cloth. Linen embroidery (white on white). Altenberg an der Lahn, Germany, early 14th century. The Cleveland Museum of Art, Purchase from the J. H. Wade Fund, Acc. 1948.352.

Figure 60a. Detail of Lenten Cloth (previous illustration).

Saxony, and Lübeck. This involved embroidering white linen with white linen thread and sometimes a small amount of colored silk thread in a variety of stitches. Early examples of "whitework" survive in many European countries. Lenten cloths (Fastentuch) once covered most crucifixes and altars in German and Austrian Catholic churches in the weeks leading up to Easter. A superb example of a Lenten cloth is in the collections of the Cleveland Museum of Art *(figs. 60, 60a)*.

The oldest Lenten cloth produced in Austria can be seen in the Gurk Cathedral in Carinthia. Painted in 1458, the cloth measures about 90 square meters and contains around one hundred panels depicting scenes from both the Old and New Testaments. Klagenfurt also has a Lenten cloth with forty-one images from 1593 that can be seen in the Church of Christ the King.

A major phenomenon in medieval textile history was opus anglicanum, or "English works," a name applied to a particular type of embroidery. These comprised works of supreme technical skill produced in England, especially from 1250 to 1350, the greatest treasures of which are vestments

Figure 61. **Orphrey with the Tree of Jesse (detail).** Embroidery (opus anglicanum), silk, gold, and silver threads on linen. England, mid-14th century. The Cleveland Museum of Art, Purchase from the J. H. Wade Fund, Acc. 1949.503.

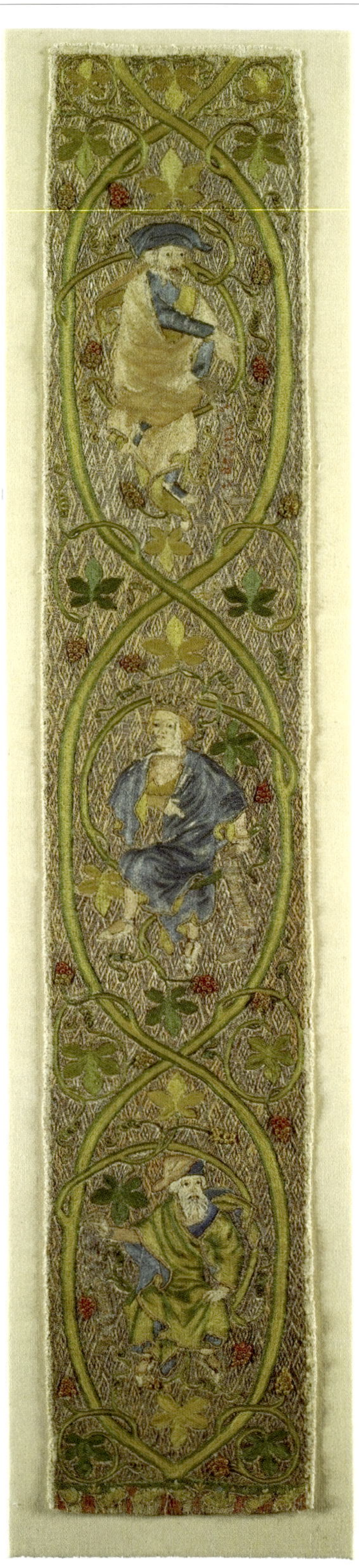

(fig. 61). Opus anglicanum was greatly prized for the quality of its work and the delicacy of its colored figurative images set against gold-embroidered silk or velvet grounds.[13]

Many of these embroideries came from monasteries and convents. For example, Christina of Huntingdon, the first prioress of the Saint Albans cell at Monkyate, was famed as an embroideress.[14] Her work was of such fine quality that of all the precious gifts offered to Pope Adrian IV (1154–59), he accepted only hers: three miters and a pair of sandals.[15] Pope Clement V (1305–14) also possessed at least three English embroidered copes that were probably received as gifts. In the Vatican inventory of 1295, opus anglicanum is mentioned 113 times. So famous was English medieval embroidery internationally that the monk Matthew Paris recorded in 1246, "The Lord Pope, having observed that the ecclesiastical ornaments of some Englishmen, such as the choir copes and miters, were embroidered in gold thread after a very desirable fashion, asked where these works were made, and received an answer, in England. 'Then,' said the Pope, 'England is surely a garden of delights for us. It is truly a never failing spring; and there where many things abound, may much be extorted.'"[16]

At the Benedictine nunnery at Langley in Leicestershire, an inventory of 1485 reveals an entire sacristy full of embroideries, including altar frontals and assorted vestments. Records exist of a vestment of black damask embroidered with roses and stars as well as a white beautifully worked with "rede trewlyps" (lovers' knots).[17] Like the art of manuscript illumination, opus anglicanum undoubtedly began in the cloister and eventually passed into the hands of lay craftspeople. These beautiful and expensive embroideries would have been preserved in the sacristy or within a secured treasury in major medieval churches wealthy enough to own them.

CHAPTER FIVE

Service Books for Mass and Office

The history of manuscript illumination corresponds almost exactly with the epoch we know as the Middle Ages, a vast period of about a thousand years. Manuscripts that were copied and decorated by hand were an important part of the medieval treasury, where the service books for the altar were often stored. Though great cathedrals and monasteries possessed libraries that housed most books, the sacristy held the sacramentaries, missals, lectionaries, graduals, antiphonaries, and other service books that priests used daily. Even after the invention of printing technology in the middle of the fifteenth century, illuminated manuscripts, particularly those destined for liturgical use, continued to be made in Italy and elsewhere through the end of the Renaissance.

An illuminated manuscript's texts were written on parchment, or animal skin, not paper. Functional texts were often enlivened with colorful painted decoration *(fig. 62)* and exquisite bindings *(fig. 49)*. In antiquity,

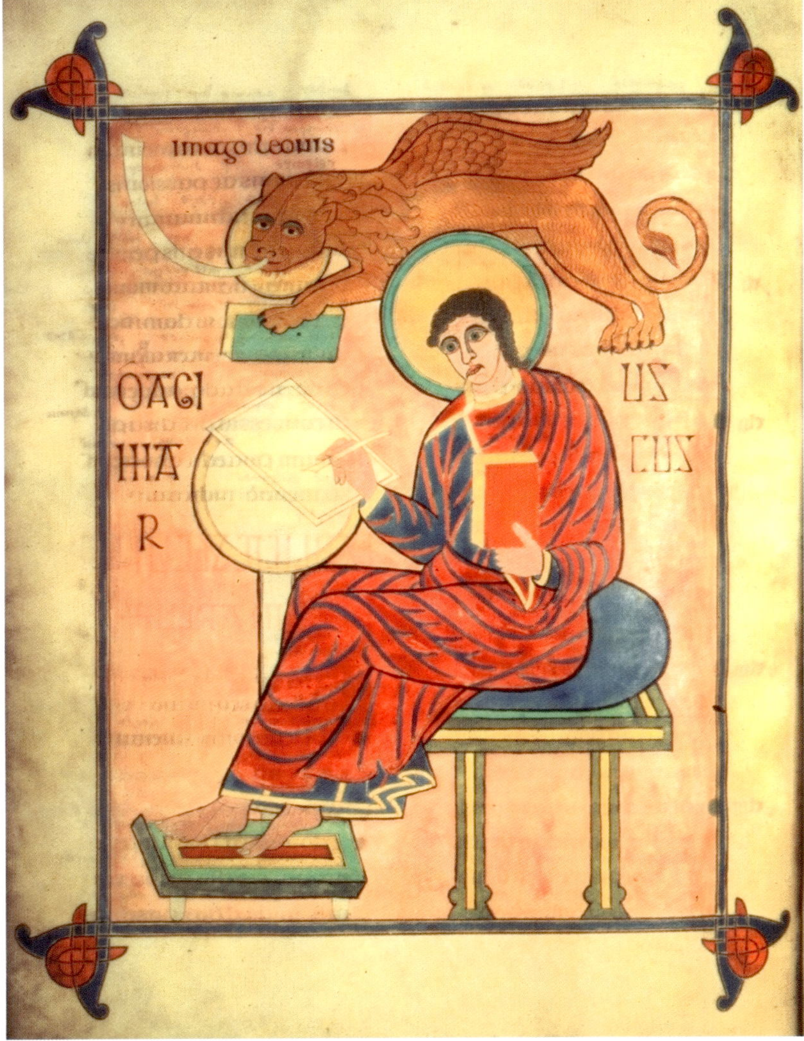

Figure 62. Saint Mark Writing. Fol. 93v. From **The Lindisfarne Gospels.** Tempera on parchment. England, ca. 698. The British Library, London, MS Cott. Nero.D.IV. This manuscript is traditionally thought to have been written and illuminated by Eadfrith, Bishop of Lindisfarne.

Photo: HIP/Art Resource, New York

Figure 63 (facing page). **The Nativity and Annunciation to the Shepherds.** Fol. 16v. From **The Berthold Sacramentary.** Tempera on parchment. Abbey of Weingarten, Germany, ca. 1215. The Pierpont Morgan Library, New York.

Photo: The Pierpont Morgan Library/Art Resource, New York

literature was primarily an oral tradition, and the papyrus scroll was read aloud. The Middle Ages broke with this tradition by treating the text as something to be revealed visually to the understanding through the written word. Often elaborately decorated with colorful pigments and gold leaf and in a multitude of styles and formats, illuminated manuscripts flourished in ecclesiastical, monastic, devotional, courtly, legal, and academic contexts throughout the Middle Ages and Renaissance. They are today readily admired in libraries and museums for the virtuosity of their miniatures, decorated letters, and elaborate marginal decoration.

Copying texts and making books have always been requisites to the practice of Christianity. Without books, services could not be conducted, laws codified and promulgated, and doctrine espoused. Above all, without books, the written word — the teachings and commandments of God himself, as conveyed in the Gospels and biblical texts — could not be made available to the faithful. From the earliest days of the church, the copying of books went on continuously in scriptoria scattered throughout Christendom. Throughout medieval Christendom, the embellishment of books was just as important in the visual projection of the sacred word as were luxurious vestments and liturgical vessels. From an early date, these books often contained decoration, either enlarged initials, pictures, or elaborate borders, which we know as illuminations.

Visually stunning books were frequently produced on the fringes of Christian Europe, but the intellectual epicenter of the faith was Rome. It was the papacy that historically assumed the greatest responsibility not only for collecting books but also for commissioning their production. And it was Rome that attracted many of the leading scribes and illuminators seeking the patronage of the papal court. Other gifted illuminators found commissions in wealthy abbeys or cathedral chapters seeking to produce stunning service books for their altars. Quite often, at least through the thirteenth century, such scribes and illuminators were talented members of the religious orders. Others were itinerant lay artists. Many of the most talented book illuminators gravitated to cathedral cities like Winchester, Paris, Rouen, and Cologne, the important production centers of the time, for the sole purpose of eking out a living in the service of the church.

The process of making a single codex, or book — from the preparation of the parchment to the mixing of inks and paints to the final binding — was expensive and laborious. Before a scribe could begin to write a book, he needed an original copy of the text, or an exemplar, to serve as a model for the new manuscript. Monasteries and cathedrals often loaned exemplars to each other for this purpose. On other occasions, it is likely that scribes and illuminators were sent to the host church in order to copy a book on the site. These activities account for the transmission of styles in book illumination.

A dense script was hard to read and was therefore broken up by decoration *(fig. 21)*. The decorated initial emerged as an accentuated first letter of script. Its function was utilitarian: to provide a marker for the reader's eye. Initials mark the beginnings of books and chapters and provide a visual gateway to the more important parts of text. Such initials became the focus of exceptional decoration, clearly to draw attention to and help classify the

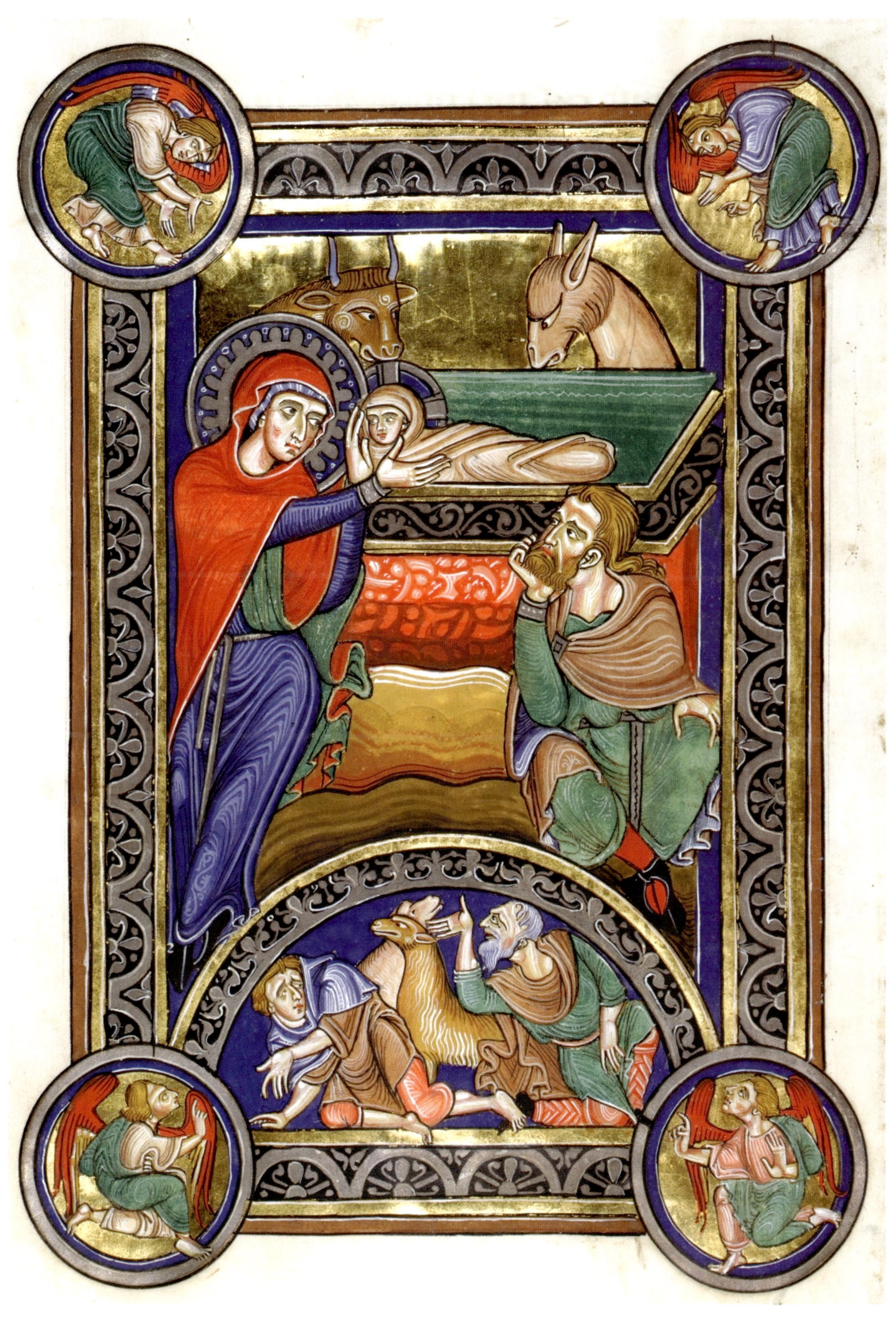

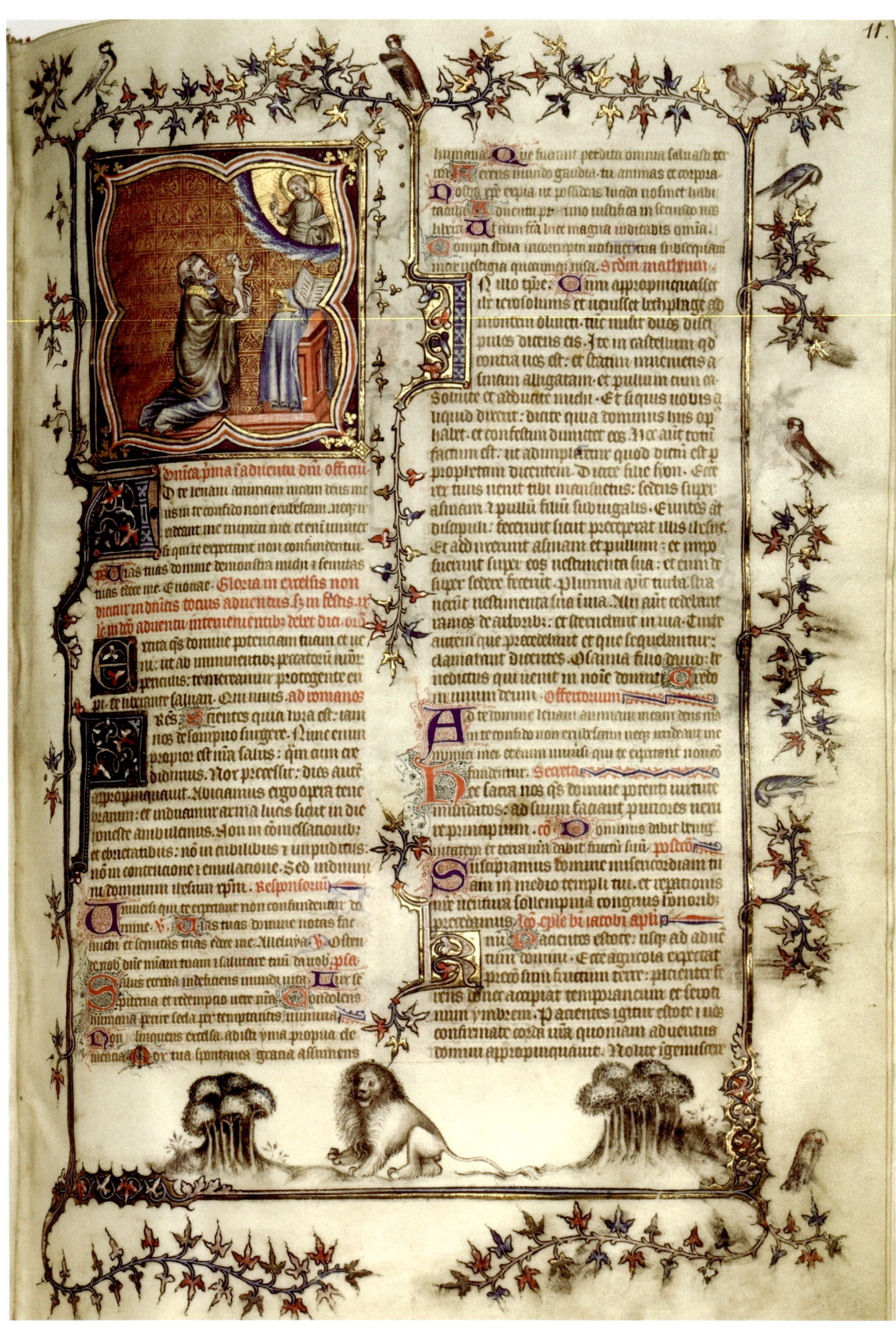

priorities of the text. Familiar images within an initial's decoration (called historiated initials) further assisted in explaining the text visually. In an era when books contained no page numbers, decorated letters made a text easier to find. Large decorated letters also enhanced a manuscript visually by providing a look of great luxury, a quality frequently sought by the book's owner.

Figure 64. A Priest Presenting a Soul to Christ. Fol. 11r from The Gotha Missal. Tempera on parchment. France, Paris, ca. 1370–72. The Cleveland Museum of Art, Purchase, Mr. and Mrs. William H. Marlatt Fund 1962.287. The opening text reads: *Ad te levavi animam meam* . . . (Unto thee have I lifted up my soul . . .). This text begins the Introit to the Mass for the first Sunday in Advent.

Cycles of Worship within the Liturgical Year

A fundamental distinction in the services of the late medieval church exists between the Mass and the Daily Offices. These were completely different in function and form. The Mass is the communion service, or Eucharist, one of the most solemn and important sacraments of the church. It was celebrated at the altar and its service books were the missal, sacramentary, and gospel lectionary. The musical counterpart to the service books for the Mass was the choral book, known as the gradual, usually made as a multivolume set to cover the entire liturgical year.

The Mass should not to be confused with the Daily Offices performed in the choir. The Daily Offices, or Divine Office, is the series of services for the hours of prayer. They are not sacramental services but prayers and anthems in honor and praise of Christ and the saints, either sung or recited at the eight canonical hours: Matins, Lauds, Prime, Terce, Sext, None, Vespers, and Compline. Their service book was the breviary, which was read privately by the clergy, especially in smaller parish churches. The musical form of the breviary was the antiphonal, a large multivolume choral book. Antiphonals were used for services in the choir by religious orders, cathedrals, collegiate churches, and perhaps a few large urban parish churches. Medieval churches and monasteries were expected to own a gradual and an antiphonal (in several volumes), but the poorest parish churches probably did not have a set of choir books.

The church year is based on two simultaneous cycles of services. The first is the Temporal cycle, or Proper of the Time, which observes Sundays and festivals commemorating the life of Christ. It opens with the first Sunday in Advent (the Sunday closest to November 30) and continues with Christmas, Lent, Paschal Time (from Easter to Ascension eve), and the season of Ascension (which includes Pentecost, Trinity Sunday, Corpus Christi, and the Sundays after Pentecost). The second quite distinct cycle of services is the Sanctoral, or Proper of the Saints, which celebrates the feast days of saints, including those of the Virgin Mary, and opens with Saint Andrew's Day (November 30). Some saints' names could be assigned to every day of the year. Local observances varied from place to place, and the calendars in liturgical manuscripts classified saints' days according to their importance: ordinary days; important, or semi-duplex, days; and days of exceptional importance, or totem duplex. The Sanctoral and the Temporal cycles were kept distinct in medieval service books and sometimes even formed separate volumes. The clergy would have easily distinguished between them.

Overleaf Figure 65. The Crucifixion and Christ in Majesty. Fols. 177v-178r. Missal from the Sainte-Chapelle in Paris. Tempera on parchment. Paris, late 14th to early 15th century. Bibliothèque Royale de Belgique, Brussels, MS 9125.

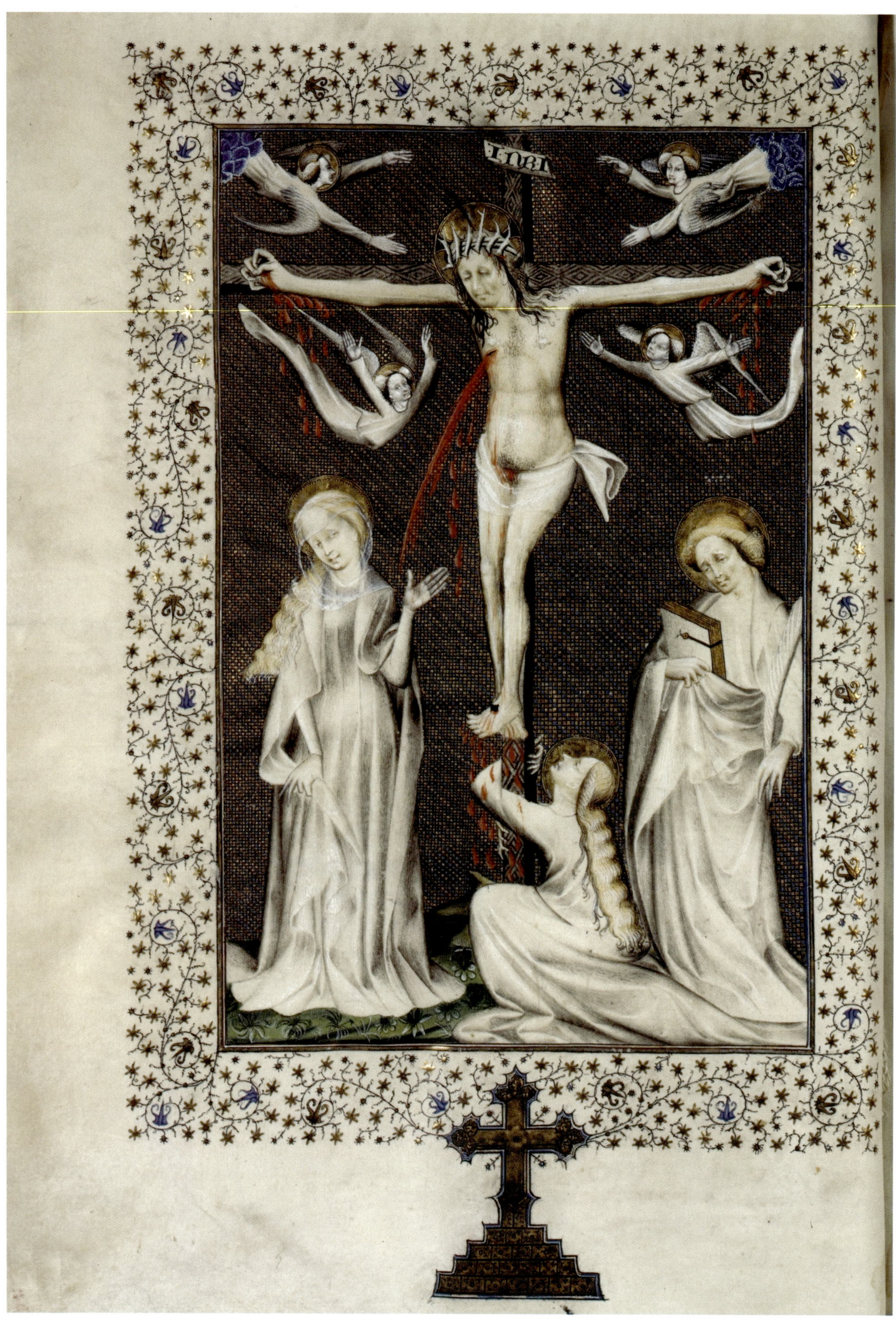

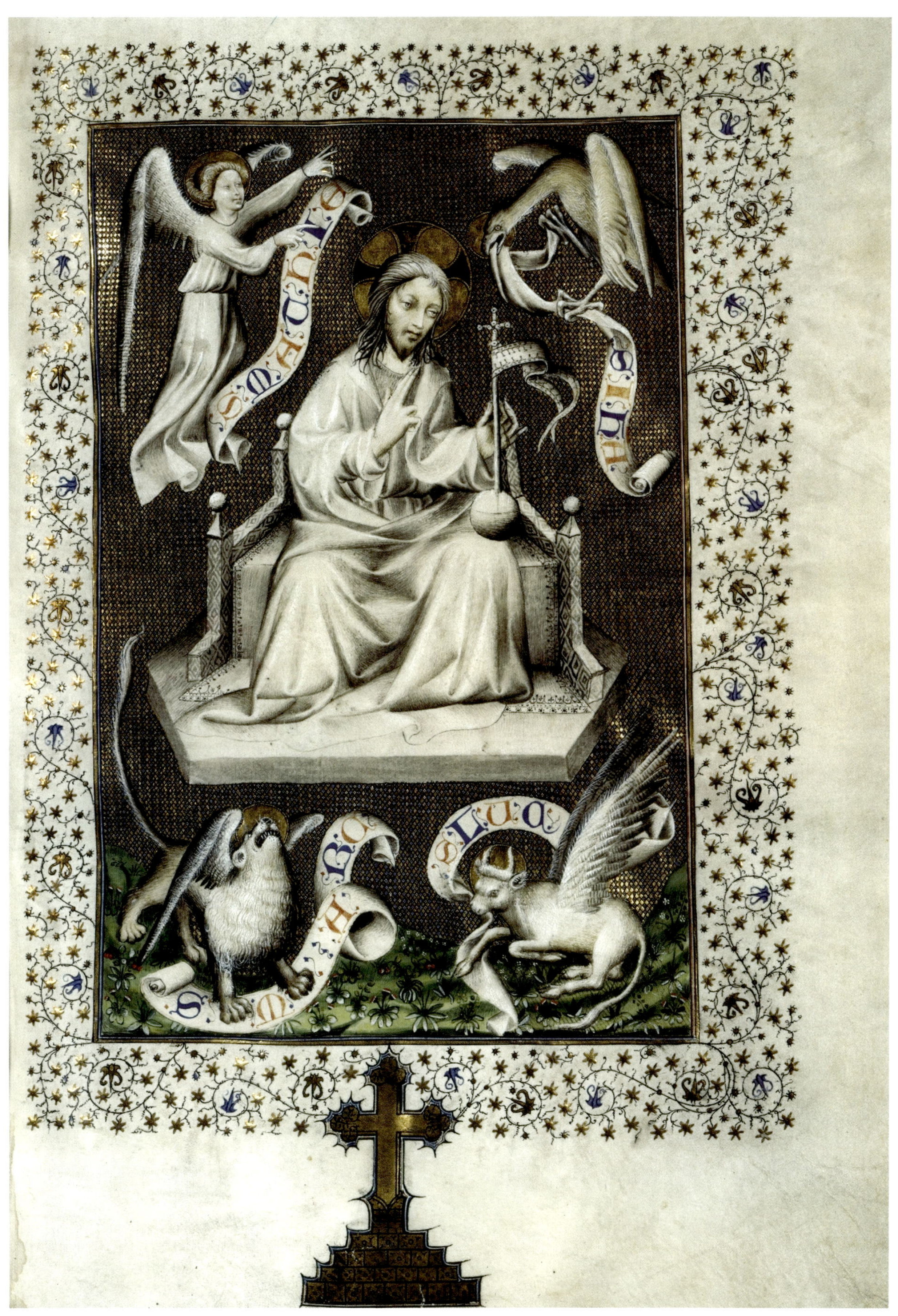

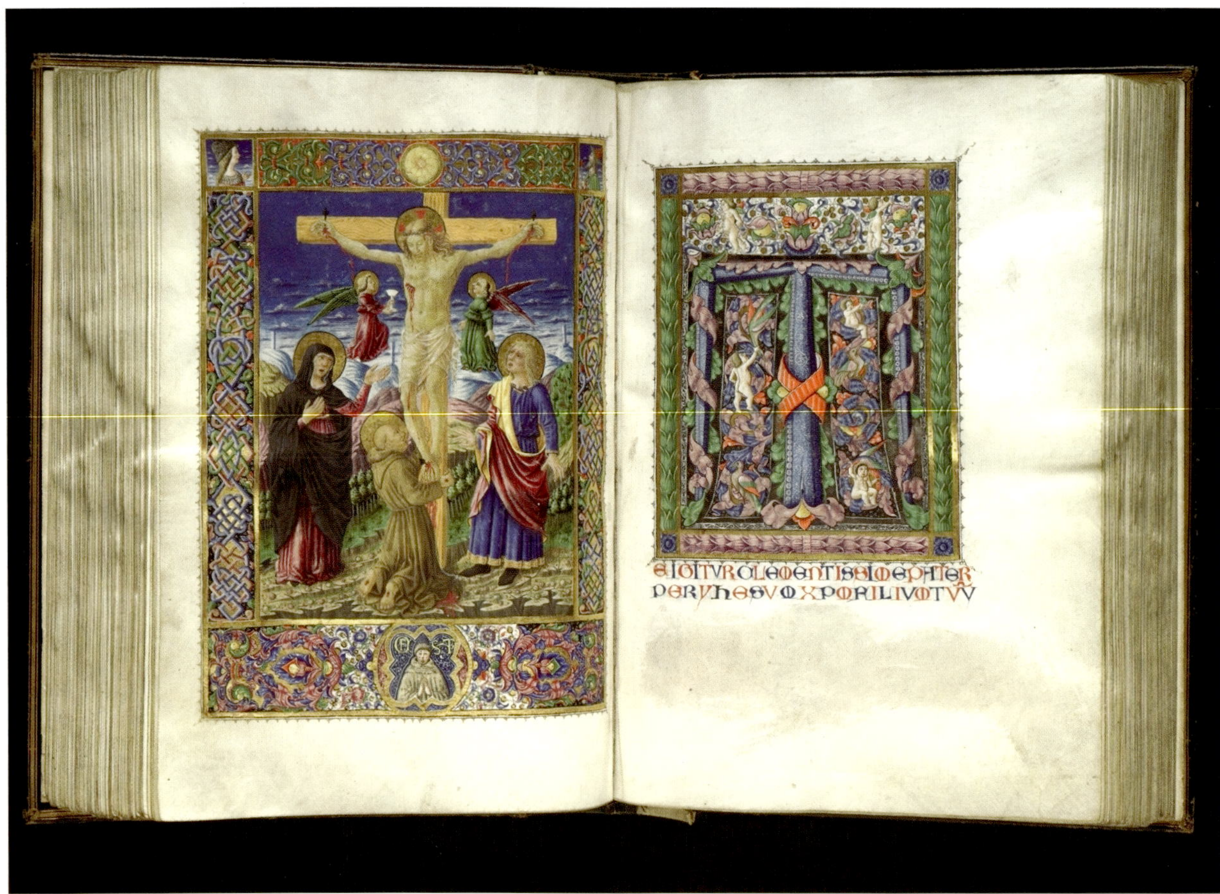

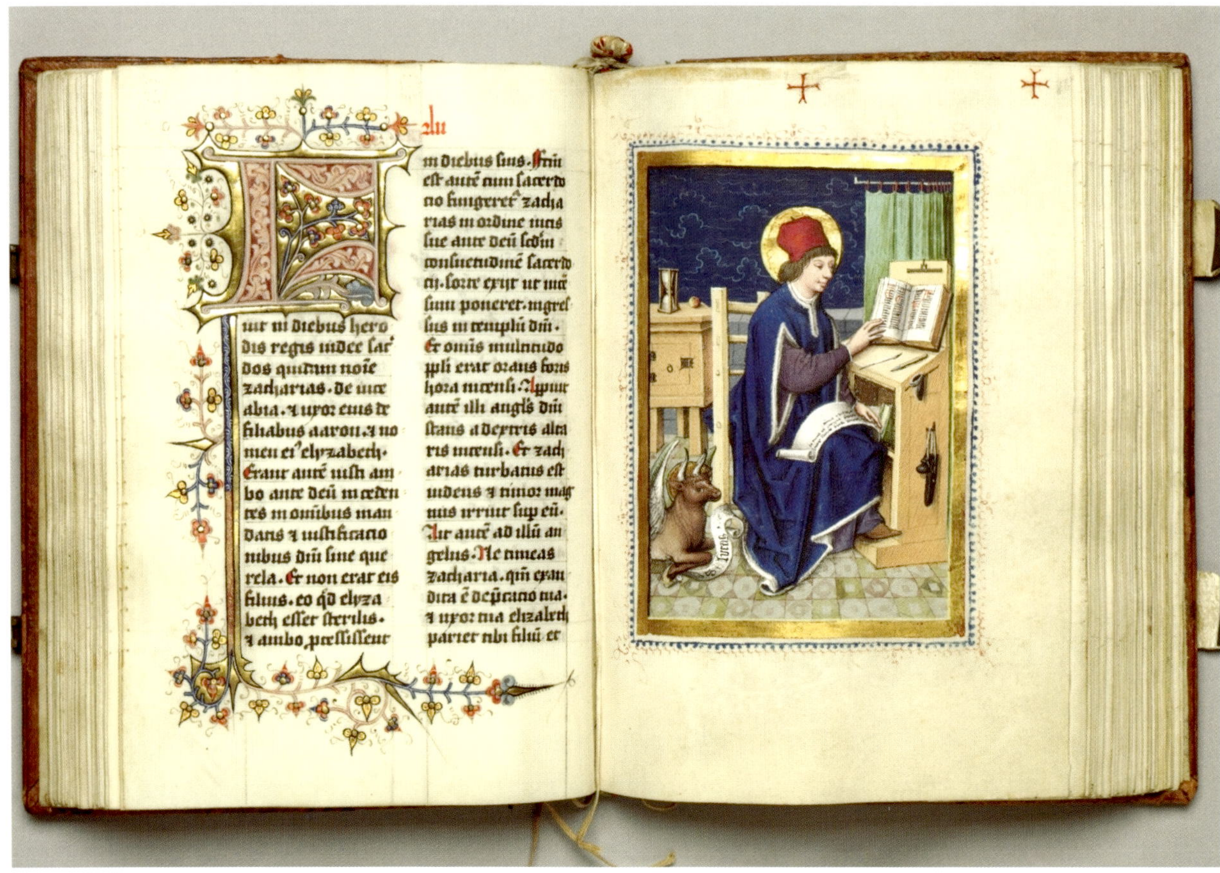

The Sacramentary

The sacramentary was the most important liturgical book used in the early church by the priest for the celebration of the Mass. It contained the prayer texts for the Mass (collect, secret, postcommunion, and the canon) and texts used for other sacramental and liturgical rites, such as baptism, ordination, penance, benediction, exorcism, and the dedication of churches. The sacramentary lay open on the altar where it was used by the priest and observed from afar by the worshippers.

Many sacramentaries, like the thirteenth-century Berthold Sacramentary *(fig. 63)*, were beautifully and extensively decorated. Unlike later missals, sacramentaries did not include Mass lections, ceremonial or vesting directions, or musical texts; these were stored separately in other liturgical books. Other parts of the Mass not in the sacramentary appeared in the Gospel Book, or evangelary, the epistolary, and the gradual. The earliest examples reflect the varying rites within the Western church, mainly the Roman and the Gallican. The Roman sacramentary had been spuriously attributed to Pope Gelasius I. In an effort to standardize the Roman sacramentary for use throughout the Empire, Pope Hadrian I sent Charlemagne the Gregorian Sacramentary in 785–86. By the late thirteenth century, the missal had replaced the sacramentary.

Figure 66 (facing page, top). The Crucifixion and Initial T. Fols. 185v-186. **The Caporali Missal from the Convent of San Francesco di Montone, near Perugia.** Tempera and burnished gold on vellum. Miniatures by Bartolommeo Caporali (ca. 1420–1505) and his brother, Jacopo (Giapeco) Caporali (died 1478). Perugia, Italy, dated 1469. The Cleveland Museum of Art, John L. Severance Fund, 2006.154.

The Missal

The Mass is celebrated at the altar by an ordained priest (or higher cleric). During the early Middle Ages, there were many books for the Mass. From the twelfth century onward, these became amalgamated into a single book: the missal. Introduced during the Carolingian period, the missal had completely replaced the older sacramentary by the thirteenth century. The missal, therefore, is the service book for the altar and contains the texts recited or sung by the priest during the Mass as well as chants, prayers, readings, biblical passages, invocations, and ceremonial directions. The missal includes texts that are used in the same form throughout the liturgical year and others that change from day to day, such as different saints' feast days or special feast days in the Temporal cycle *(fig. 64)*.

Figure 67 (facing page, bottom). Evangelary. Fols. 87v-88r with **Portrait of Saint Luke.** Tempera on parchment. Miniatures by the Hausbuch Master. Middle Rhine, Germany, ca. 1480. The Cleveland Museum of Art, Mr. and Mrs. William H. Marlatt Fund, 1952.465.

Because missals included instructions and required texts for the Mass, every priest had one. However, not every church in medieval Europe could afford to own a magnificently decorated missal. The principal fields of decoration were the canon pages. Lavish illuminated examples from the Middle Ages or Renaissance, many of which survive today in libraries and museums, were produced for wealthy monastic foundations, large cathedral churches, and, in some instances, private chapels, where a benefactor bore production costs *(fig. 65)*.

A spectacular example of a Renaissance illuminated missal is the Caporali Missal now in the Cleveland Museum of Art *(fig. 66)*. According to the colophon on folio 400, this illuminated missal was executed for the Franciscan convent of S. Francesco di Montone near Perugia in Italy's Umbria region. The buildings of this male convent still exist, and the present volume, a liturgical service book for the Mass, very likely was intended for use on the church's high altar. The colophon provides the name of

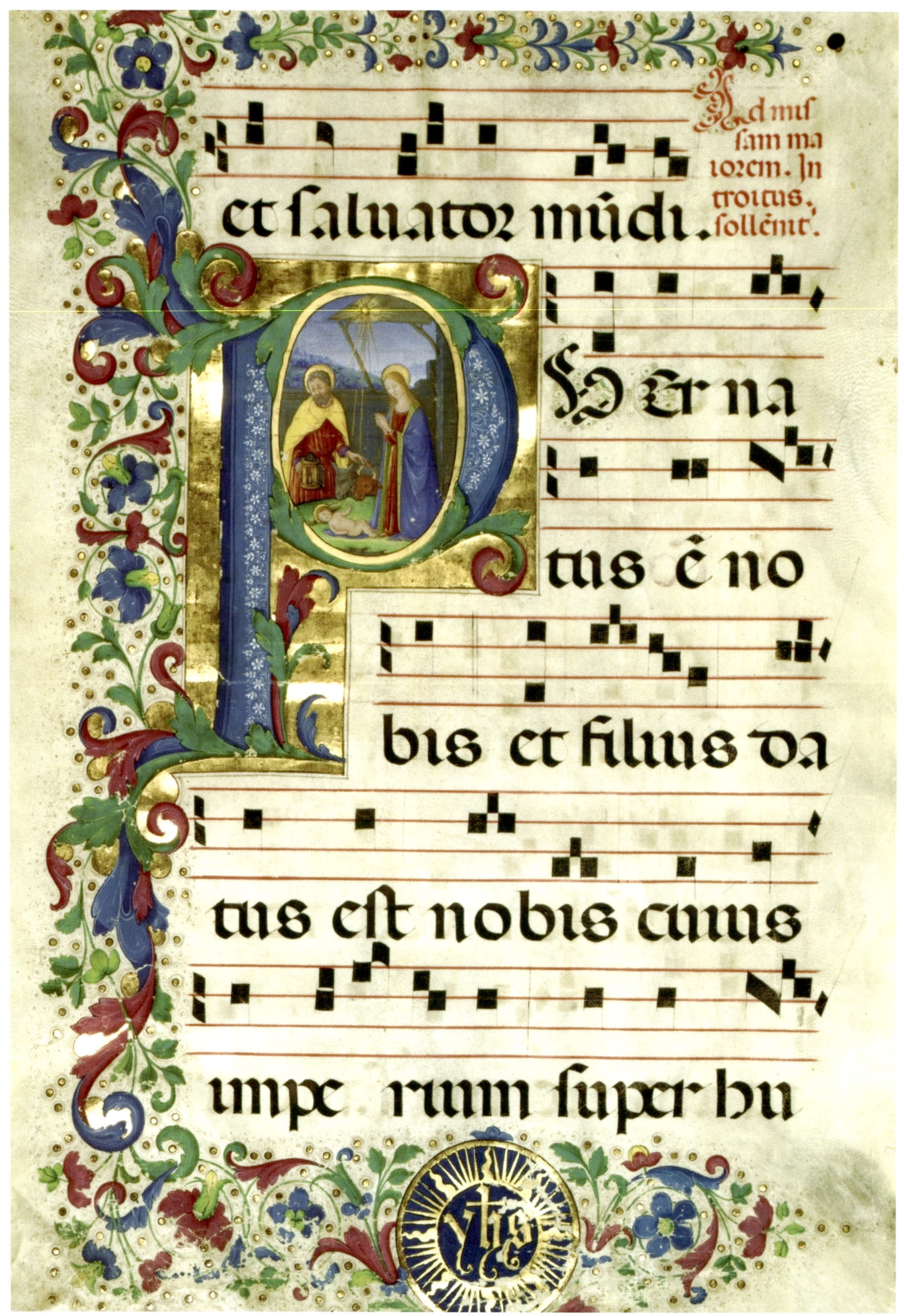

Ad mis sam ma iorem. In troitus. sollēnit'.
et saluator mūdi.
Uer na
tus ē no
bis et filius da
tus est nobis cuius
impe rium super hu

the German scribe, Henricus Haring, and the precise date of completion, October 4, 1469. Also identified are the names of the convent's guardian, Presbiter Frater Stephanus Cambi, and two procurators who commissioned the missal, Franciscus Ser Johannis de Ciurellis and Petrus Paulus de Miraculis. These individuals are represented within the borders of the Canon illustration on folio 185v. Such details identifying the date, place, commission, and scribe are exceptionally rare.

Of principal interest are the illuminations, extensive for a manuscript missal, which include a luxuriously decorated opening page (ordo missalis) with elaborate borders of naturalistically rendered animals, putti, and roundels, showing Saint Francis displaying his stigmata and King David in prayer. Folios 185v–186 reveal the volume's masterpiece, a two-page deluxe opening to the Canon of the Mass with a Calvary scene (verso) and an elaborate Te igitur (recto). The latter is composed of a large, decorated T with highly involved foliate decoration, putti, and birds. The former is a magnificent rendering of a traditional Calvary scene with a crucified Christ flanked by the Virgin and Saint John with two angels. Saint Francis kneels at the foot of the cross (attesting to the Franciscan usage of the volume). Elaborate use of burnished gold exists throughout. Scattered through the volume are thirty-one small historiated initials with various scenes, including a Nativity scene, Pentecost, Saints Peter and Paul, and more. Each of the small initials is further embellished with marginal floral extensions and filigree fillings within some letters.

The most outstanding part of the illumination is due to the work of Bartolommeo Caporali, an important panel and fresco painter and miniaturist. His hand may be perceived first and foremost in the monumental full-page miniature of the Crucifixion. The central element of the crucified Christ, including Saint Francis kneeling at the foot of the cross, is a masterpiece of rare quality. The corpus of Christ with its imposing musculature is carefully modeled in subtle shades of ochre, yellow, and brown and attests to intensive anatomical studies and a highly developed sense of naturalism on the part of the artist. The head of Christ rests on his chest to the right capturing the moment of death (Christo Morto), and his face mirrors exhaustion. He wears an almost translucent loincloth (perizonium) draped in fine folds suggestive of a soft tactile character. Bartolommeo was likely assisted by his brother, Giapeco, a Perugian miniaturist, who completed the remaining illuminations of the Caporali Missal.

Figure 68 (facing page). Initial P with the Nativity: Leaf from a Gradual. Tempera on parchment. Attavante degli Attavanti and Workshop, Florence, ca. 1500. The Cleveland Museum of Art, the Jeanne Miles Blackburn Collection, 2003.173. The opening text reads ***Puer natus e[st] nobis, et filius datus est nobis*** (For a child is born to us, and a son is given to us) and represents the opening of the Introit for Christmas Day.

The Evangelary

The evangelary, also known as the Gospel Lectionary or book of pericopes, contained the Gospel readings for the Mass *(fig. 67)*. Before the twelfth century, the Gospel readings at Mass were usually not arranged in an evangelary but read directly from a text of the four Gospels. In that sense, the Gospel Book, richly decorated with evangelist portraits, was the antecedent for the evangelary. Since the evangelary provided the full gospel reading in liturgical order for each feast, it was a more practical volume for the altar than the Gospel Book.

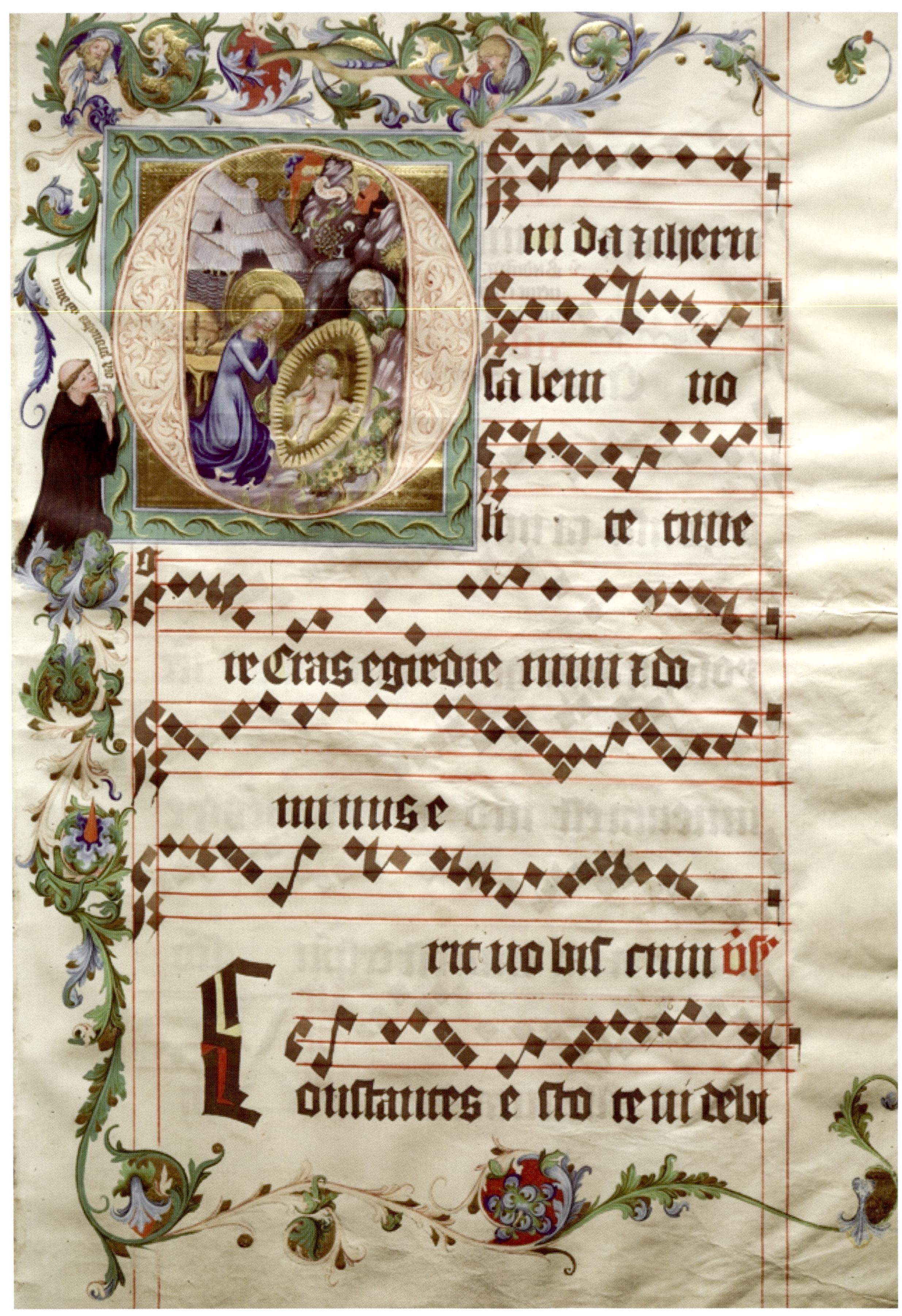

By the seventh century, the practice of continuous readings of the Gospels at the altar during church services was replaced by the assignment of specific passages (pericopes) for each day. Thus the evangelary gradually replaced the Gospel Book at the altar following the Carolingian period. For practical purposes, Gospel Books ceased to be produced entirely after the twelfth century. Because these volumes symbolized the word of God, evangelaries, like the earlier Gospel Books, were not only lavishly illuminated with authors' portraits of the four evangelists but were also often bound into beautiful gilt-silver covers, sometimes inset with gemstones and carved ivory plaques.

Figure 69 (facing page). Initial O with the Nativity: Bifolium from an Antiphonal. Tempera on parchment. Prague, Bohemia, ca. 1405. The Cleveland Museum of Art, Andrew R. and Martha Holden Jennings Fund, 1976.100. The opening text reads ***O iuda et iherusalem*** (Oh Judea and Jerusalem). The antiphonal was made for an unknown Benedictine monastery.

Choir Books

A variety of music or choral manuscripts were used throughout the Middle Ages and Renaissance for the practice of the Christian liturgy and the singing of the Daily Office. Some of the most spectacular and largest illuminations found in medieval manuscripts derive from choral books. Choir books were usually made in large format in order to be placed on a lectern and viewed simultaneously by the members of a choir *(figs. 68, 69)*. They sometimes reached huge proportions (up to 40 by 26 inches) and represented the extreme limit of scale reached by books during the Middle Ages and Renaissance. Such enormous books were frequently embellished with enlarged decorated letters containing sacred figures or religious scenes. These large initials not only illustrated liturgical feast days within their texts but also served as visual aids that enabled the user to navigate through the volume's texts and music. The addition of lavish marginal ornamentation also added luster and rich visual interest.

Though choral books were produced all over Europe during this period, the finest and most ostentatious were those illuminated in Italy. The commissioning of large multivolume sets of choral books often attracted the most talented illuminators. Such well-known artists as Lorenzo Monaco and Fra Angelico are known to have illustrated liturgical books in addition to their traditional painting on wood panel or fresco. These beautiful books then ranked among the most prestigious treasures of a church.

Every church, chapel, and community of monks or nuns needed liturgical manuscripts, including choral books, in order to maintain the elaborate services of the church. Because of this large demand, the copying and "noting" (supplying the music) of manuscripts went on continuously throughout Europe, even beyond the invention of printing in the 1440s. It is believed the origins of liturgical music date to Saint Gregory the Great (d. 604), who is credited with recording the principles of Gregorian chant. Noting and illuminating these service books were arduous tasks that required great care and precision. It is an expense often found in medieval accounts.

Notes

Preface

1. Abbot Suger, "De Administratione XXXIII," in *Abbot Suger on the Abbey Church of St.-Denis and Its Art Treasures,* ed. and trans. Erwin Panofsky (Princeton, N.J.: Princeton Univ. Press, 1946), 66–77 and 62–65, respectively.

1. The Medieval Liturgical Treasury

1. "Suppression of English Monasteries under Henry VIII," in *The Catholic Encyclopedia* (New York: Encyclopedia Press, 1913), 3:562–63.
2. Paul Williamson, ed., *The Medieval Treasury: The Art of the Middle Ages in the Victoria and Albert Museum* (London: Victoria and Albert Museum, 1986), 14. See C. E. Woodruff and W. Danks, *Memorials of the Cathedral and Priory of Christ in Canterbury* (London: Chapman and Hall, 1912), 82.
3. Patrick M. de Winter, *Sacral Treasure of the Guelphs* (Bloomington: Indiana Univ. Press, 1985), 128–37.
4. Timothy Husband and Julien Chapuis, *The Treasury of Basel Cathedral,* exh. cat., Metropolitan Museum of Art (New York, 2001). For the history of the treasure, see Chapuis, "A Treasury in Basel," 11–23.
5. See William D. Wixom, "For the Service of the Table of God," in *The Royal Abbey of Saint-Denis in the Time of Abbot Suger (1122–1151),* exh. cat., Metropolitan Museum of Art (New York, 1981), 101–5.
6. Elisabeth Taburet-Delahaye, *Paris 1400: Les arts sous Charles VI,* exh. cat., Réunion des Musées Nationaux (Paris, 2004), 310–11.

2. Liturgy and Ritual

1. I am indebted to Rev. David A. Novak for supplying information on this point.
2. This belief is shared by Orthodox Christians, High Church Anglicans, and certain Lutherans, but for most Protestants the bread and wine are nothing more than symbols of Christ and not his actual presence. Catholics and the Orthodox have very different ways of expressing this.
3. Theodor Klauser, *A Short History of the Western Liturgy: An Account and Some Reflections,* trans. John Halliburton (London: Oxford Univ. Press, 1979), 9. I am indebted to Rev. David A. Novak for calling my attention to this.
4. More properly the priest does not pray with his back to the people but faces the same direction as the people. Thus, priest and congregation are all oriented toward the East—from where Christ will appear at the end of time. My thanks to Rev. David A. Novak for this clarification. See His Holiness Benedict XVI (written as Joseph Cardinal Ratzinger), "Sacred Places: The Altar and the Direction of Liturgical Prayer," *Sacred Architecture 11* (2006): 27–30.
5. Organs only appeared as fixed elements in medieval churches and in the liturgy during the fifteenth century. Organs are known, however, to have occasionally existed in some ecclesiastical settings, especially monastic, as early as the eleventh century. I am indebted to Paul Cox for this information. The world's oldest playable church organ apparently survives in Switzerland and is said to date to about 1390. I thank Rev. David A. Novak for calling my attention to this.
6. Until the Second Vatican Council (1962–65), the liturgical language of the Roman Catholic Church remained Latin. Following the reforms to the liturgy undertaken by the Council, the liturgy was afterward permitted to be celebrated in the local vernacular language.

3. Artistic Metalwork for the Altar

1. A detailed technical discussion of enameling falls outside the scope of this publication. Numerous studies exist for both the general reader and the specialist. Good general introductions to medieval enameling include Marian Campbell, *Medieval Enamels* (Owings Mills, Md.: Stemmer House, 1983); Hanns Swarzenski and Nancy Netzer, *Enamels and Glass* (Boston: Museum of Fine Arts, 1986); Barbara Drake Boehm and Elisabeth Taburet-Delahaye, *Enamels of Limoges, 1100–1350,* exh. cat., Metropolitan Museum of Art (New York, 1996).
2. D. R. Dendy, *The Use of Lights in Christian Worship* (London: SPCK, 1959), 17–44.
3. Augustine, Bishop of Hippo, *Contra Crescon.*, c. xxix and Hom. 1 in Matt. See also the *Catholic Encyclopedia*, 3:562–63.
4. The fistula did survive into the twentieth century for papal use and is mentioned in the *Praenotanda* of the Roman missal of Pope Paul VI of 1969. It has been abandoned in the current *Missale Romanum* (1983).
5. *Corpus Juris Canonici*, ed. Emil Friedberg (Leipzig, 1876–82; repr. Graz, 1955), cap. Xlv, dist. I de consecratione.
6. This stricture was rescinded after Vatican II in order to permit the use of relatively nonbreakable materials such as special glass, stone, and ceramics. It was reinstated with the current *Missale Romanum* (1983), which requires the use of "noble materials."
7. Marlia Mundell Mango, *Silver from Early Byzantium: The Kaper Koraon and Related Treasures*, exh. cat., Walters Art Gallery (Baltimore, Md., 1986), cat. 60, p. 230.
8. See Williamson, ed., *The Medieval Treasury,* 208–9.
9. Patrick M. de Winter, "The Sacral Treasure of the Guelphs," *Bulletin of the Cleveland Museum of Art* 72 (Mar. 1985): 86–87. An inscription on parchment placed behind the monstrance reads: ista[m] patena[m] fecit s[anctus] ber[n]wardus. (This paten was made by Saint Bernward.) Though this saint had a reputation for his metalworking skills, the inscription may mean that Bernward was not the actual goldsmith but that he commissioned and paid for the making of the paten. It clearly would have been made to accompany a now-lost chalice. The niello decoration on the paten was applied around 1185 and is attributed to the Saint Oswald Reliquary Workshop of Hildesheim.
10. *Catholic Encyclopedia*, 6:89.
11. Eucharistic doves are available today from some suppliers of liturgical furnishings. At the Cathedral of Amiens the continuous historic tradition of using doves still survives. I am indebted to Rev. David A. Novak for this information.
12. *Eucharistic Vessels of the Middle Ages*, exh. cat., Busch-Reisinger Museum (Cambridge, Mass., 1975), 87.
13. *Catholic Encyclopedia*, 5:144–45.
14. Jacques-Paul Migne, *Patrologia Latina*, 149, cols. 722–23; as cited in *Eucharistic Vessels*, 87.
15. See also Archdale King, *Eucharistic Reservation in the Western Church* (London: A. R. Mowbray, 1965), 57–60.
16. *Catholic Encyclopedia*, 4:533.

4. Objects for Procession and the Vesting of the Priest

1. For a complete discussion of the Gertrude Cross and the similar Liudolf Cross, both commissioned by Countess Gertrude around 1040, see de Winter, "The Sacral Treasure of the Guelphs," 30–36.
2. R. W. Southern, *Western Society and the Church in the Middle Ages* (Harmondsworth, Eng.: Penguin Books, 1970), 31.

3. In recent times the use of relics in altars was made optional by the liturgical reforms of Vatican II.
4. Abbot Suger, "The Other Little Book on the Consecration of the Church of St.-Denis," in *Abbot Suger on the Abbey Church of St.-Denis and Its Art Treasures*, ed. and trans. Erwin Panofsky, 2nd ed. (Princeton, N.J.: Princeton Univ. Press, 1979), 87–89.
5. "Gods as Magical Charms: The Use of Ancient Gems in the Medieval Christian West," in *Survival of the Gods: Classical Mythology in Medieval Art*, exh. cat., Brown University (Providence, R.I., 1987), 185–92.
6. Ibid., 185.
7. Ibid., 186.
8. Suger, "De Administratione XXXIII," in *Abbot Suger,* 1946, 63–65.
9. Ibid., 79.
10. See Herbert Norris, *Church Vestments, Their Origin & Development* (London: J. M. Dent, 1949) 8–9; Joseph R. Strayer, ed., *Dictionary of the Middle Ages* (New York: Charles Scribner's Sons, 1989), 12:397.
11. An account of the vesting of the priest for the Mass is included in the Ordo Romanus I. In the Middle Ages, the word *ordo* referred to a ritual book containing directions for liturgical functions. The prayers recited by the celebrant or his assistants appeared in separate books, such as the Sacramentary, Antiphonary, and Psalter, while the Ordo concerned itself only with the ceremony. A considerable number of Ordines are preserved among manuscripts from the eighth to the twelfth centuries. The first printed in modern times was the so-called "Ordo Romanus Vulgatus" which, after an edition published by George Cassander at Cologne in 1561, was reprinted by Hittorp in his "De divinis catholicæ ecclesiæ officiis" (Cologne, 1568) and is hence often known as the "Ordo Romanus of Hittorp."
12. Extraordinary examples of papal vestments are preserved in the Museo Sacro at the Vatican. See, for example, the dalmatics, chasubles, cope, stole, and maniple made for Pope Clement VIII (1592–1605) in Robert P. Bergman and Diane De Grazia, *Vatican Treasures, Early Christian, Renaissance, and Baroque Art from the Papal Collections*, exh. cat., Cleveland Museum of Art (Cleveland, 1998), 71–91. Other examples from the Middle Ages and Renaissance are preserved in the Schatzkammer in Vienna and other European treasuries.
13. For a general discussion with numerous examples, see Donald King, *Opus Anglicanum: English Medieval Embroidery*, exh. cat. (London: Arts Council, 1963).
14. Janet Mayo, *A History of Ecclesiastical Dress* (London: B. T. Batsford, 1984), 50.
15. Thomas Walsingham, *Gesta Abbatum Monasterii Sancti Albani a.d. 793–1290*, ed. H. T. Riley, Rolls Service I (London: Longsman, Green, 1867), 127.
16. Mayo, *Ecclesiastical Dress*, 50.
17. Sachervell Sitwell, *Monks, Nuns and Monasteries* (New York: Holt, Rinehart and Winston, 1965), 39.

5. Service Books for Mass and Office

1. Abbot Suger, "De Administratione, XXXIII," in *Abbot Suger*, 1979.

Glossary

acanthus: Plant from the Mediterranean region with fleshy, curling, large-lobed leaves that, more or less stylized, are often used as ornamentation in manuscript painting, especially for border decoration.

alb: A white, ankle-length, sleeved tunic, generally, beneath other vestments, worn by the celebrant of the Mass.

amice: A white cloth with two long ribbons worn over the priest's shoulders beneath the outer vestments at Mass.

antependium: A hanging of cloth, metal, or wood that covers the front of an altar.

antiphonary (also antiphonal): A choral book containing the music used in the Divine Office, or the cycle of daily devotions of the year; the musical counterpart to the breviary.

aquamanile: A metal ewer, or vessel, for both liturgical and secular use. In liturgical applications, aquamanilia held the water used to wash the celebrants' hands during Mass.

aspergillum: A rod with a brush or perforated globe at the end used for sprinkling holy water at the asperges.

balducchino: A canopy over an altar.

bas-de-page: Lower margin of a manuscript; area below the text block.

basse-taille: An enameling technique in which a gold or silver plaque is incised with a design in low relief, covered completely by translucent enamel, and fired to fuse the enamel to the metal.

bifolium: In a manuscript, a single sheet folded in half to form two folia, or four pages.

book of hours: Prayer books intended for lay use in private or family devotions and that typically contain a compendium of prayers and devotions dedicated to the Virgin Mary and recited at the canonical hours of the day (formularies recited or sung at eight designated periods of the day). To this core were appended other elements such as a calendar, Penitential Psalms, litanies, and suffrages. Elaborate versions contain a full cycle of miniatures as well as involved marginal decorations. Books of hours form the most popular and abundant of all surviving medieval manuscripts.

brandea: Cloths that were touched to a saint's shrine or relic to absorb its sanctity and later venerated as relics themselves.

breviary: Liturgical book comprising hymns, readings, psalms, anthems, and other prayers for the reading of the Daily Office, required of all priests, monks, and nuns.

cabochon: An unfaceted, polished gem.

calamarium: A pouch used by medieval scribes for the storage of pens and related writing instruments, such as penknives, styli, awls, needles, and pumice stones.

cameo: A precious or semiprecious stone, usually with more than one layer of color, carved in relief.

catchwords: The first word or words of the next quire written below the text block on the verso of the last leaf of the preceding quire. Catchwords functioned as guides to the scribe and binder.

censer: A portable vessel used for the burning of incense and known today as the thurible.

chalice: The cup or goblet used to hold the Eucharistic wine during the Mass. Usually made en suite with a paten for holding the Eucharistic wafer.

champlevé: An enameling technique in which hollows, or grooves, are scooped out from a copper plaque to create a design. The hollows are filled with opaque glass paste and fired in order to fuse the glass to the metal. The surface is then polished until flush and smooth.

chasuble: The primary vestment worn by officiating priests or bishops at Mass. They were typically made of the most expensive and precious material and were sometimes decorated with bands called orpheries. In the Middle Ages, chasubles were conical in shape.

choral books: Music manuscripts containing the chants of the Latin liturgy and arranged according to the church calendar and their various functions within the liturgy; chiefly the antiphonary and gradual.

chrism: A mixture of olive oil and balsam, blessed by a bishop, and used in the administration of certain sacraments and other church functions.

ciborium: A covered vessel used for storing the reserved consecrated Eucharistic wafers in the tabernacle behind the altar.

cincture:. A cord used as a girdle to bind the loose flowing alb around the waist of the priest.

cloisonné: An enameling technique in which cloisons, ribbonlike strips of metal, are fixed to the surface of a metal plate to create cells, which are then filled with enamel paste of different colors. Once fired, the piece is polished and the design of the cloisons appears.

codex: A manuscript handwritten on individual leaves of vellum that can be turned and read in succession. Succeeded the scroll as the main support for handwritten script in Western Europe; another term for book.

collation: Analysis of the makeup, or sequential arrangement of the quires, which constitutes a codex.

colophon: A passage appearing at the end of a manuscript, recording information about the text, place, date of execution, and occasionally the name of the scribe.

Compline: See *Daily Office*.

cope: Cape worn in processions by the celebrant of the Mass; a semi-circular vestment fastened across the chest by a brooch, or morse.

corporal: A white linen cloth, symbolic of the shroud of Christ, on which the host and the chalice are placed during the Mass.

crosier: A staff resembling a shepherd's crook that a bishop or abbot carried as a symbol of pastoral authority.

Daily Office: A complex round of prayers and readings formulated for recitation at the canonical or liturgical hours of the day and required of all clergy, monks, and nuns. They are *Matins* (about 2:30 A.M.), *Lauds* (5:00 A.M.), *Prime* (6:00 A.M.), *Terce* (9:00 A.M.), *Sext* (noon), *None* (3:00 P.M.), *Vespers* (sunset), and *Compline* (9:00 P.M.).

dalmatic: A sleeved, tuniclike upper garment worn principally by deacons as their liturgical dress but also by bishops and priests. The celebrant of the Mass wore this vestment under the chasuble.

diptych: An object, usually an ivory or painting, in the form of a two-panel construction attached with a hinge, which allowed it to be folded, or closed.

drollery: Animal and human hybrids that inhabit the initials and foliate borders of Gothic manuscript leaves.

evangelary: A book containing the Gospel readings for the Mass, arranged according to the liturgical year.

Evangelists: Saints Matthew, Mark, Luke, and John, the four authors of the Gospels whose portraits usually precede their respective texts in certain manuscripts, such as the Gospel Book and the book of hours.

excised: Cut or removed; a leaf detached from a manuscript.

exemplar: A corrected original text from which a duplicate is copied.

fanon: A shoulder cape worn only by the pope.

Fastentuch: A German word for Lenten cloths, which were used to cover crucifixes and altars in German and Austrian churches in the weeks leading up to Easter.

filigree: Ornamental threads of metal composed of fine grains or beads.

fistula: A small hollow tube used to communicate the Eucharistic wine to the people from the ministerial chalice.

flabellum: A liturgical fan used during the Middle Ages to keep the flies away from the Eucharist.

folio: The leaf of a manuscript or codex, usually numbered only on the front side and referred to by its two faces: recto and verso (front and back). In a manuscript it is customary to count leaves, or folia, and not pages. May also refer to a large-format book.

formata: A bold, formal Gothic bookhand, more elegant than textualis, also known as Gothic Black Letter.

frontispiece: An illustrated leaf preceding the title page of a book.

gathering: See *quire.*

gloss: A commentary on a text, located in the margins or between the lines in smaller script.

Gospel Book: Liturgical book containing the complete text of the Gospels of Saints Matthew, Mark, Luke, and John. Used on the medieval altar in conjunction with the sacramentary, but after the eighth century they were partially replaced by evangelaries.

Gospel lectionary: See *evangelary.*

gradual: Liturgical book containing the noted music and chants for the Mass sung by the choir in response to the celebrant.

grotesque: See *drollery.*

historiated initial: An enlarged initial containing individual figures or groups that interact; these often form narrative scenes that illustrate or refer to the text it introduces.

humanistic codex: A book that reflects the conscious reformation of script and book design promoted by the Italian humanists of the fourteenth and fifteenth centuries. The book aesthetic of this period reflecting the revival of classical learning.

illuminator: The decorator or painter of a vellum codex.

incense boat: A boat-shaped vessel used to store the incense.

incipit: The opening words of a text in Latin.

incunabulum: A book printed before 1500.

initial: An emphasized letter at the beginning of a text; used in medieval manuscripts to form breaks within a text and to prioritize the components of the text by drawing the attention of the reader; a purely medieval invention and often lavishly decorated. See *historiated initial.*

intaglio: The art of engraving stones or gems in negative relief; the opposite of a cameo.

knop: A decorative knob, typically spherical; a protuberance found on the stems of chalices, crosiers, and candlesticks.

Lauds: See *Daily Office.*

litany: A form of prayer consisting of a series of invocations for deliverance or intercession. These were addressed in a formal and hierarchical sequence to the Trinity, the Virgin, the angels, and then the saints, according to their rank as apostles, martyrs, confessors, and virgins.

liturgy: The form(s) of the church's public worship; ritual.

maniple: A narrow strip of material worn over the left forearm by a priest, deacon, and subdeacon.

Matins: See *Daily Office.*

miniature: A picture, frequently narrative, used as illustration in a manuscript. Derived from the Latin minium, a red pigment used in manuscript painting.

missal: The service book of the altar. A book used by the celebrant at Mass; contains all spoken and chanted texts for the celebrant with directions. Arranged according to the liturgical calendar.

miter: A cap with two points worn by bishops and abbots.

monstrance: A vessel designed to carry and display a relic or the consecrated host; designed to be carried in ritual procession or to stand on an altar.

morse: A clasp or brooch, often highly ornate, used for fastening a cope.

niello: A decorative technique used to enrich an incised design on silver by filling it with a black metal alloy of silver sulfide and lead. When fired, the substance turns black and contrasts with the silver.

None: See *Daily Office.*

opus anglicanum: Embroidery crafted in England, mainly between 1100 and 1350, and of a standard unsurpassed elsewhere.

opus teutonicum: Also called "whitework" or white stitching on a white ground, the term denotes a technique popular in the German lands from about 1100 to 1400.

orphrey: Decorative bands, usually embroidered, applied to copes, dalmatics, or chasubles.

ostensorium: An elaborate vessel, similar to a monstrance, but used generally for the display of the consecrated host; traditionally made from gold or silver with a glass or crystal insert for displaying the host.

parchment: The skin of animals, usually cattle, sheep, or goats, prepared by soaking and stretching, for use as manuscript leaves. See *vellum.*

paten: A circular, slightly concave plate, typically of silver or gold, used for the Eucharistic wafer.

pectoral cross: The cross suspended on a chain and worn on the chest of a bishop or abbot.

phylactery: In the Middle Ages, a small container holding a relic or texts and worn around the neck for personal protection.

prickings: Holes formed by a stylus along the edge of a sheet of vellum or parchment; used as an aid in ruling in preparation for copying.

Prime: See *Daily Office.*

Psalter: A book containing all 150 biblical psalms.

pyx: A small cylindrical box used to store the consecrated host, especially to provide communion to the sick.

quire: A group of leaves folded in half to form bifolia and inserted one inside the other. These were then collated with other quires and stitched together to form a codex or book.

recto: In a bound open manuscript, the right side of a leaf.

reliquary: A receptacle such as a coffer, shrine, or monstrance used for keeping or displaying a sacred relic.

repoussé: A metalworking technique in which relief is achieved by hammering out a thin sheet of metal, usually silver or gold, from the reverse side.

rubric: Headings and explanatory notes written in red ink.

sacramentary: Service book containing the prayers recited by the priest (or bishop) at Mass at the altar. Later superseded by the missal.

sardonyx: A semiprecious stone with variegated colors of red, brown, and white.

scriptorium: A room used for writing or copying books.

Sext: See *Daily Office*.

situla: A bucket used for holy water.

staurotheca: A reliquary designed to contain fragments of Christ's cross, one of Christendom's most sacred relics.

stole: A narrow textile strip worn over the shoulders by priests and deacons and extending to at least the knee.

stylus: A pointed instrument used for inserting prickings in vellum and for drypoint ruling and drawing.

suffrages: Prayers of petition to the saints for intercession or aid; found in the books of hours.

surplice: A half-length tunic with large sleeves made of fine linen or cotton and worn by all clergy; especially worn by priests when administering the sacraments. It is never girded.

tabernacle: A fixed and locked container usually above and behind the altar for the secure containment of the reserved Eucharist.

Terce: See *Daily Office*.

textualis: Standard Gothic bookhand of the thirteenth century and later.

thurible: See *censer*.

thurifer: The service or acolyte who carries the censer in a liturgical service.

tunicle: A short vestment worn by a subdeacon over the alb during Mass or by a bishop under the dalmatic during pontifical ceremonies.

use: Variations within the text of manuscript, such as calendars or litanies, peculiar to a diocese, town, or religious order. An aid to scholars in localizing a manuscript.

vellum: A general term for animal skin and often used interchangeably with parchment. Also used to refer to prepared calfskin, a thinner and finer support used for leaves in smaller manuscripts like books of hours, Psalters, and octavo Bibles.

verso: Reverse side of a leaf or folio. In a bound open codex, that on the left.

Vespers: See *Daily Office*.

viatic pyx: A pyx, or small cylindrical container, used by the priest for carrying communion to the sick; generally not used to contain the reserved hosts between Masses.

Selected Bibliography

General Surveys and Sources

Becks, Leonie, and Georg Hauser. *Die Schatzkammer des kölner Domes*. Cologne: Kölner Dom, 2000.

Chartraire, Eugene. *Inventaire du trésor de l'église primatiale et metropolitaine de Sens*. Paris: Picard, 1897.

Crosby, Sumner McKnight, and Jane Hayward. *The Royal Abbey of Saint-Denis in the Time of Abbot Suger (1122–1151)*. New York: Metropolitan Museum of Art, 1981. An exhibition catalog.

Elbern, Victor H. *Dom und Domschatz in Hildesheim*. Hildesheim: Karl Robert Langewiesche Nachfolger Haus Koster, 1991.

Evans, Joan. *Monastic Life at Cluny, 910–1157*. Oxford: Oxford University Press, 1931.

Frazier, M. E. "Medieval Church Treasuries." *Metropolitan Museum of Art Bulletin* 43 (1985–86): 3–56.

Gerson, Paula Lieber. *Abbot Suger and Saint-Denis: A Symposium*. New York: Metropolitan Museum of Art, 1986.

Lasko, Peter. *Ars Sacra, 800–1200*. 2nd ed. New Haven, Conn.: Yale University Press, 1994.

Panofsky, Erwin, trans. *Abbot Suger on the Abbey Church of St.-Denis and Its Art Treasures*. 2nd ed. Princeton, N.J.: Princeton University Press, 1979.

Taralon, Jean. *Treasures of the Churches of France*. New York: Braziller, 1966.

Theophilus. *On the Various Arts*. Translated by C. R. Dodwell. Oxford: Clarendon Press, 1986.

Ultee, Maarten. *The Abbey of St. Germain des Prés in the Seventeenth Century*. New Haven, Conn.: Yale University Press, 1981.

de Winter, Patrick M. *The Sacral Treasure of the Guelphs*. Cleveland: Cleveland Museum of Art, 1985.

Zarnecki, George. *The Monastic Achievement*. London: Thames and Hudson, 1972.

Exhibition and Collection Catalogs

Age of Chivalry: Art in Plantaganet England, 1200–1400. London: Royal Academy of Arts, 1987.

Archibald, Marion, and D. H. Turner, et al. *The Golden Age of Anglo-Saxon Art*. London: British Museum Publications, 1985.

Bergman, Robert P., and Diane De Grazia. *Vatican Treasures: Early Christian, Renaissance, and Baroque Art from the Papal Collections*. Cleveland: Cleveland Museum of Art, 1998.

Boehm, Barbara Drake, and Jiri Fajt, eds. *Prague: The Crown of Bohemia, 1347–1437*. New York: Metropolitan Museum of Art; New Haven, Conn.: Yale University Press, 2005.

Brandt, Michael. *Bernward von Hildesheim und das Zeitalter der Ottonen*. 2 vols. Hildesheim: Bernward Verlag; Mainz: P. von Zabern, 1993.

Calkins, Robert G. *A Medieval Treasury: An Exhibition of Medieval Art from the Third to the Sixteenth Century*. Ithaca, N.Y.: Cornell University Press, 1968.

Casalini, Eugenio M., et al. *Tesori d'arte dell'Annunziata di Firenze*. Florence: Alinari, 1987. An exhibition catalog.

Deuchler, Florens, ed. *The Year 1200*. 2 vols. New York: Metropolitan Museum of Art, 1970.

Eucharistic Vessels of the Middle Ages. Cambridge, Mass.: Busch-Reisinger Museum, 1975.

Les Fastes du Gothique: le siècle de Charles V. Paris: Réunion des Musées Nationaux, 1982.

Fliegel, Stephen N., and Sophie Jugie. *Art from the Court of Burgundy, 1364–1419*. Paris: Réunion des Musées Nationaux, 2004.

Husband, Timothy, and Julien Chapuis. *The Treasury of Basel Cathedral*. New York: Metropolitan Museum of Art, 2001.

Nielsen, Christina M. *Devotion and Splendor: Medieval Art at the Art Institute of Chicago*. Chicago: Art Institute, 2004.

Ornamenta Ecclesiae: Kunst und Künstler der Romanik. Cologne: Joseph-Haubrich-Kunsthalle, 1985.

Puhle, Matthias. *Otto der Grosse: Magdeburg und Europa*. 2 vols. Mainz: Philipp von Zabern, 2001.

Rhein und Maas, Kunst und Kultur 800–1400. Cologne: Joseph-Haubrich-Kunsthalle, 1972.

Schroder, Timothy. *Treasures of the English Church: Sacred Gold and Silver, 800–2000*. London: Goldsmiths Company, 2008.

Taburet-Delahaye, Elisabeth, et al. *Paris 1400: Les arts sous Charles VI*. Paris: Réunion des Musées Nationaux, 2004.

Transformations of the Court Style: Gothic Art in Europe, 1270–1330. Providence, R.I.: School of Design, Brown University, 1977.

Les Tresors des églises de France. Paris: Caisse nationale des monuments historiques, 1965.

Williamson, Paul. *The Medieval Treasury: The Art of the Middle Ages in the Victoria and Albert Museum*. London: Victoria and Albert Museum, 1986.

Zarnecki, George, Janet Holt, et al. *English Romanesque Art, 1066–1200*. London: Arts Council of Great Britain, 1984.

The Arts of Byzantium

Evans, Helen C., ed. *Byzantium: Faith and Power (1261–1557)*. New York: Metropolitan Museum of Art, 2004. An exhibition catalog.

Evans, Helen C., and William D. Wixom, eds. *The Glory of Byzantium: Art and Culture of the Middle Byzantine Era, A.D. 843–1261*. New York: Metropolitan Museum of Art, 1997. An exhibition catalog.

Pitarakis, Brigitte. *Les croix-reliquaires pectorals Byzantines en bronze*. Paris: Picard, 2006.

Safran, Linda, ed. *Heaven on Earth: Art and the Church in Byzantium*. University Park: Pennsylvania State University Press, 2000.

Vikan, Gary, ed. *Silver from Early Byzantium*. Baltimore, Md.: Walters Art Gallery, 1986. An exhibition catalog.

Weitzmann, Kurt, ed. *Age of Spirituality: Late Antique and Early Christian Art, Third to Seventh Century*. New York: Metropolitan Museum of Art, 1979. An exhibition catalog.

Enamels

Brandt, Michael, ed. *Abglanz des Himmels: Romanik in Hildesheim*. Regensburg: Diocesan Museum, 2001. An exhibition catalog.

Campbell, Marian. *An Introduction to Medieval Enamels*. Owings Mills, Md.: Stemmer House, 1983.

Enamels of Limoges, 1100–1350. New York: Metropolitan Museum of Art, 1996. An exhibition catalog.

Gauthier, Marie-Madeleine. *L'art de l'email champlevé en Italie à l'époque primitive du gothique*. Rome, 1972.

———. *Emaux meridionaux: catalogue international de l'oeuvre de Limoges*. Paris: Éditions du Centre National de la Recherche Sciѐntifique, 1987.

———. *Emaux du moyen âge occidental*. Fribourg: Office du Livre, 1972.

Swarzenski, Hanns, and Nancy Netzer. *Catalogue of Medieval Objects in the Museum of Fine Arts, Boston*. Boston: Museum of Fine Arts, 1986.

Ivories

Barnet, Peter, ed. *Images in Ivory: Precious Objects of the Gothic Age*. Princeton, N.J.: Princeton University Press, 1997. An exhibition catalog.

Gaborit-Chopin, Danielle. *Ivoires du Moyen Age*. Fribourg: Office du Livre, 1978.

Longhurst, M. H. *Catalogue of Carvings in Ivory*. 2 vols. London: Victoria and Albert Museum, 1927–29.

Oikonomides, N. "John VII Palaeologus and the Ivory Pyxis at Dumbarton Oaks." *Dumbarton Oaks Papers* 31 (1977): 329–37.

Randall, Richard H. "An Eleventh-Century Ivory Pectoral Cross." *Journal of the Warburg and Courtauld Institutes* 25 (1962): 159–71.

St. Clair, Archer, and Elizabeth Parker McLachlan, eds. *The Carver's Art: Medieval Sculpture in Ivory, Bone, and Horn*. New Brunswick, N.J.: Rutgers University Press, 1989. An exhibition catalog.

Williamson, Paul. *An Introduction to Medieval Ivory Carvings*. London: HMSO, 1982.

Liturgy

Bock, Nicolas, and Peter Kurmann, et al. *Art, Cérémonial et Liturgie au Moyen Âge: Actes du Colloque de 3e cycle romand de lettres, Lausanne-Fribourg*. Rome: Viella, 2002.

Davies, J. G., ed. *A Dictionary of Liturgy and Worship*. New York: Macmillan, 1972.

———. *A Select Liturgical Lexicon*. Richmond, Va.: John Knox Press, 1965.

Hughes, Andrew. *Medieval Manuscripts for Mass and Office: A Guide to Their Organization and Terminology*. Toronto: University of Toronto Press, 1982.

Kennedy, V. L. *The Saints of the Canon of the Mass*. 2nd ed. rev. Vatican City: Pontificio Istituto di Archeologia Cristiana, 1963.

King, Archdale. *Eucharistic Reservation in the Western Church*. London: A. R. Mowbray, 1965.

———. *Liturgy of the Roman Church*. London: Longmans, Green & Co., 1957.

Klauser, Theodor. *A Short History of the Western Liturgy*. Translated by John Halliburton. Oxford: Oxford University Press, 1969.

Palazzo, Eric. *A History of Liturgical Books from the Beginning to the Thirteenth Century*. Translated by Madeleine Beaumont. Collegeville, Minn.: The Liturgical Press, 1993.

Pfaff, R. W. *Medieval Latin Liturgy: A Select Bibliography*. Toronto: University of Toronto Press, 1982.

Steiner, Ruth. *Monasticism and the Arts*. Edited by Timothy Gregory Verdon. Syracuse, N.Y.: Syracuse University Press, 1984.

Manuscripts

Alexander, Jonathan J. G. *Medieval Illuminators and Their Methods of Work*. New Haven, Conn.: Yale University Press, 1992.

———, ed. *The Painted Page: Italian Renaissance Book Illumination, 1450–1550*. Munich: Prestel, 1994. An exhibit catalog.

Brown, Michelle P. *Understanding Illuminated Manuscripts: A Guide to Technical Terms*. Los Angeles: J. Paul Getty Museum in association with the British Library, 1994.

Calkins, Robert G. *Illuminated Books of the Middle Ages*. Ithaca, N.Y.: Cornell University Press, 1983.

de Hamel, Christopher. *A History of Illuminated Manuscripts*. 2nd ed. London: Phaidon, 1994.

Needham, Paul. *Twelve Centuries of Bookbindings, 400–1600*. New York: Pierpont Morgan Library, 1979.

Pächt, Otto. *Book Illumination in the Middle Ages: An Introduction*. Oxford: Oxford University Press, 1986.

Palladino, Pia, ed. *Treasures of a Lost Art: Italian Manuscript Painting of the Middle Ages and Renaissance*. New York: Metropolitan Museum of Art, 2003.

Relics and Reliquaries

Battiscombe, C. F. *The Relics of Saint Cuthbert*. Oxford: Oxford University Press, 1956.

Bentley, James. *Restless Bones: The Story of Relics*. London: Constable, 1985.

Bozóky, Edina, and Anne-Marie Helvétius. *Les Reliques: Objets, cultes, symbols*. Turnhout: Brepols, 1999.

Frolow, A. *Les reliquaries de la Vraie Croix*. Paris: Institut français d'études byzantines, 1965.

Gauthier, Marie-Madeleine. *Les routes de la foi; Reliques et reliquiares de Jérusalem à Compostelle*. Fribourg: Office du Livre, 1983.

Grimme, Ernst Gunther. *Goldschmiedekunst im Mittelalter: Form und Bedeutung des Reliquiars von 800 bis 1500*. Cologne: M. DuMont Schauberg, 1972.

Hahn, C. "The Voices of the Saints: Speaking Reliquaries." *Gesta* 36 (1997): 20–31.

Legner, Anton. *Reliquien in Kunst und Kult; zwischen Antike und Aufklärung*. Darmstadt: Wissenschaftliche Buchgesellschaft, 1995.

Sox, David. *Relics and Shrines*. London: G. Allen & Unwin, 1985.

van Os, Henk. *The Way to Heaven: Relic Veneration in the Middle Ages*. Amsterdam: de Prom, 2000. An exhibition catalog.

Metalwork

Calkins, Robert G. "Metalwork of the Church Treasuries," in *Monuments of Medieval Art*. Ithaca, N.Y.: Cornell University Press, 1979. See also "Mosan Metalwork" in the same volume.

Cotsonis, John A. *Byzantine Figural Processional Crosses*. Washington, D.C.: Dumbarton Oaks, 1994.

Kitzinger, Ernst. "A Pair of Silver Book Covers in the Sion Treasure," in *Gatherings in Honor of Dorothy E. Miner*. Edited by I. E. McCracken, L. M. C. Randall, and R. H. Randall Jr. Baltimore, Md.: Walters Art Gallery, 1974.

Longhurst, M. H., and C. R. Morey. "The Covers of the Lorsch Gospels." *Speculum* 3 (1928): 64–74.

Taburet-Delahaye, Elisabeth. *L'Orfèvrerie Gothique (XIIIe début XVe siècle) au Musée de Cluny*. Paris: Réunion des Musées Nationaux, 1989.

Willberg, A. *Goldschmiedekunst des Mittelalters*. Cologne, 1998.

Wolfson, Michael, et al. *Der grosse Goldkelch Bischof Gerhards: Geschichte, Frommigkeit, und Kunst um 1400*. Hildesheim: Olms, 1996. An exhibition catalog.

Textiles

Christie, A. G. I. *English Medieval Embroidery*. Oxford: Clarendon Press, 1938.

Dearmer, Percy. *Linen Ornaments of the Church*. Oxford: Alcuin Club Tracts, 1929.

Dolby, Anastasia. *Church Vestments: Their Origin, Use and Ornament*. London: Chapman and Hall, 1868.

King, D. *Opus Anglicanum: English Medieval Embroidery*. London: Arts Council of Great Britain; Victoria and Albert Museum, 1963. An exhibition catalog.

Lesage, Robert. *Vestments and Church Furniture*. Translated by Fergus Murphy. New York: Hawthorn Books, 1960.

Mayo, Janet. *A History of Ecclesiastical Dress*. London: Batsford, 1984.

Norris, Herbert. *Church Vestments: Their Origin & Development*. London: Dent, 1949.

Pocknee, Cyril E. *Liturgical Vesture: Its Origins and Development*. London: Mowbray, 1960.

Santangelo, Nino. *Tessuti d'arte italiani dal XII. al XVIII. secolo*. Milan: Electa, 1959.

Young, B. "Opus Anglicanum." *Metropolitan Museum of Art Bulletin* 29 (March 1971): 291–98.

Index